WRITERS
IN CONVERSATION
VOLUME TWO

JOHN ASHBERY
PAUL AUSTER
JOHN BARTH
ROBERTSON DAVIES
JOAN DIDION
JOHN FOWLES
URSULA LE GUIN
ARTHUR MILLER
ALICE MUNRO
MORDECAI RICHLER
W.G. SEBALD
ISAAC BASHEVIS SINGER
GEORGE STEINER
PAUL THEROUX
ALICE WALKER
TIMBERLAKE WERTENBAKER
ARNOLD WESKER
TOM WOLFE

WITH
CHRISTOPHER BIGSBY

WRITERS IN CONVERSATION
VOLUME TWO
WITH CHRISTOPHER BIGSBY

First Published in 2001 for The Arthur Miller Centre,
by EAS Publishing.
In conjunction with Pen&inc.
University of East Anglia, Norwich, NR4 7TJ.

A CIP record for this book is available from the British Library.
ISBN: 1-902913-09-4

Production: Julia Bell/Christopher Bigsby
Typesetting: Julian p Jackson
Copy Editing: Emma Hargrave
Cover Design: Julian p Jackson
Cover Illustration: Bella Bigsby

WRITERS IN CONVERSATION is typeset in Bembo and **Hoefler Text** on
acid-free paper.

Distribution by Signature Books, Sunhouse, 2–4 Little Peter Street,
Manchester, M15 4PS.
T: +44(0)161 834 8767
E: admin@signature-books.co.uk

Printed and bound by Biddles **Ltd, Guildford and Kings Lynn.**

WRITERS
IN CONVERSATION

VOLUME TWO

ARTHUR MILLER CENTRE FOR AMERICAN STUDIES

CONTENTS

INTRODUCTION

This is the second volume of conversations that I have conducted with writers over a period of some twenty years. Many were recorded for the BBC; that with Timberlake Wertenbaker took place at the British Council's Cambridge Seminar; still others were the product of personal research.

There is a legitimate question to be asked about why we read such interviews and why writers submit to them. The latter is seemingly more easily answered: it is part of the promotion business. Sell the author and you will sell the book. It is a chore, a faustian pact with a publisher who in return promises – sometimes even meaning it – advertising, display stands, enthused reps spreading the good news through chains of eager bookstores. Yet, I suspect it is more than that.

The interviewer is a surrogate reader. He or she represents the otherwise anonymous consumer of the book who rarely communicates with the author, unless through on-line reviews, often themselves cynical products of bored publicists, or postcards with green ink messages pointing out factual errors. Of course, public readings offer something in the way of contact and, indeed, frequently include opportunities for questions from the floor. But a one-on-one interview permits of a greater intimacy, a more systematic enquiry.

There is no reason, of course, why authors should be analysts of their own work. Indeed, there are cogent reasons why, for their own creative health, they should not be. But in the process of answering questions I suspect there are occasions when the formulation of a response involves revelation not only for the interviewer but for the writer him or her self. Just as it is possible to discover what one thinks through the process of writing, so it is through speaking. Psycho-analysis, deeply problematic is it might be, also turns on questions and answers, though I am not suggesting that what follows is psycho-analysis. If it were I would have charged.

As with all conversations, there are revelations and concealments in the following pages. These days we are alert to the casuistry of interrogators and aware of the necessity for self-protection. The greater surprise, then, is how open these writers proved, in talking of their craft and their lives, or at least how adroit in appearing to be so because there is a theatricality to public encounters of this kind.

For my own part, though, I came away from these interviews knowing a great deal more than I had before and at least with the illusion of understanding more, not only about the individuals concerned and their work, but the context in which they wrote. We are, doubtless, all voyeurs, who find other people's lives fascinating, why else the popularity of autobiography and biography. But such curiosity may also betoken that same interest in entering the sensibility of others that takes us to literature in the first place. We turn to it to learn more about ourselves by discovering more about others, more about our time and place by visiting other times and places.

Read W.G. Sebald's account of his own upbringing and you understand something not only about him and his work but also about the times he and we live in, the anxieties, guilts, aspirations that have defined a generation. And what is true of him is true of others in the following pages who explain not only the nature of their craft but what it has been to be alive in a century of radical change, violence, shifting patterns of belief. Creative writers are not historians but there is a history contained in their work and, of course, in their lives. The story of story making is also a story worth reading.

I would, finally, like to acknowledge the generosity of the BBC and of the writers contained in this book for their kind permission for me to publish these interviews. I would also like to thank the many BBC producers with whom I have worked over the years.

Christopher Bigsby
Norwich
2001

IN CONVERSATION
WITH
JOHN ASHBERY

John Ashbery was born in 1927. He studied at Harvard University, where he began to write. His first substantial collection of poetry, *Some Trees*, appeared in 1956, and took eight years to sell eight hundred copies. Ashbery spent much of the following decade working as an art critic in Europe, remote from the New York literary scene. In 1962, however, *The Tennis Court Oath* served both to put Ashbery on the map and to raise a question that has never quite gone away, that of the difficulty of some of his poetry. It was a volume that seemed to release language from its presumed responsibility to communicate with clarity. His reputation continued to grow and *Self-Portrait in a Convex Mirror* (1975) won a series of awards, including the National Book Critics Circle Award, the National Book Award and the Pulitzer Prize. Ashbery has a fondness for the long poem: *Flow Chart* (1991) is more than two hundred pages long. It was followed by *Hotel Lautrèamont* (1992), *And the Stars Were Shining* (1994), *Can You Hear, Bird* (1995) and *Wakefulness* (1998). This interview was conducted when *Flow Chart* was published in 1991.

Bigsby: When you started *Flow Chart* did you know what direction it would take?

Ashbery: As usual, I didn't know what I was going to do when I set out to do it. I had been writing some longish poems, and an English friend of mine, who lives in New York and who designed the jacket for *Flow Chart*, said to me, 'Why don't you write a hundred page poem about your mother?' – my mother having died recently. It seemed a rather unlikely project. But then I thought about it and I said, 'Maybe I will try to write a hundred-page poem.' I had written long poems before and indeed have become known – even notorious – for them. So I wrote that poem and it wasn't about my mother, though she makes a few appearances along with lots of other people and things. I just worked until I had written a hundred pages. In the end it turned out to be over two hundred pages long when the book was published.

Bigsby: Two hundred and sixteen, which is a long, long poem.

Ashbery: I cut some, too.

Bigsby: What is the attraction to you of writing long poems?

Ashbery: It is something that I work on over a long period of time, obviously. Most of my poems I write all at once, at one sitting, so one attraction is the fact that the poem will reflect different frames of mind over a period. It will take on another kind of dimension. Also, the built-in anxiety of not knowing whether I will be able to finish it may well inject a poignant note which may be for the better.

Bigsby: How do you know when you have finished? How do you know when to put the last full-stop?

Ashbery: In this case it was easy because I had set myself to write at least a hundred pages before I started. In other cases I think you trip a switch that turns off the poem. Usually when that happens if I try to continue writing the poem it just doesn't work. It is some kind of instinctive thing. I don't know whether I have always had it, but I certainly have ever since I can remember.

Bigsby: With a novel you can put it down and pick it up and because of the narrative drive, because of the characters, you can get back into the text again. Even with a long poem, with a strong sense of metre and rhyme, you can do that. But *Flow Chart* is not really in strict metre and doesn't deploy rhyme. How content are you for people to read the poem in a very fragmented way – to put it down, pick it up, forget where they were?

Ashbery: That doesn't bother me in the least because I have an idea that that is the way we all behave. That is a part of our reading habits. There may very well be people who pick up a book of poetry and read it through from the beginning to the end but it is not what I do and I have a feeling it is not general practice.

Bigsby: Does that in some way reflect your own method of composition? Do you allow outside events to force their way into the poem?

Ashbery: That is certainly true of life itself and it seems to me that this way of perceiving it is a true way of reflecting how we go about our days.

Bigsby: At times it seems to be a poem that reads something like a literary testament. Certainly it is partly autobiographical, and yet you have always reacted against confessional poetry. Is there a contradiction there?

Ashbery: There are some autobiographical moments in it and other moments which are invented autobiography. I never felt that my autobiography was interesting to anybody but me. It turns out I am wrong – confessional poetry is very popular – and so that is why, I suppose, I invent some autobiographical passages here and there and then when some real ones happen along I use them too.

Bigsby: Can you explain what you mean by inventing an autobiographical passage?

Ashbery: There is a passage in *Flow Chart* which seems to be taking place in the lower forms of an elementary school. The voice addresses a Miss McGregor but I never had a teacher named Miss McGregor. That is as good an example as I can think of.

Bigsby: In so far as you do look backwards in this poem, perhaps I could do the same. You were born and brought up in Rochester in New York, right on the edge of Lake Ontario.

Ashbery: I was born in the city of Rochester because that is where the best hospital nearest to us was. But my father was a farmer. We had a farm on Lake Ontario, or very close to it, and my grandparents lived just a few miles away down the lake.

Bigsby: Has anything of that early experience found its way into your poetry?

Ashbery: I think so. I have been reading Hermann Broch's *The Sleep Walkers*. It mentions living near a mountain and suggests that the mountain invades every single part of your life. It is the same way with people who live by the ocean or, as in my case, the lake. Their lives are not their own because they are invaded by the ocean or the lake, which is a large body of water. You can't see across it. It was like that for me; the rhythm of the water was something that I probably absorbed very early. In fact, many of my titles are very watery.

Bigsby: Such as, *A Wave*.

Ashbery: Yes, and also *April Galleons*, *Flow Chart* and an earlier one called *Clepsydra*, which is a water clock.

Bigsby: You were one of only two children and your brother died when you were very young.

Ashbery: I was twelve and he was nine.

Bigsby: What impact did that have on you?

Ashbery: I felt very guilty. I felt that I had caused his death because we used to fight all the time, although basically we were very close. But it also made for a more isolated life since we lived out in the country and I didn't really have any friends who I could play with when I was growing up; they all lived too far away or back in the town. Although when I was very young I lived with my grandparents in the city of Rochester where I had a lot of little playmates, when I was about seven I went back to live with my parents in an isolated, rural part of the country and I always longed to be back in the city.

Bigsby: How did you deal with that? Did you turn to books?

Ashbery: I read all the time, which upset my parents because they thought I should go outdoors and enjoy the fresh air and get some roses in my cheeks! I really escaped into a fantasy world of books.

Bigsby: Did poetry play any part in that?

Ashbery: Yes, mostly the Victorian poetry that we had around the house and *The Book of Knowledge* that I read over and over when I was a child. My grandfather had a lot of nineteenth-century novels and volumes of poetry which I read without really understanding or enjoying them too much. At that time I didn't really have any intention of writing poetry myself. The poems that struck me most were the popular recitation pieces of the nineteenth century, such as the 'The Curfew Shall Not Ring Tonight', 'High Tide in Lincolnshire' and Tennyson's 'Eagle', which I remember I recited in some grade-school programme, which is quite easy as it is only eight lines long.

Bigsby: You also turned to painting and, of course, you have gone on to involve yourself with painting as an art critic. How far are the roots of your poetry in art? A number of your poems have been inspired by the titles of paintings, but how far have the aesthetics of art influenced your verse?

Ashbery: It is hard for me to judge. I did want to be a painter, but when I got caught up with poetry I gradually lost interest in painting and only started writing about art when I was already thirty, and then only kind of accidentally. I needed to pay the rent and so I managed to get an assignment from *Art News* magazine, which liked poets to write for them even if they didn't know anything about art. I gradually got better at it and a friend of mine has commented that I backed into a brilliant career as an art critic. But although art has frequently come into my work and the poem I seem to be best known for is 'Self-Portrait in a Convex Mirror', I have always felt that most of my ideas came out of music. I know you are going to ask me how that can possibly be and I won't be able to answer it.

Bigsby: I won't ask you that, but music has been important to you, hasn't it?

Ashbery: I listen to music all the time and especially when I am writing. I always have a record on or I listen to the classical radio station.

Bigsby: Have you collaborated with musicians?

Ashbery: Not really, though several of my poems have been set to music.

Bigsby: Was music in any sense a trigger to your writing? Or was it just a parallel interest?

Ashbery: It is a trigger in some sense, but I would really be at a loss to say how.

Bigsby: John Cage is a name that comes to my mind as someone whose approach to music in some ways parallels your approach to poetry. He was concerned to force people to listen more carefully, to listen to those things that we don't perhaps define as music. Wouldn't that be true of your writing?

Ashbery: Yes. Once in my early twenties – when I felt that writing had become very difficult and almost impossible – I was inspired by hearing a long piano piece of his. It is a very uncompromising work that lasts almost an hour and is called *Music of Changes*, and I thought that I could try to do something like that in poetry. It helped me over a dry period.

Bigsby: At the beginning of your career, I suppose almost before your career had really begun, you went to France and stayed there on and off for quite some time. You would imagine for a poet – particularly for one who relies on hearing language, the sound of language – that expatriation would carry problems. Did it?

Ashbery: It did for a while. Much of my poetry comes out of the cadences of American speech as I hear it around me, especially in New York City where you hear it for better or for worse. I found it very difficult to write at first in France. It was not until I had been there for two and a half years or so that I began to feel easy about writing again. It was about five years before I found I could get along well writing there, without the American 'surround'.

Bigsby: Your interest in spoken language, which forces its way into some of your poems, led you in a logical direction, namely to the theatre. You wrote a number of plays. But since the 1950s you have left that on one side. What drew you to the theatre and why did you abandon it?

Ashbery: I abandoned it because it seemed very unlikely that anyone would ever produce the plays – they were not closet dramas but were actually meant to be staged. It was quite difficult to write them and so I decided to use the effort for poetry. I wasn't yet known as a poet either, but at least it was easier to write a poem than a play. I always meant to go back to writing plays but somehow whenever I try to write something other than a poem it always turns into a poem, or I think of it as a poem. But even at this late date I suppose I could always try it again.

Bigsby: You didn't only turn to drama. You also wrote a novel, but just the one.

Ashbery: That was a collaboration between me and my friend James Schuyler, the poet, who died recently. It wasn't really a novel. We wrote it as a kind of game to amuse ourselves, never thinking that anyone would publish it. We didn't finish it until about eighteen years after we began writing it and only then because a publisher expressed interest and so we put on a burst of energy. It has no real plot; it is mostly conversations. We were both influenced by Ivy Compton Burnett and Ronald Firbank and some of those novels which are nothing but dialogue, such as *The Awkward Age* by Henry James.

Bigsby: What is the difference between a piece of prose which may have a poetic ring to it and a prose poem of the kind you have written?

Ashbery: I don't think anyone has ever decided this question satisfactorily. Many critics would insist that there is no such thing as prose poetry, even though we have had it since at least the nineteenth century, particularly in Baudelaire. I started writing a series of three long prose poems, called *Three Poems*, I think because I wanted to decide for myself whether such a thing did exist and, if so, what it would be like, how it would differ from prose. In fact, I wondered whether prose itself, I mean really prosaic prose, might not take on a poetic context if it were looked at from a certain angle. As far as I know, the jury is still out on whether there is such a thing as prose poetry, but I and other poets continue to work at it.

Bigsby: I suppose the contrary question is, what is the function of rhythm and metre?

Ashbery: I don't employ them often in my own poetry.

Bigsby: But you do from time to time.

Ashbery: Yes, but just because I try to think of different things to do. When I was still in my teens I wrote rhyming sonnets and heroic couplets, that sort of thing, and when I found that I could do this, that it wasn't beyond my capabilities, I began to lose interest. So I tried to find the things that did test my capabilities.

Bigsby: Surely rhythm and metre do give you certain constraints, certain parameters, certain disciplines, within which you then have to work? Are those constraints something that you resist?

Ashbery: They are constraints, yes, but for readers they can be a security blanket. You know you are going to land comfortably on the next rhyme and the line will work in the way that the previous lines have done. There is certainly no reason not to use them, if one is inclined to do so. As Schoenberg said, 'A lot of music remains to be written in the key of C major.' There are some people today who do it well and with great originality, but I don't think it matters really what form the poem takes as long as it can be identified by a few people as a poem.

Bigsby: When you started to write as a poet what sort of poet did you imagine that you were going to be?

Ashbery: The first poets I read in high school were Robert Frost, Edwin Arlington Robinson and Edna St. Vincent Millay, all rather traditional poets. At the same time I was very interested in surrealist art, which I had discovered in the library and in magazines. Although I hadn't yet read any surrealist poetry, I was obviously ripe to be influenced by it when I eventually did come upon it. I think the first time I did was when a cousin of mine, who knew I was interested in poetry, gave me a little magazine which had a lot of Latin American surrealist poems translated into English. At that point I realized there were kinds of poetry I didn't yet know about, which would probably interest me more than the kinds that I did know.

Bigsby: And that led to a certain reaction to your earlier poetry. *The Tennis Court Oath*, for example, was seen as excessively difficult, a word which crops up frequently in criticism of your work. Indeed, that volume *is* difficult, sometimes almost to the point of opacity. It is very, very gnomic. What led you to write that book?

Ashbery: Those are poems that I wrote after I had gone to live in France and I was very much at sea about what I wanted to write. My first book had been published. It had been accepted just before I left America and it came out the following spring. Although I liked the way I was writing in that book I wanted to try to do something different, but I didn't know what. So I did a lot of experiments with collage and a kind of automatic writing, just to see what could be done. And since my first book had been a total flop, so far as I could tell, and I thought no one would ever publish another book of mine, I decided to write as a way of finding out what I could do. Then I had the chance to publish a second book of poetry, so I put a lot of things into it that should probably have remained in my drawer: sketches, experiments and so on, as well as a few more finished poems which I had written at the same time. But it is quite a jumble and I regret having published some of the poems that are in there, though a few are still interesting.

Bigsby: What do you make of this response to your poetry, that it is difficult?

Ashbery: It is a kind of self-fulfilling prophecy: I have become so noted for being difficult that every interviewer always asks me the same question and the answer gets repeated.

Bigsby: Let me refine it a little, then. There are some lines in your 1972 book *Three Poems*, which seem to me to bear on this. You say there, 'I know that I braid too much of my own snapped off perceptions of things as they come to me. They are private and always will be. Where then are the private turns of event destined to boom later like golden chimes released over a city from a highest tower.' That is the problem, isn't it, bridging the gap between private perception and public meaning?

Ashbery: Yes, but that's a problem every writer is faced with. Another writer could mean those lines to be a sort of *ars poetica*. I was talking about poetry but thinking more about writing a poem when I wrote them. Recently there was an article about me in a New York magazine written by a lady who I had met recently, but who had known my poetry for a long time and who very much admired it. Nevertheless, she felt that she couldn't just leave it at that, but had to point out the difficulty of it.

She said, 'A lot of this book is very tough', meaning it is hard to understand. So I said, 'Well, show me some that you don't understand and I will try to tenderize it for you.' Then she got very frustrated because she was looking through the book and suddenly it didn't look difficult to her. However, your question is certainly a valid one and I don't know what to say in response. When I first began reading twentieth-century poetry I found it difficult too. I couldn't make head nor tail of Wallace Stevens, for instance, or even Auden, who was the first major influence on me. I found it very difficult at first. Just the fact that he used a colloquial matter-of-fact voice disconcerted me – I didn't think you were supposed to do that in poetry. I realized afterwards that the rules are there to be broken. But the fact is that what we think of as modern poetry is hard to understand, for a while at least, and I didn't think that my own was going to be any more difficult than anybody else's. I thought I was in the mainstream of modern poetry. It turned out that I was mistaken and that my poetry gives many people a lot of difficulty and raises many hackles. Just the sound of my name can do that in certain quarters.

Bigsby: You once said that the lines of poetry that mean the most to us are the ones that don't make sense in a conventional way. If that is so, why? Why are the memorable lines the lines that don't make sense?

Ashbery: I don't remember putting it as baldly as that, but certainly there are lines of poetry which we can't fathom but which haunt us like dreams we can't understand. I am trying to think of an example right now. Tennyson is a poet I like very much and one of my favourite lines of poetry is from his poem 'Mariana' which, although not obscure, nevertheless seems very mysterious. It is, 'The broken sheds look sad and strange.' I always thought that was a very beautiful line without knowing why. I mean, what is so beautiful about a broken shed? Or what is beautiful about the fact that it looks sad and strange? Although the line is pretty straightforward, its resonances are mysterious.

Bigsby: Is that the essence of poetry, as distinct from prose, that it contains an element of the mysterious, the unknown, something that doesn't bubble entirely to the surface? Is that what you look for?

Ashbery: I don't think you have to look for it. It is everywhere; it bubbles up by itself into one's writing.

Bigsby: In the 1950s and the early 1960s, when you were writing about art at the same time as you were writing poetry, were you struck by the difference between those two areas? After all, American art was very self-confident in the 1950s and early 1960s. American poetry wasn't really, was it?

Ashbery: It wasn't just a question of that. It was that the art was defiantly experimental and convinced people, whereas poetry always seems to be somewhat behind the other arts. Probably the best-known poet of the period was Robert Lowell, who was not really a modernist like Pollock or Cage. I thought there was something that I could do which would be in the same sort of reckless spirit of the art that I admired at the time.

Bigsby: On the other hand, talking of the 1960s in *Flow Chart*, you say:

> *My imagination was trying to get its act together, I mean really see/ itself. But . . . it could not really accept itself for all it was because of the/ possibility that a trick was involved. And yet . . . it also knew it wasn't/ nothing.*

What on earth did you mean by that?

Ashbery: I have no idea, I don't remember.

Bigsby: At the very least it suggests a level of self-doubt.

Ashbery: I am full of self-doubt. I have no idea whether what I am doing is viable or should even be attempted, but I seem to have no choice but to do it or try to do it. As to the passage you quote, of course this is a very long work and I don't remember many passages. But yes, it does indicate my anxiety.

Bigsby: You have said that the artist's chief concern should be to create a work of art that the critic can't ever begin to talk about. Is that wilful perverseness?

Ashbery: Yes, I think it is wilful perverseness. But at the same time what makes poetry for me is what can't be paraphrased. For instance, in the Tennyson line I quoted, if you put that line another way you would have a very boring statement about some sheds. What is lost in translation is just what makes it so beautiful.

Bigsby: One of your works which had the greatest success was *Self-Portrait in a Convex Mirror*, in the mid-1970s. But you have said that it isn't a favourite of yours. Why?

Ashbery: I don't know. I was quite surprised that it was successful. When I wrote it I felt even more unsure than I usually do when I am writing and I felt I was writing at a really low level of energy. Once I had written it, I tinkered with it endlessly, making all sorts of changes, most of them not really important ones, but I was never quite satisfied. I shifted commas and changed prepositions, that sort of thing. I think the deliberate essayistic tone of the poem, which may be what makes it more congenial to readers, is a kind of put-on. Really, underneath, it is as irrational as my other poetry. Perhaps I feel that this is a fraud I have perpetrated and that it simply *seems* to make more sense than it actually does.

Bigsby: You have been using words such as unsure and self-doubt, and that feeling is there in *Flow Chart*. You say:

> *though reams of work do get done,*
> *not much listens. I have a feeling my voice is just for me,*
> *that no one else has ever heard it.*

You can't really think that, can you?

Ashbery: Why not? When one sits at one's desk spinning reams of poetry there is no certainty that there is ever going to be an echo outside your room of what you are working on. Although my poetry has received a lot of attention, some of it positive, I still can't help but feel doubtful about it. And I suppose I wouldn't want to feel otherwise.

Bigsby: There is another moment in *Flow Chart* when you ask, 'How far did I go wrong?' Do you have a sense that your career may have had wrong directions built into it?

Ashbery: That does sometimes occur to me; the idea that maybe I took a wrong turning somewhere and have been, as someone said of Zola, 'laboriously toiling up the wrong road to art' all the while.

Bigsby: You had one chance to reconstruct that career. When you published *Selected Poems* you got a chance to go back through your career, pull out the poems you wished to gather together and sculpt something new, something that was not there before. Did you have a feeling of consciously creating another version of yourself when you produced the *Selected Poems*?

Ashbery: No, not really. I was always against the idea of having a *Selected Poems*. It seemed too much like being buried alive. I wanted to make sure I could go on afterwards. I think I made the selection in an afternoon by just going through the tables of contents of my books. I omitted some poems that I like because I forgot about them or their names escaped my attention, and I put in some that I didn't like as much as others. Some were left out because, though I like them, they seemed to be repetitive of other poems that I like slightly better. But I didn't mean this to be my final word on my work. I didn't mean to imply that whatever was excluded from the book was something that I wanted to be forgotten. Not at all.

Bigsby: One line from *Flow Chart* says, 'All writing is putting aside something in one's lap like a sandwich juggling priorities.' Writing has obviously had its rewards for you. Have those rewards been bought at a significant cost? Has there been a price to pay?

Ashbery: Yes, I think so. I have often felt that being a poet has dis-equipped me for doing anything else. I can't seem to do the things that one is supposed to: like answer letters or balance one's cheque book or use the empty time between poems to accomplish something in some other line. I think that is probably the cost of being a poet.

Bigsby: That is a relatively trivial price to pay. Have there been any more profound prices?

Ashbery: I don't know that they are trivial. There seems to be a lot of life that escapes one. One sees happy families going about their lives and one wishes one could be part of that life and yet one somehow seems excluded from it, or I do anyway.

Bigsby: So writing is a withdrawal?

Ashbery: It is also the only thing that really gives me pleasure, which is why I do it. I don't think of it as a withdrawal in the sense that I am writing for my own private consumption. I write with the hope that at least somebody is going to read my work and like it, otherwise there would be no point. But I don't tailor it to a reader. How could I – one never knows who is going to pick up one's work and start reading it? To quote Gertrude Stein, 'I write for myself and for strangers.'

Bigsby: Towards the end of *Flow Chart* you talk about the figure of the writer and you say, 'His literature would have performed its duty by setting you gently down in a new place.' Is that what the writer's job is?

Ashbery: In so far as a writer has a job, I suppose that could be one example of it. I am not sure I wanted that to be the definitive word on writing but, now that you mention it, sure, why not?

Bigsby: Something else occurs to me while we are talking about that function in relation to your work. The name that comes to mind is Walt Whitman, not just because of the lists you offer in *The Vermont Notebook*, but because I sense that there are no privileged moments in your work, as there weren't in Whitman's, that all moments have their rights and their values and are worth exploring.

Ashbery: I think that's the kind of democratic notion that I have found in Whitman. However, when I was young I believed in privileged moments. I thought that I should only write when I felt a certain moment of inspiration or ecstasy. These turned out to be very few and far between and I also became someone who worked for a living, so I realized I would have to use whatever time was at my disposal and forget about the privilege if it wasn't there at the time.

Bigsby: The moment is privileged not only in the sense of inspiration coming to you, the writer. It is also writing about moments which appear ordinary and banal but which, by being addressed, become something less than banal.

Ashbery: And those are most of the moments that are in our lives; they are obviously very precious just because they are part of our lives, indeed what is most characteristic of our lives. The peaks, when they are there, are wonderful but uncharacteristic.

Bigsby: You once said that 'poetry is a hopelessly minor art and I am really glad it is'. Is that true?

Ashbery: I think, as my friend Kenneth Koch once said, 'Poets are in the enviable position of being unloved.' The fact that not much attention is paid to us, at least in terms of other branches of the arts, is galling to us but at the same time probably lucky: you don't often get the feeling that someone is breathing down your neck, trying to determine what your next move is. You can work it out for yourself.

IN CONVERSATION
WITH
PAUL AUSTER

P aul Auster, born in 1947, is best known for *The New York Trilogy* – *City of Glass* (1985), *Ghosts* (1986) and *The Locked Room* (1986) – works which deploy aspects of detective fiction as part of novels which explore language, identity and time. In *City of Glass* the protagonist masquerades as a detective called Paul Auster. Subsequent works include *The Invention of Solitude* (1982), *In the Country of Last Things* (1987), *The Music of Chance* (1990), *Mr. Vertigo* (1994) and *Timbucktu* (1999). Paul Auster has worked as a translator and has published several volumes of poetry, including *Unearth: Poems 1970–1972* (1974) and *Wall Writing: Poems 1972–1975* (1976). The following interview was conducted in March, 1991.

Bigsby: Chance seems to recur in your work.

Auster: It occurs in my own life with some consistency and to such a degree that I feel that if I did not actually incorporate it into the work I am doing I would not even come close to embodying the real as I experience it. I know people often say of my work that it is improbable and crazy and unrealistic but I consider myself a realist, an absolutely rock bottom, nuts-and-bolts man of the earth. I am not making it up.

Bigsby: *The Music of Chance* seems to me to be in large part a debate about freedom.

Auster: I think this is a crucial element in the book. It is about freedom and responsibility and whether there can be such a thing as freedom without responsibility. At the beginning of the book Nash is a so-called responsible citizen. He has a family, a child and an important job. He is a fireman, and that is not some casual occupation. He gives it all up and is, in a sense, running away from his life, running away from responsibility. So he is freed from things, but I do not know if that's really freedom. In the end he arbitrarily decides to take a stand, to accept the given, which is something that is very difficult for people to do, I think. We all struggle against it, simply saying: 'This is my life. I am living it now. The present exists.' That seems to be the greatest kind of responsibility anyone can assume. I think only the experience of that so-called freedom can bring someone to the point where that decision can be made.

Bigsby: A number of your books seem to be written in what I might call a parenthetical style, that is to say the main story contains other stories which spin out of it. But *The Music of Chance* is not quite like that; it has a very direct, natural narrative track. The reader is accelerated through the story by the original narrative explosion.

Auster: It is certainly the most straightforward narrative I have ever come up with. It is not usually a matter – or not ever a matter, of intentionality, though. The stories impose themselves on me in a certain way and I simply follow them. It seems to me now, having written a number of novels, that in some way they alternate between rather labyrinthine structures and rather simple ones. The book that preceded *The Music of Chance*, *Moon Palace*, was quite complex in its structure. The book before that, *In the Country of Last Things*, was not; it was very straightforward and did not loop around. But *The Locked Room*, before that, had many stories within stories, anecdotes, digressions. I suppose that when you sit down to write a book, you want to write against the book you wrote before. I think this is some kind of dialectic that has been set in motion in my work.

Bigsby: This is your latest book but I would like to take you back not only earlier in your career but earlier in your life. You have said that you were brought up as an American boy who knew less about his ancestors than he did about Hopalong Cassidy's hat. What did you mean by that?

Auster: I just meant to say that I did not have a Jewish upbringing in any religious sense. My parents were the second generation to live in America. By then the Old World had been severed from our everyday reality. I was brought up just as an American kid and I was immersed in American law and American myths rather than Jewish or European myths.

Bigsby: Have you subsequently set out to reconstitute those ancestors?

Auster: To some degree, yes, I think so. My adult life has been seeking to put these two parts of myself back together. But, again, it is not untypical for American immigrant families to forget where they came from. That has always been the impulse: to erase what happened before, to start all over again.

Bigsby: I wonder if that absence with respect to your Jewish identity doesn't emerge in terms of the themes of your books. For example, you have characters with very unsure identities. You have people who are the victims of arbitrary fate. Other characters struggle to survive. Survival seems an important issue to you.

Auster: Yes. I am sure that if I could have my brain opened up and examined nearly everything I write about would have some connection with personal experience in some way. But when I am writing a novel I don't analyze it so much as race after the images that are coming to me. It is only in the most oblique and obscure ways that these hidden traumas or memories break surface. Often I can finish a passage in a book, or even an entire book, and not really know what it means, be no closer to solving whatever question it is that I posed for myself, perhaps because I wasn't even posing it in terms which could be answered.

Bigsby: You began your writing career as a poet, though I imagine you were writing prose alongside the poetry. Why did it take such a long time for you to work your way towards the novel?

Auster: First, it is quite true what you say. I was doing both for a long time. I was very dissatisfied with the prose I was producing in my twenties. I could not see my way around certain problems, certain narrative problems, and there was a period when I just stopped. I said, 'I am not going to do this any more. It is a waste of time and I will just continue to write poems because they are small and I can encompass them. I can work on them.' I finally started writing prose as an everyday occupation in about 1979. That is when I got serious about it. I think I had reached a point of such indifference to the whole question that I wrote out of a kind of passion, even anger, and formal questions did not matter to me any more. Critical problems were totally irrelevant and I just wanted to go blindly ahead and see what happened. I lost my self-consciousness to the degree that I was able to finish a page and go on to the next page without wanting to cross everything out.

Bigsby: It surprises me that you use the word anger because I don't find that in your prose. If anything, there is a kind of detachment.

Auster: Curiously enough, I think I have only been able to write well under a kind of passionate excess. It does not sound that way. I don't want the writing to sound angry but there is a kind of pot boiling away when the work is going well, and I am beyond questions of literature at that point. Writing is linear: language unfolds sequentially. You can't put it all in at the same time. That is the problem and that is where the real work comes.

Bigsby: What is the source of the anger?

Auster: I don't know. In a way I think it is frustration over the very limitations of languages as I experience them. I sometimes feel that I am wandering in a haze of things that cannot be articulated and the struggle to put things down clearly is so enormous that I think at times my brain is damaged. I do not think as clearly as other people. The words don't come when I want them. I can spend fifteen or twenty minutes trying to decide between prepositions and then I have no idea which is right any more; absolutely stupid basic stuff, basic grammatical questions. It is just a tremendous puzzle for me all the time. I think the anger comes out of that. The words are not there and I get so frustrated that I get angry and then the words start to come.

Bigsby: Your father was something of an absence in your life. Why did you make him in large part the subject of your first prose book, *The Invention of Solitude*?

Auster: When I started writing that I was not even writing a book. I just sat down and again this anger, this passion, whatever you want to call it, that seems to set me going, energized me. My father had dropped dead and I was shocked and felt compelled to sit down and try to write things down before I forgot them. I assumed I was going to write three to five pages but it just kept going. I kept doing it day after day and it eventually grew into a book. That is the first part of *The Invention of Solitude*. That hundred pages, or whatever it was, then needed a response. And that became the second half of the book.

The question of voice was difficult for me. The first part was written quite naturally, without any reflection, in the first person. It came to me that way and that is the way I did it. When I started doing the next part I started it in the first person, too, thinking that it would be the same as the other. But I worked and worked for several months and was very displeased with what I did. I could not understand what was going wrong. The tone of the first part had seemed correct to me, but I was not getting it in the next and it finally hit me, as a kind of revelation, that the first part had been about someone else. The second part was really about myself: myself as subject, not biographically so, but as thinking subject. I was examining myself in the way maybe you examine a laboratory rat. My own thoughts. To talk about myself in the first person was impossible so I had to step back and treat myself as though I were someone else. I finally figured out that I had to do it in the third person. After that decision, things came rather quickly. Everything seemed to fall into place and I could go on with it and finish it. Ever since then the question of first-person or third-person narration has been a major preoccupation and I have often had a lot of trouble with it. In some of my books it slides a bit.

Some books are in the first person and then lapse into the third, or vice versa. It is a question that concerns me a great deal.

Bigsby: This is partly true of *The Music of Chance*. It is a third-person narrative and yet I wonder why, given that we are so close to the sensibility of the central character?

Auster: It is almost a pseudo first-person novel. Yet there is a certain sense of detachment and distance, as though the narrative voice was unfolding maybe three inches above Nashe's head. It is not an omniscient narrator: we are very close but not quite inside him, the way a first-person novel would sound. The book before that, *Moon Palace*, is written in the first person, but there are enormous chunks of it which are told in the third; for example, when the narrator disappears and tells stories of other people. My original thought about that book was that it should all be in the third person, but that gave me tremendous problems. I finally shifted to the first person, which is obviously the opposite solution from the other book. So each book has its own set of problems to be solved.

Bigsby: This sense of distance and detachment doesn't seem to go together with anger.

Auster: I think what I meant by anger is an anger at language, the frustration of saying the things that you have to say. You are correct, though, to point out that distance and detachment contradict passion and anger or any other strong emotion. So, both are happening at the same time.

Bigsby: How far was *The Invention of Solitude* a bridge between poetry and the novel?

Auster: I think it was a bridge. In retrospect I can see that everything I have done has come out of that book. The problems and questions and experiences that are examined there have been the meat of what I have done since.

Bigsby: *The Invention of Solitude* was evidently a crucial book for you. It seems to have opened up something, given birth to something. Even the word 'solitude' in the title identifies what has become a central concern, doesn't it?

Auster: Yes. Unquestionably. I think it was also a central concern in my poetry before then. Solitude is not loneliness. It is simply the state of being alone. For me it is a neutral term, one with no gloomy or lugubrious associations. And what I have discovered, in the moments of my own life when I have been most intensely alone, is that it is precisely then that you discover your connection to other people. Even in isolation you understand that you cannot separate yourself from your past, your parents, all your experiences and, most importantly of all, from your ability to think about yourself. What you experience is heavily, if not entirely, dependent on language and language is something we make together. Nobody makes up his own language and so your ability to think about your own solitude means that you are not alone. In the second part of *The Invention of Solitude*, 'The Book of Memory,' the reason I quote so liberally from other writers is because I wanted it to be a collective work. This is the hoard of voices which inhabits my skull. These are the voices that I live with, and I wanted them to come out and share the work with me.

Bigsby: I find that very interesting because one of the things the novel can do, that poetry on the whole cannot, is offer us a range of voices. There is a social density in the novel. But you seem to keep your cast quite small. Why is that?

Auster: I suppose I am doing what I am able to do. I am hoping to broaden the canvas. I always push it a little further but maybe I am just not able to do it yet. I hope some day I will. The book I am trying to write now is more heavily populated and I am actually making great efforts to talk about people who live, so to speak, in groups, in terms of friendships, social circles and so on. Those people out there in the real world. I am more interested in how men and women get along and how women get along with each other. Obviously there is a lot I haven't even begun to get close to in my books, but at each step I'm doing what I can and not what I would wish to be able to do. The wishes are the things that are struck from the book in the end because it just does not work. You do what you can do.

Bigsby: You have worked as a translator. How far has this helped in terms of your own writing?

Auster: I used to make my living translating books and I think that helped a lot in terms of craft: just being able to analyze sentences, think about alternatives. The funny thing about writing fiction – the most daunting problem beyond all the others I have been talking about – is simply, what is the next sentence? Every idea seems to engender fifty other ideas. The next sentence can spring out in any one of those fifty directions. So the problem is, which one are you going to choose? I think translating was helpful to me simply in teaching me how to think about the sentence as something in and of itself, as separate from its surroundings.

Bigsby: So the sentence is almost like an object?

Auster: Yes.

Bigsby: As a translator you must have developed a kind of mental thesaurus, constantly trying out the appropriateness of this word or that phrase to convey exactly the nuance you want to capture. Translation presumably requires a degree of revision and reworking. Does that carry over into your writing?

Auster: Yes. I write quite slowly, as you can imagine from what I have been telling you, and if I produce a page after a day's work I feel reasonably satisfied. Sometimes I can manage two, but sometimes it is only half a page. That means that by the time I type them up, this paragraph or these two paragraphs have been rewritten many times during the day, sometimes twenty times. I write in a notebook and that is where all the scribbling and scratching take place. Then, just in order to read it, I have to type it up. So I keep a running typescript of every book as I am going along. I pretty much leave it until I have done the first draft and then I start going through the typescript and marking it up again. Every sentence is probably written fifteen times on average.

Bigsby: Is there also a carry-over from the poetry into your prose? Your poetry itself seemed to change. Your poems were tight, compacted, almost like a nut. Sometimes they were opaque. Then as you went on they seemed to unfurl and move towards prose.

Auster: I agree that that is the movement in those poems. The early ones were clenched like little fists. They were very gnomic and difficult to penetrate. I was doing my best at the time but they certainly opened up and became more discursive. When I look back on it now I can see that the next step had to be prose or at least narrative poetry, which did not really interest me. So I was going back to prose whether I knew it or not.

Bigsby: You had an *annus mirabilis*, which was 1985–86, when you published the three novels that formed *The New York Trilogy*. How far did you think of them as a trilogy when you wrote the first word of the first book?

Auster: I can tell you very definitely that when I was beginning *City of Glass*, the first book, I had no idea it would be a trilogy. It was just a book. But as I was getting on with it, maybe halfway or two-thirds of the way through, I suddenly remembered a play that I had written about seven or eight years before. It was a little play that I had written and not been satisfied with. I had put it in the drawer and forgotten all about it, but now it started to bounce around in my head again. I pulled it out, looked at it and, sure enough, it was about many of the same kinds of things as the novel I was writing. So I thought, 'Mmm, this play is no good but there is still something there, so I am going to rework it as a story not as a play any more.' Once there were two; suddenly there were three. The third book was composed of rejected material from the first. There was a whole set of concerns around the question of biography that I wanted to talk about: whether anyone can accurately depict another's life, for example. This question is also, in a sense, about the issue of solitude and I wanted to attack it again.

Bigsby: You had a hard time publishing the first volume of *The New York Trilogy*. Why was that?

Auster: God only knows. I did not know what to think. I kept sending it out and it kept getting rejected. There were some people who could not make head nor tail of it. Others seemed to like it to a certain degree, but then got mystified by the end. A couple of editors said: 'Well, we would be happy to publish it if you would just change it, if you would just make the ending more comprehensible, expand it here and there.' I really didn't want to touch it. I thought it should be exactly the way it was. I waited and finally a small press decided to do the books but they didn't start getting published until they were all finished. So the books were actually written between 1981 and 1984.

Bigsby: You have written a detective novel under a pseudonym and you used the form of the detective novel in *The New York Trilogy*. Why are you drawn to that genre, not inhabiting it so much as using it?

Auster: In a very good detective novel every sentence is boiling with possibilities and you have to read it very attentively. It demands the kind of attention that every story should be given, but you are extra alert. You are constantly being compelled to ask questions and I think this is fascinating. The typical crime story itself does not interest me very much. I think the reason I used it in *The New York Trilogy* was because when I got a series of telephone calls from the Pinkerton Agency I began to think of the book in terms of detectives.

Bigsby: As you imply, you have a walk-on part – or, rather, something more than a walk-on part – in *The New York Trilogy* in that the central character in *City of Glass* is mistaken for somebody called Paul Auster and goes to meet him. Why did you choose to introduce this character, Paul Auster, into the novel?

Auster: I would not have begun to think about it if it had not been for the phone calls from the Pinkerton Agency. But there is a curious thing about all novels which utterly fascinates me. On the cover of the book is the author's name – Nathaniel Hawthorne, for example. And you open the book and suddenly someone is talking to you. It is not really Nathaniel Hawthorne, though it is Nathaniel Hawthorne's narrative voice. It is a voice not even pretending to be Hawthorne. There is a gap between Hawthorne the writer and Hawthorne the man, and that gap, that space, is something that interests me. I thought, if I could take my name off the cover of the book and put it inside the book as well maybe something interesting would begin to happen. It was also a way of taking more responsibility for what was happening, in a very basic personal way. Me, the person sitting here in front of you right now, moves into the book in part, I suppose, to make fun of myself. This Paul Auster is not such a smart guy. He is a kind of ludicrous character who misreads the situation entirely. This, in turn, was a way of saying that, finally, you are not responsible for what you do because you don't even know what you are doing when you write a novel.

Bigsby: You followed *The New York Trilogy* with *In the Country of Last Things*, which is ostensibly a futuristic novel but really seems like an echo chamber of twentieth-century horrors.

Auster: That is certainly the way I thought of it and I was surprised, to tell you the truth, when reviewers talked about it in terms of science fiction or the future. It seems to me absolutely about the present and the immediate past. I had a subtitle that I walked around with in my head as I was composing the book: *Anna Bloom Walks Through the Twentieth Century*, Anna Bloom being the name of the central character. It was not the twenty-first century, but the twentieth century. There are many things in that book that are lifted right out of history books and newspaper articles. I know it is all told from rather an oblique angle but it is not so distorted as you might think. There are people living in those kinds of circumstances even as we speak today. Right now.

Bigsby: That did seem to be a novel where I could feel anger.

Auster: It also took me a long time to write. Fifteen years. I started hearing her voice way back in 1970. I was just finishing being a student when all of a sudden there was this woman's voice talking through my head. It was Anna Bloom. I wrote a bit of it and then felt embarrassed. I asked myself, who is this and isn't it rather presumptuous of me to write through a woman's persona? So I put it aside and hoped it would not come back. Then two or three years later I started hearing her again. I started writing again and waited for the impulse to die out. It finally did. This went on, back and forth, for a long time and finally – as I was writing *The New York Trilogy*, I think it was probably between the second and third books – she came back and I sat down and wrote, maybe the first forty pages of the book as they are now. I gave them to my wife and I said, 'Isn't this garbage? Don't you think I should just stop doing it?' And she said, 'Oh, no, I like this very much. In fact I like this better than anything you have done before. You have to finish the book as a present to me. You just have to promise.' So I did, and I think if she had not pushed me to do it I would not have continued. In a way it is the book I am most attached to and in a way the one I am proudest of.

Bigsby: Why are you so attached to it?

Auster: I think it is the best. It came to me as a kind of inspiration and I don't know if I will be able to do such a thing again: something which floats like that, the narrative moving almost by itself, just generated by a voice. I certainly find her the most interesting character I have ever written about.

Bigsby: In the novel, Anna Bloom is reduced at one point to near-starvation and degradation. That is a state that a good few of your characters have to confront at one stage or another. In fact, one critic talked of your 'existential derelicts'. Is that a phrase that has some meaning, do you think?

Auster: It is a pretty phrase. I don't think I have ever heard it before. So many *i*'s in those words. It is good.

Bigsby: But those characters do recur. There are such figures in *Moon Palace*, *City of Glass* and, to some degree, *The Music of Chance*.

Auster: Well, with this difference: Anna Bloom doesn't choose it. These men in the other books have chosen it as a kind of test, a game that they are playing with themselves. It is a kind of inner brinkmanship to see how much they can start shoving overboard and how much they need to continue the voyage through life: what is necessary and what isn't necessary. And in almost every case they go too far. They push themselves beyond the point where they can recuperate their past lives.

Bigsby: Anna Bloom's name crops up in *Moon Palace* and there is a link, too, between *Moon Palace* and *The Music of Chance*, in the form of a car. It is almost as though you are forging a link between your books. Do you see your novels as standing separately or do they all add up to one huge novel?

Auster: For me it is one huge novel taken from different perspectives, different angles. I have this feeling that my imaginary universe, or my imagination pure and simple, has its limits. Everyone's does, in some way. You can think of it as a continent, a big mass of land. So far I have filled in a few little provinces here and there but if I can keep going long enough maybe some of these provinces will be contiguous and will begin to create a continent. I always feel that I have not even begun, that this is all just the preliminaries and maybe something really good is going to come later if I keep working hard enough.

Bigsby: If language is a thing that brings your characters together, something that they share whether they are aware of it or not, there is another aspect of your characters which seems to pull them apart, and that is that they seem to inhabit their own stories. They all have a story of their life that they have created, and that story, plausible as it is in terms of their own experience, is not the same as the story told by other characters in the book. So that while story brings people together, requiring somebody to speak and somebody to listen, it also separates people as they generate their narratives.

Auster: That is interesting. I had never quite thought of it in those terms: narratives intercepting, so to speak. Yes, there is something to what you say. Yet, at the same time, each person's story involves other people so that those other characters, in their individual stories, have to meet and form something else. I do feel that everything is connected, that every gesture made by every human being affects everybody else at the same time. There is a tremendous rippling effect that goes through the universe. When you are very alert you feel it, you feel all those vibrations around you. But there are times when you are not so alert, when you feel walled off. The important thing about novels, and why I want to keep writing them, is that they allow me to express my own contradictions, which maybe you could describe as my many voices or stories. This means that one does not have to be consistent. This is a means of accepting one's multiplicity. I think we are all many; we are all inhabited by several selves and in any given moment we will respond to a situation differently. The same thing which one day will make us weep, the next day will make us laugh and the third day leave us utterly indifferent. Yet each time it is the same person responding. That interests me.

Bigsby: Sometimes, disturbingly, your characters find themselves in somebody else's story.

Auster: I think so, yes. Again, interestingly, you are expressing things in ways that I haven't really considered before. I suppose you could say that Pozzi in *The Music of Chance* becomes part of Nashe's story and then the two of them become part of Stone's story. Yes, that is an interesting way to look at the book.

Bigsby: Did you raid your drama for *The Music of Chance*?

Auster: Yes. In the mid-1970s I wrote a few plays. They were pretty terrible. One of the plays was about two men building a wall. In fact, the entire play consisted of two men building a wall. By the end they were walled off from the audience. That was the entire action. It was not very good and so I put it away. But the wall was in my mind all those years afterwards and I wanted to attack it again. I had to do it better the second time and so that is where all of that business comes from in *The Music of Chance*, from that earlier play.

Bigsby: There is a sense in which *The Music of Chance* seems to be a mixture. It has echoes of a road movie at the beginning, while the poker game at its centre is almost a genre piece. But it also has overtones of fable and fairy story.

Auster: You mentioned fairy stories and that is, I suppose, how I would describe this book now. When I was writing it I was so immersed in the reality of the situation, the everydayness of what was going on, that I did not think of it in any terms other than a step-by-step progression of events. As I was getting towards the end of the book, however, it suddenly dawned on me that what I was doing was writing a fairy tale; it is almost classically simple and self-evident. A wanderer goes off on the road seeking his fortune. He meets up with another wanderer and they go to the ogre's castle and engage in a contest which they lose. Then, in order to win their freedom, they have to perform a certain task, like spinning gold out of straw. It is the structure of a Grimm's fairy tale, of a Hans Christian Andersen story, but I did not know that until it was finished.

Bigsby: In *The Locked Room* you say of a character who is a writer that the severity of his inwardness seemed to demand that particular profession. Would that be a description of you?

Auster: Probably. Yes, I wouldn't deny it. We all live alone inside ourselves. Our lives are unfolding inside our heads. Our bodies are in the world but the world is in our heads and that is where we experience it really. And I suppose that is where I have placed my books. We do have the possibility of connecting with other people; I don't deny that, but it is rare. It does not happen very often. I think it gets back to passion and love, and people loving each other. This is the greatest thing we can do and it is a way of overcoming that solitary singleness that everyone feels. I don't mean to be too pompous about it but in a way that is what books do, too. Maybe that is why I care about books so much. When you read something that is really good – not just run of the mill but something really good that marks you for the rest of your life – you feel in that narrative voice, on that page, the existence of another mind, another human being sitting behind that book, and a connection is made. It is a beautiful thing. It is one of the great experiences that we can have as people. Beyond that I don't know what there is. It's the best thing that we can possibly do.

Bigsby: How far do you feel that your work fits into an American tradition?

Auster: I feel that in many ways I am absolutely immersed in the American tradition and that I am writing about the same things that my American ancestors wrote about. The fact is, though, that the American novel changed. The novels of Melville and Hawthorne, the stories of Poe and the writings of Thoreau, for example, all of whom I am passionately interested in, were not about sociology, which is what the novel has come to concern itself with in the United States. Those writings had a metaphysical dimension, a philosophical dimension to them, which I think has been forgotten and ignored.

Bigsby: What does seem to be firmly in the American vein in your writing is the way in which characters tend to read every event, every conversation, as a clue to some sort of hidden meaning. Yours is a world of hieroglyphs and ciphers and clues.

Auster: You find that an American trait?

Bigsby: It is very powerfully there in Melville, Hawthorne and Poe.

Auster: Yes. I think so. I loved *The Narrative of Arthur Gordon Pym*. The other writer who I suppose had a tremendous impact on me was Dostoevsky. I read *Crime and Punishment* at the age of fifteen and that novel convinced me that what I wanted to do with my life was to write, because if there could be books like this then writing was the best thing you could possibly do. So I suppose it was a Russian novelist who knocked me down first and hardest.

In Conversation
with
John Barth

John Barth was born in Maryland in 1930 and educated at Johns Hopkins University in Baltimore. Maryland and its eastern shore feature in a number of his books. His first novel, *The Floating Opera*, was published in 1956 and followed by *The End of the Road* (1958). In 1960 he published The *Sot-Weed Factor*, a large-scale pastiche of an eighteenth-century novel. *Giles Goat-Boy* (1966) is an allegorical story in which the university campus becomes an image of the wider world. *Lost in the Funhouse* (1968) has a metafictional quality also present in *Chimera* (1972), which won the National Book Award, and *Letters* (1979). *Sabbatical* (1982) is set in and around Chesapeake Bay, as is *The Tidewater Tales: A Novel* (1987). *On With The Story* appeared in 1996. This interview was conducted at John Barth's home in Baltimore in 1982.

Bigsby: The Chesapeake Bay area provides the setting for a number of your novels.

Barth: I think we invent ourselves after the fact. One looks for metaphors in the things that one wants to write about anyhow. The notion of a border state, in its metaphorical sense, appeals to me: the business in fiction of tampering with, of negotiating, the borders between certain kinds of forms. I like to interpolate lines of verse and sometimes pieces of musical score and so forth into my novel. The novel as a form, like immigrant America and like a border state, is a permeable and malleable genre whose boundaries are always open to negotiation, I believe. I like the tide-water image, because of the haunting metaphor of things that come and go and come and go and recycle. I have done that for Maryland, and my fiction comes and goes now and then.

Bigsby: You are a twin.

Barth: Opposite-sex twin.

Bigsby: There is always something fascinating to people about twins, as though in a way you were in a position to see yourself from the outside, as though there is another model of you, the seeds of another model of you. Do you ever feel anything like that?

Barth: No, but that must be an occupational hazard of being an identical twin, where that sense of what Aristophanes, in Plato's *Symposium*, says is true of all of us, that we are the sundered half of a once primordial whole. In later life, when the normal course of maturation and differentiation separates people like myself and my sister, one is likely always to feel like half a person, and not in a crippled or a disabled sense. I understand profoundly the reason why twins have been used by almost every culture on the planet as a metaphor for whatever dualisms they had to deal with. I learned recently from *Scientific American*, or the science page of the *New York Times* – those dual organs of truth – that the sun may be a twin. Our sun may be a twin. The sun in the centre of our solar system may have a lost partner which recycles through our orbit every twenty-six million years or so, deflects a certain number of comets from their course which then smack our half of that twinship and change the course of evolution.

Bigsby: That is a useful theory. You would have to stick around for a long while to prove it.

Barth: Well, you know, as with Shakespeare's witches and fairies, for a writer it is enough that these things be metaphorically fecund; whether they turn out to be fact or not the case is of secondary importance.

Bigsby: When you were young, indeed right up to the time you went off to college, you were more interested in music than in literature.

Barth: Much more so.

Bigsby: Can you see the remnants of that in your work?

Barth: I can, though not in the sense that my fiction is especially musical. My early ambition to be a musician was not to be either a composer or a performer, but an orchestrator – what in those days of Big Band jazz we called arrangers – and there is the remnant I find in my work. I am most comfortable as a writer taking, as it were, a received melody line and a myth, or a worn-out literary convention like the epistolary novel – even an old mode like the eighteenth-century episodic Fieldingesque novel – and then reorchestrating it to my present purpose. That is what arrangers do and I find myself still doing that in my fiction, even sometimes just to the extent of taking a theme, a melody line, from my own previous fiction and feeling that I want to play that in another key, or fake it in a different tempo. Re-enactment is a theme that gets re-enacted ad nauseum in my books.

Bigsby: With two novels written and accepted for publication 1955 was a remarkable year for you. But your publisher didn't exactly take them as is, particularly *The Floating Opera*.

Barth: The first nine publishers didn't take it at all.

Bigsby: But it is not only that one that has been revised. Are novels ever finished in your mind?

Barth: They certainly are. In the case of my first novel, I was a very young man with a family, and ambitious as well as needy, and in the academic world, as in the world of the Muses and the world of landlords and grocery men, one needs a book out in order to go on and do the next thing, or even to survive in what one is doing. The first nine publishers who saw that novel didn't want it – I'm making up a number but it was something like that – the tenth, let's say, wanted it all right but didn't like something about the ending, in fact they didn't like the way it ended. I changed the ending to get the thing published. I don't like the idea of writers going through their works, poking at them and never having done with them after they are in print. They are done. You have had your say. But when the book, which had quickly gone out of print, later surfaced in paperback and hardcover editions, I took the opportunity to stick the right ending on, the one I had had in the first place, and take out the odd infelicity here and there. You don't want to be a Soviet historian about your own bibliography and go about changing it. Sometimes you are likely to muck it up. I had a grandfather-in-law, a Methodist minister, who was a Sunday painter and, as he got older and his vision began to fail, he recalled all his paintings – a very easy thing to do because they were held by his relatives – and repainted them all in gaudier colours, which he could still see in his failing years. There's a cautionary lesson there, I think, for a writer.

Bigsby: There was in those early novels a strong nihilistic strain.

Barth: So I thought at the time, in my innocence. The first novel, *The Floating Opera*, I think of as being a nihilist comedy; and the second, *At the End of the Road*, if not a nihilist tragedy then at least a nihilist catastrophe because it ends up with the female lead dead and everybody else more or less wrecked. When I began to write the third novel in what I had thought – again in that sort of arrogant, large-visioned way that many a youngster begins in the medium – was the last part of a trilogy, it ended being a pseudo-historical novel, *The Sot-Weed Factor*. This was to complete that trilogy on nihilism, as I brashly thought of it. I realized early into that book that what I had been really writing about all along was innocence, a subject more to my liking than philosophy in any of its forms. And that has, I believe, remained a kind of cardinal subject of mine ever since.

Bigsby: One thing you have done for the most part is avoid realism. I think you once said that realism is an aberration in the history of literature. And yet realism has a kind of gravitational pull. What is the appeal of that siren call?

Barth: Especially in the novel, we ought quickly to add. Of course, the novel itself is a Johnny-come-lately among literary forms and its appearance on the literary scene, if I remember from my student days, coincides roughly with realism as a predominant mode. In the history of the novel – and since it is the genre I mainly practise it is a genre whose history I respect and whose origins in the popular culture I respect as well – realism is more the norm, and irrealism the aberration. But in the history of tale-telling, it is my impression that the opposite can be argued. In any case, the pendulum does swing back and forth between those two and there are all sorts of compromises that writers make with these two antitheses. After doing a series of so-called mythological stories – some of the stories in *Lost in the Fun House* and the novellas in *The Chimera* series – I saw coming both a return to the state of Maryland, out of which I had dwelt for quarter of a century and, happily coinciding with that, a kind of *detente* with the realistic tradition. And in that large, fat novel, *Letters*, which everybody has so much trouble finishing and loving, except its author, there is a kind of extended hand offered again to realism. This runs through *Sabbatical* and indeed persists in the one now in progress. However, just as with locating the action in the state of Maryland, so locating it in realism is not something I regard myself as being stuck with for the rest of my life, any more than I was stuck with it in the middle.

Bigsby: As you suggest, *Letters* is a long novel. So is *The Sot-Weed Factor*.

Barth: So is *Giles Goat-Boy*. Three extended impositions on civilized attention.

Bigsby: Does length come from the form that you are using, in that the eighteenth-century, nineteenth-century novels you are parodying or pastiching were indeed long; or does it come from something else? Is it a sense of trying to embrace a totality of experience?

Barth: All of the above, plus half a dozen other things that probably even such a conscious, self-conscious writer as myself may be unaware of. I remember William Gass saying to my advanced apprentice writers at Johns Hopkins, who really are pre-professional people publishing their homework as they write, that his first loyalty as a writer is not to the readers – that is pandering, he says, self-indulgence – it is to the verbal object trying to get itself born. I like to remind people who think of me as being an extraordinarily long-winded novelist that I have also written what surely must be one of the shortest literary objects in the English language, the first story in the *Lost in the Fun House* series. It is ten words long but since it loops back on itself, it is also the longest story.

Bigsby: On the other hand, you have a character in *The Sot-Weed Factor*, Henry Burlingame, whose problem is that he doesn't know what to exclude. Is that an illness you suffer from?

Barth: It may be an illness; it is certainly an illness that not a few of my critics have felt that I suffer from. Sometimes in fiction, of course, they are in a spirit of exorcism, you know; there, but for the grace of the Muses, go I. I remind you, too, that coming to my undergraduate education as a rather callow and unread fellow it was my good luck to help to defray my tuition not only by playing jazz in Baltimore clubs, but by filing books in the Hopkins library stacks, and my stacks were the stacks of the classics library and an oriental seminary. We were given our cart of books and it was implied, though not overtly said, that we needn't be in a great hurry to get back. It was really just to help us pay off our tuition. So we would take our cart of books and we would disappear in the stacks for four or five hours and read what we were refiling. This is what I think of as my à la carte education. It was right off the book-filing cart. What I happened to be filing was not just Homer and Virgil and Ovid and Dante and the *Decameron*, the *Heptameron*, the *Pentameron*, and all those things, but also the wonderful, enormously long Sanskrit and Arabic works – *The Thousand and One Nights*, in Burton's ten-volume edition with seven supplemental volumes, the Sanskrit *Ocean Historian*; the *Pantatantra*. Early on I learned that whatever the modernist rage for economy of means there are other ways of going at the medium and that Orientals, at least, and our ancestors can sometimes have an astonishing patience with the very long narrative.

Bigsby: In a sense, your novels are less an imitation of life than they are an imitation of literature. That's to say they are full of documents and stories, some of them real, some of them not. Why are you interested in experience as it is refracted through other documents, other stories?

Barth: Damned if I know. I could give a spiel but it would only be a spiel. I suspect it is simply part of my temperament as a writer, but I have become sensitive to the subject since the belief seems to be abroad – and I find it simply mistaken – that fiction about fiction or language about language is somehow therefore not about life in our house. Aristotle's dictum that the proper subject of literature is human experience, its happiness and its misery, is not questioned. I second that motion promptly. But, after all, in most other aspects of human experience – in everything from having a conversation to walking upright or welding automobile frames with robot machines – feedback loops and a kind of consciousness of what we are doing while we are doing it is taken for granted. That is how we function as human beings. That is how most animals function as animals. Language is almost never just about itself, but in my view it is almost always also about itself. If you strip that notion of its by now unpleasant modernist associations, it quickly becomes apparent that it is as old as literature itself. It is so true that I am convinced that if the first story ever told began with the words 'Once upon a time . . .', the second story ever told probably began with the words, 'Once upon a time there was a story that began with the words "Once upon a time . . ."' We go through life telling stories, listening to stories. Listen to us now. We are listening to what we are saying as we are saying it, making mid-course corrections sentence by sentence. We go through our lives the same way, reviewing what we have done. The metaphor I like to use comes from coastal piloting – I am an amateur sailor too. In deduced reckoning, one determines where to go by determining where one is by reviewing where one has been. And that, of course, involves an element of self-consciousness. That is the self-consciousness or self-reflexiveness that I find in my fiction to be simply imitative of life, of living life.

Bigsby: If experience is a kind of fiction and history is certainly a kind of fiction, are some fictions more equal than others?

Barth: I suspect that some fictions are a good deal more equal than others. I suspect that the final measure for that, along with the artist's energies and skill, is the power and depth of a moderately knowledgeable reader's response to them. Quite so.

Bigsby: Were you surprised when *Giles Goat-Boy* appeared in the best seller list in 1966?

Barth: Astonished.

Bigsby: Why do you think it provoked the popular response that it did?

Barth: Because *The Sot-Weed Factor* should have been on the list. That was its predecessor, and it should have been, but I think it was inattentively published and then the word got around that it was not an uninteresting novel. And so people who buy books and sell books looked with more anticipation, more eagerness, for its successor than they had looked for it. Its successor came along: a much more difficult novel and tiring to read, I think. It also happens to be the least favourite of my novels for me to remember. I am more unhappy with more things about *Giles Goat-Boy* than I am about any other book that I have published, including *Letters*, which is a much longer and more difficult read than I had meant it to be. It just came out that way.

Bigsby: What are you unhappy with in *Giles Goat-Boy*?

Barth: Part of it is the plan of that novel: it figures the universe under the figure of a big university, not very much of a metaphor in the American 1950s and early 1960s when academic gigantism was at its most rampant. Part of the game was that the allegory would not be very sophisticated; it would be sophomoric. But of course it is bad strategy to play that game for very long. It is a novel that I could not have made shorter, and yet I think it is a novel that is regrettably long. The brightest critic I read on that novel said, after all, that the allegory there is just a manner of speaking. And of course that is exactly what I intended, that it be just a manner of speaking. The most tiresome aspect of allegory is to be taken as a joke, as part of the joke. But it was also a joke that many people found tiresome and that in memory I find a little tiresome myself.

Bigsby: You are, as you say, an old-fashioned storyteller. That is the tradition you are picking up and the unravelling of a story clearly matters to you, as does character. What is the relationship between that side of you and the very self-conscious game-player who intervenes in that process?

Barth: Probably the difference between left brain and right brain. Of course, that kind of thing comes naturally to one who has been a twin:

one is used to being two things at the same time, or half of one. The storytelling I suckled from Scheherazade and I circle back to it again and again. The formalism probably comes from nothing more interesting than the fact that when I was a young apprentice and a student it was my generation who did their university work and did their serious reading and orientation as prospective writers by cutting their teeth on the high modernists, on Joyce and Pound and so forth. So, not a few of us thought that literature ought to be tricky. And I haven't repudiated that at all, though I do have great respect for the other swing of the pendulum, which dominates American fiction now. The pope of that church is Raymond Carver, whose advice to my students was – no tricks.

Bigsby: Saul Bellow once said that to be technically up-to-date is the least important attribute of a writer, to which you added, yes, but it may nevertheless be essential. Why?

Barth: Quite so. When I made that remark the 'why' was because it seems to me that we are living in high-tech times. Modernism never took that much hold, I guess, in the United Kingdom and in America as it did in South America and Europe. But we don't object to high-tech athletics, for example. We don't object so much to high-tech music, certainly not to high-tech performers of music. But when a writer comes on, particularly in this country, as less than straightforwardly rural, almost folksy in his or her approach, they suspect him of being tricksy, and tricksiness won't do. But, God knows, when you look at Homer and Virgil and Dante and Ovid – who wears his tricks so lightly that you scarcely know them – you are in the presence of formally very cunning and even crafty art. Bellow himself has never been innocent of that kind of knowledge, but he has chosen, for reasons of his own, to look suspiciously at the whole phenomenon of literary modernism. I believe Bellow would trace his spiritual ancestry much more directly from the nineteenth century, from writers with high moral concern, writers who – in the unsympathetic words of my colleague Hugh Kenner giving advice to anybody who wants to win a Nobel Prize – write elevated moral sentiments in language easily translated into Swedish.

Bigsby: Your career stretches over a period in which there have been fundamental changes in American society. Has that entered into your work?

Barth: My work hasn't been very much socially responsible, that's for sure. I have said somewhere that I think any writer – if he or she is not living in a cave – is likely to be responsive to changes in his or her society. I don't think he or she need feel responsible to such changes. You don't have to write about them any more than I have to try consciously to be American, you know. I am that and I am a novelist and not a short-story writer.

Bigsby: I wonder, though, if your response to what was going on in American society doesn't spill over into *Sabbatical*?

Barth: It spills over into *Letters*, too, of course.

Bigsby: Exactly. It begins in *Letters* and intensifies in *Sabbatical*, where plot, fiction and character aren't only literary constructions, because the CIA also has its plot; the CIA has its fictions and it creates identities as well.

Barth: Quite so.

Bigsby: Am I right in thinking that you are interested in that novel in the nexus between a writer's fictions and public fictions?

Barth: You are right. And the equation of two different kinds of plots also informs *The Sot-Weed Factor*, long before Vietnam and the CIA in its more egregious aspects had hit the fan of public attention. It is resurrected very much for that reason. But I can't even say now whether *Sabbatical*, and I hasten to add its successor in the works, is preoccupied, sometimes even a little bit obsessed, with the CIA – which is, after all, rather small potatoes as American intelligence and paramilitary institutions go – because it is a metaphor for other things that I am interested in, or vice versa. It was impressive to me, coming back to the Chesapeake Bay area after being away from it for so long, to be reminded that when one lives here one lives very near the seat of power. That is why the British fought here in 1812. To take a simple example, one that runs through *Sabbatical* and its successor, if one is simply bopping around in a sailboat on Chesapeake Bay, you are likely to run into dead KGB agents or CIA agents or atomic submarines cruising up to the Naval Academy. There is probably more firepower, in addition to nerve-gas establishments and every other sort of frightful thing, around these placid waters that James Mitchener writes about than there is almost anywhere else on the globe. We are living in a bloody powder-keg here. The great decisions are made not far down the road from where you and I are sitting and speaking right now. That sense of them mucking up my Chesapeake Bay with their bloody submarines and aircraft carriers and underground agents and hanky-panky is strong. I am not innocent about it. I know it has gone on at least since Benjamin Franklin and Thomas Jefferson were on the scene. But I was reminded of it in that forcible way by coming back here. Just as one was reminded by the Vietnam War of the political aspects of many features of our life that we had perhaps been less than perfectly conscious of before the radical students and the radical teachers rubbed our noses in them. That was an innocence well lost.

Bigsby: I notice that in the course of this interview you have referred to Scheherazade, who becomes a patron saint of writers. Is that because she had no choice but to spin stories?

Barth: I keep changing my mind about what the image of Scheherazade means to me. At first it seemed that she is a kind of obvious metaphor for the condition of all writers, particularly writers in universities. It is publish or perish. She is the very paradigm of that state of affairs. And that is true, by extension, of all writers – and all entertainers, for that matter – and literature surely is a variety of entertainment. We all sleep with an audience that we may at any time fatally cease to please. The relation of Scheherazade to the king is a terrifying one. He holds her future in his hands, as do the audiences of us all. But, at the same time, it is important to notice that that no doubt terrifying relationship is at the same time inspiring and fertilizing in both senses. The woman does publish a whole lot of stories. *A Thousand and One Nights* of them. And at the end she trots in three children, who she has born to her imperious auditor over that period. I have just written an essay in which I have cracked the secret of Scheherazade's menstrual cycle, which nobody even knew was a problem until it occurred to me that it was. Just how did that get done? And why are there a 1,001 nights rather than 999 or 2,002 or some other neat number? I have figured out why, but I am not going to tell you. You will have to go read the essay.

IN CONVERSATION
WITH
ROBERTSON DAVIES

Robertson Davies was born in Thamesville, Ontario, in 1913 and educated at Queen's University and Balliol College, Oxford. He lived for a time in England where he worked as an actor, before returning to Canada. He worked as editor of *Saturday Review* and later as a publisher. He subsequently became Professor of English at the University of Ontario. This interview was conducted in September 1991, in the library of Massey College, of which Davies was once Master. His first book, *Tempest Tost*, appeared in 1951, part of a trilogy including *Leaven of Malice* (1954), and *A Mixture of Frailties* (1958). Subsequent works include *Fifth Business* (1970), *What's Bred in the Bone* (1986), which was shortlisted for the Booker Prize, *Murther and Walking Spirits* (1991), and *The Cunning Man* (1994). Robertson Davies died in December, 1995.

Bigsby: It has always struck me that there is a theatrical quality to many of your novels.

Davies: The theatrical way of looking at life was one with which I had been acquainted from my childhood. My parents were very literary people and crazy about the arts. They were both extremely fond of music; they both played things and sang. They read a great deal and were mad about the theatre, so that the conversation in my family home when I was a little boy was all about these things. They just sort of soaked in without my being aware of them. Long before I had seen a theatre I knew about theatres and it seemed to me that people identified themselves and explained themselves a great deal through dialogue. I was very interested in that and tried to get as much as possible of that into my books. When I was a boy and about to read a book I leafed through it and if there was a lot of dialogue I knew it was a good book, and if it was thick, thick, thick, with pages of description, then I did not want to read it.

Bigsby: The theatre offers something that the novel doesn't; it offers a sense of community, of working together with people to create something. On the other hand there is a negative side to that because the work is not entirely your own. Is that perhaps why you moved away from theatre?

Davies: The work is not entirely your own and it can be extremely wounding and disappointing to discover how little your work counts for in the totality of a theatrical production. I got a heavy dose of that when finally a play of mine was produced and went to Broadway. By the time it got there the stars, the director and the principal actors had mauled it around so much, and played with it so greatly, that it lost any colour or flavour or form that I had given it. I thought, 'This is the life of a dog. I am through with it.'

Bigsby: That production went to New York, but on the whole your plays have not exported, not travelled, whereas your novels most definitely have.

Davies: I tried to get people interested when my plays were on. I remember that the chief reader for H.M. Tennant and Company, who I won't identify, wrote me a letter finally saying, 'Mr Davies, you must understand that nobody, *but* nobody, is interested in Canada.' I thought, 'So, they are just interested in about two square miles of the West End. Well, to hell with them.' And that was that.

Bigsby: Your first novel, *Tempest Tost*, is actually about an amateur production of a play. It almost seems to me that it could have been a play.

Davies: It was originally intended to be a play but when I became so browned off with the theatre I thought I would try my hand at doing it as a novel. I did, and it was accepted right away and published both in England and the United States. It is still in print. That is a lot better than a couple of weeks in the West End, you know.

Bigsby: It strikes me that the theatre has never entirely gone out of your system, not just because of this business of an emphasis on dialogue but because of a fascination with the process of disguise, of appearing to be what you are not, of magic, of conjuring acts on the stage, as subject matter and as process. Isn't it, in part at least, that which interests you?

Davies: It does, because what you encounter in the theatre is people, characters, who change very radically in the course of the play and that is something which is observable in life. The theatre, in other words, is a paradigm of ordinary life and as such is intensely interesting and very, very useful. Everyone is acting a part most of the time, and the work of the perceptive literary artist is to find them in the dressing room and see what they are doing, what costume they are issuing, what make-up they are putting on, what lines they read, what is really going on inside them. The primary thing, though, is what it always was, to get your audience and hold them.

I don't want to be a bore about this but I have always said to young, would-be writers who come to me and say, 'What do you think the writer's position should be on this, that or the other?', that the writer's position is what it was in the Middle Ages when a man went into the market place and sat down on a mat and beat on a copper bowl and said, 'Give me a copper coin and I will tell you a golden tale.' And when he had collected enough people and enough copper coins he told them his golden tale. Most of them were illiterate. He might himself have been illiterate but this was still drama and the novel and the romance. That is what lies at the bottom of the whole thing. You can be as refined, as splendid, as delicate as you wish but it must be on top of some strength or you have got nothing.

Bigsby: That suggests that story and narrative are fundamental to you.

Davies: Narrative is very, very important; without narrative you are nowhere. Unless you have got a story you might as well close up your shop.

Bigsby: The first novel turned out to be the first of a trilogy. Now there are three trilogies and that suggests that you feel the need for space. You are not a great believer in the slim volume. You were a journalist. Hemingway's experience of being a journalist was to produce a minimalist prose. Your response has been completely different.

Davies: I hope I don't produce extravagantly over-written novels. I try to be as compressed as possible because as a journalist, as Hemingway said, you can't twaddle on eternally. You must get your piece said and that is the end of that. There seems to be quite a lot to be said about the kind of themes that I tackle but I try to say it as concisely as is consistent with not writing a kind of telegraphic narrative.

Bigsby: Did you know in any of those cases that there were going to be three parts to the story?

Davies: No, never. It was simply that having written that first novel some of the characters in it attracted me so strongly that I thought there was more to be said about them. So I got them into a second novel with some new characters and then it seemed to me that there was still a third novel to be written about that particular Canadian town that was really a kind of English Georgian town transferred to Canada. I ended up with three novels, but they were not linked except by a few characters and the examination of that particular kind of provincial life.

Bigsby: This trilogy is *Tempest Tost*, *Leaven of Malice* and *Mixture of Frailties*. But isn't the essential story the education of its central character, the opening up of a life for her?

Davies: It is that German thing, the *Bildungsroman*, except that, perhaps unusually, it is about a girl rather than a young man.

Bigsby: She is a musician, like the character in your later novel, *The Lyre of Orpheus*. Is music important to you in terms of your prose style as well as subject matter?

Davies: Yes, immensely, because I have a very keen ear for the rhythm of music and also of prose. I am a great supporter of what Thomas Mann said when he explained that he did not write poetry because he was interested in the infinitely more sophisticated and difficult rhythms of prose. I follow along in that line and I write my novels – as many people have commented, some favourably, some unfavourably – to be heard rather than just be taken in by the eye. I condemn the speed-reader. You don't get the juice out of a book, certainly not out of my books, if you rush at it and gobble it.

Bigsby: Are you a believer in hearing the voice of the writer?

Davies: Yes, I am. I have, I think, shown that this works because I have been jolting around a very great deal the last few years and reading aloud from my books and a lot of people say that they find this very helpful in bringing them to life because they know how I meant them to sound.

Bigsby: So there is a touch of Mark Twain and Charles Dickens in you?

Davies: A bit of that. I have also advised readers to build up a kind of repertory company of first-rate actors in their own minds and cast books and get them performed in their minds that way. This is not my idea. The theatre critic James Agee used to say that whenever he read *Dombey and Son* he always cast John Gielgud as Mr Dombey, as he was the perfect Mr Dombey. If you go to the movies a lot you can cast a novel very readily and it gives it an enormous amount of swat when you are reading it.

Bigsby: We were commenting on the musicians in your work but in the trilogy which includes *The Rebel Angels*, *What's Bred in the Bone* and *The Lyre Orpheus*, there is also an artist who is a central figure. It seems that not only are you a writer but in your books you are fascinated with the process of producing art of one kind or another.

Davies: Yes, I am, and that has led me in some interesting directions in my reading and study and personal experience. I am very much interested in the thought of C.G. Jung and this provides an insight into the artistic process which you do not get, for instance, in the deep psychology of Sigmund Freud. Freud once said, very handsomely, that before the mystery of artistic creations psychoanalysis must lay down its arms. Jung didn't say quite as much. He had a go at offering some notion of where the well-springs of this creation come from. He had some encounters, for instance, with James Joyce, which were very, interesting in this respect. Art is not such a splendid irreproachable element in life as people suppose it. It spreads all through life like smoke or like a stain, and collecting it and turning it into a work of art is only part of the job.

Bigsby: Is there a tension between your interest in your characters' struggles to liberate themselves and forge their own identities and the Jungian notion of an archetype which would make them simply re-enactments of archetypal experiences?

Davies: No, not wholly that. Archetypal experiences seize upon people and use them sometimes in ways that are very detrimental to their happiness and wellbeing, but the Jungian approach is to suggest that until middle-life your struggle is to find your place in the world, find your orientation in your work, in your sexual life, in your attitude towards mankind; then, after that, your principal attention is devoted to discovering yourself and becoming as intelligently acquainted with yourself as you can manage. That does not mean, as many people suppose, beating yourself like a wretched slave who has been found out stealing from the till but, rather, trying to bring a quality of charity and decency and even realism to a notion of what you are.

Bigsby: Your most recent trilogy – which is now already being called the Cornish trilogy, after Francis Cornish, the central character – raises the question of pastiche, the degree to which an artist is an imitator of others, in his case a very conscious imitator of others. Where does that fascination come from?

Davies: An artist is necessarily an imitator of others. Nobody originates an entirely new style or an entirely new aspect of life which he captures in his art. For instance, the surrealists, who seemed to be such an extraordinary outburst when they first appeared in the late 1920s, were really doing something that had been done in the seventeenth century. There is literally nothing new under the sun and the artist has to decide what he is going to pick out of the toy box and use for his own entertainment. The perpetual search for something new, I feel, is extremely delusive. When people talk about the avant-garde I often wonder how many of them have had much military experience: the avant-garde are the people that you throw out in front to get killed so that the rear-guard may come up and take the fort. Who wants to be in the avant-garde? The easiest way to become old hat is to be at the forefront of the latest movement.

Bigsby: In the case of Francis Cornish doesn't this business of pastiche raise another question, a fundamental question about the nature of truth. Not only is he faking paintings, but he is also a spy. In a sense, then, his life is a lie. He is a man who is creating a semblance of a real which is not real.

Davies: I think that that is true but I think that this is simply because he could not say what he wanted to say as an artist in what would be regarded as a contemporary style, one that would be recognized by people surrounding him as 'of today'. But what he had to say was timeless; it was about himself, it was a reconsideration of his life and he could only do that in terms of an art of a bygone day.

Bigsby: Wearing a mask may actually be a way of enabling you to tell the truth?

Davies: Absolutely. When the Greek actors assumed a mask of God what they said took on godlike significance.

Bigsby: But there is a fundamental paradox, isn't there, for the writer, in that he is trying to tell the truth through lies.

Davies: But all art is paradox. You knock out the paradox from life and you pretty well get back to the cave.

Bigsby: On the face of it you appear to be a realist as a novelist. You create dense, believable, social worlds inhabited by people who speak a believable language. On the other hand, something in you seems to be in rebellion against realism.

Davies: Reality is a kind of mask people wear. We all tend to approach one another and behave towards one another in what we believe to be an acceptable manner. This is to wear a mask. We all wear masks all the time and in my novels I try to get behind the mask and ask what really is making the people behave as they do.

Bigsby: But when you introduce magic or tarot cards into your books these are not set up as Aunt Sallys. There is surely an element of deliberate disturbance in the text as though they constitute a kind of truth.

Davies: That is something I do in order to torment the extreme rationalists because what is contained in astrology and the tarot and gnosis was taken with extraordinary seriousness a few hundred years ago by people who were just as intelligent as we are. St Augustine had a lot of time for astrology. You have got to ask yourself, am I greater than Augustine? I wonder if I am. This sort of intuitive approach to the unseen world was the science of an earlier day. Nowadays we regard science as quantification. The question is whether truth is statistical, subject to experiment and proof, or whether it is moving and shifting and many coloured. We have only five senses. Suppose we had two more, what an awful lot we would apprehend that we don't see now in the world around us. But scientists – not the best ones, but some of them – behave as though the evidence of our five senses and the things we can make from them can explain the universe. They have a hope!

Bigsby: Is there an element in writing, an element in art, which cannot be accounted for: an element of mystery?

Davies: Yes, although I would not like to appear to be backing some of the nonsense that is talked about writing. People sometimes ask me if my characters ever take over and carry the story away from something I had originally intended. The fact of the matter is that they do but it isn't as if I were seized by a group of ghosts and carried into a realm utterly unknown to me; it is just that in my work I see that there are possibilities and things to be done that are much more interesting than I was able to foresee when I began.

Bigsby: The theme that lies at the root of a great deal of your writing is the isolation of the human spirit. Why that theme above others?

Davies: Because it seems to be one which we don't like to face but which we would be well advised to face and consider. We are born alone, we die alone and, to an extraordinary extent, we live alone. More than we suppose; even the most intimate human relationships have their limits and you just have to live inside yourself twenty-four hours a day for as many days as you have. If you have any sensitivity or any awareness of your own life and the life around you, you have to take your knocks, recognizing what is going on, what is happening to you, who you are, how you are affecting other people: all the extraordinary complexity of life which you have to bear as an individual. And that complexity is rooted in isolation.

Bigsby: Isn't there a sense in which art is a denial of that isolation?

Davies: Exactly, you have put your finger on it. That is why it is good.

Bigsby: I sometimes get the feeling that you have no time for small emotions, for niceness, politeness.

Davies: That reminds me of a story which is very dear to my wife because I met her at the Old Vic, where she worked for many years in close association with the great Lilian Baylis. She said that Miss Baylis had something which she said to all the people who worked for her: 'Come to me in your joys, dear, and come to me in your sorrows, but I have no time for chat.' You know, this is a very good attitude. You can wipe out an awful lot of rubbish if you have no time for chat. I have to make time for chat because not to do so is to be harsh and abrasive in a way that I don't choose to be, but, oh, one gets so tired of chat.

Bigsby: But there is a harsh and abrasive side to you. Sometimes that has been directed at your fellow Canadians and you seem to get a certain amount of pleasure out of that.

Davies: Perhaps I have tried to goad them into more mental activity. My complaint about my fellow countrymen is that they are so intellectually lazy. I would not say they have had an easy time but they have never had to reflect or take a psychological approach to their nationhood, and this is what I am always trying to get them to do. Very frequently the only thing you can do is dance around and hit them on the head with a jester's bauble and abuse them and try to goad them into some sort of response. It is not easy.

Bigsby: I am interested in that phrase 'jester's bauble' because it is your humour that really holds you back from following the logic of the critique you develop sometimes.

Davies: Yes, I know that. A story that my wife and I are extremely fond of is that some years ago, here in this college, I met a group of high-school students. Young people ask some very good questions but they had a teacher with them who was a terrible boob. He was anxious to show his students that he really could put me in my place, so he glared at me across the table and said, 'Did you ever think that your use of humour is going to keep your books from living?' And I thought, what does this man suppose that humour is, something you get out of a bottle and swig down before you write, or that it is a venom that you inject into the cookie you offer to the public? It is true that if you take a humorous attitude towards things a lot of people are going to miss what you are talking about, refuse to accept that you are serious. But I believe earnestly, as Bernard Shaw did when he said that he had learned how to write from Mozart, that you have to discover what urgently needs saying and then say it with the utmost frivolity. I can't help doing that. It is bred in the bone.

Bigsby: Do you think being a Canadian writer, living in a country which is in some way on the margin – geographically on the edge and made to feel such by the proximity of the United States – explains something of your work and your attitudes?

Davies: Yes, I think it is to a considerable extent the work of a person who is not at the very heart of the action but who gets a good view of the action by virtue of having an excellent seat.

Bigsby: Isn't there a risk, though, that that very detachment may breed a kind of sentimentality?

Davies: Yes, it can.

Bigsby: Do you think there is a sentimentalist in you?

Davies: People sometimes think so but I don't think it is sentimentality. I prefer to think of it as a gentleness which is less easily seen in modern fiction and in modern drama than it used to be. People used to delight in sentimental plays, before the First World War for instance; they don't any more. But I think they have now gone over the edge and believe that life is simply a can of worms. It isn't a can of worms. There is great beauty, great splendour to be found in it, and great nobility and a great human quality to be found in people. We should not miss this just because we have found out that a lot of people are scoundrels and that a lot of school principals are child abusers and everybody has Aids. It is so easy to make yourself seem sophisticated and highly intelligent by taking a negative view of everything. In committees it is so often the negative vote that carries the day, because negativism, to simple minds, always looks like truth and intelligence. But daring demands that you take a positive view, and I am all for daring.

IN CONVERSATION
WITH
JOAN DIDION

J oan Didion was born in 1934. Her novels include *Run River* (1963), set in the Sacramento Valley, California; *Play It As It Lays* (1970), also set in California; and *A Book of Common Prayer* (1977), in which a woman from that state is exposed to life in Central America. Didion followed this with *Democracy* (1984) which draws on another favourite location, Hawaii, and *The Last Thing He Wanted* (1996). She has also written a number of non-fiction books, including *The White Album* (1979), which features autobiographical material; *Salvador* (1983), which draws on her experiences of El Salvador's civil war; and *After Henry* (1992). This interview dates from 1984.

Bigsby: Who is the Joan Didion who introduces herself at the beginning of *Democracy*?

Didion: Well, of course, it's me. It's also not me. One of the really comforting things about writing a novel, one of the few comforting things, is that you are somebody else when you are sitting at your desk. You are not necessarily stuck with yourself all the time. You are and are not yourself. I don't think about it. It is almost a superstitious thing. You do not spend a lot of time trying to analyze why you do something or how you do it because you are afraid that you will wake up and it will go away.

Bigsby: None the less, why did you use that autobiographical third person?

Didion: I was scared to death, is why. I could not seem to get into this story and finally I thought, *just break through*. The beginning of the novel is about somebody, the author, having a hard time writing a novel.

Bigsby: I wonder if narrative doesn't become the subject of the book.

Didion: The subject of the book is narrative, that's right. I could see that once I was into it.

Bigsby: And history is a narrative, too.

Didion: The whole question of making sense of your life or making sense of what is going on, has to do with narrative, with finding a narrative.

Bigsby: The novel is called *Democracy*, which brings to mind Henry Adams's novel of the same name, which looks at the political and moral corruption of the 1860s. How far were you consciously setting out to do the same thing for the 1960s and 1970s?

Didion: Not at all. That isn't what I was setting out to do. What I was setting out to do was write a romance of the Pacific, a romance as opposed to a novel. That was the only thought in my mind. When I started it I was calling it by other names. I called it *Angel Visits* for a while, and I called it *Pacific Distances* for a while. Then, when I got near finishing it, I didn't like either one of those and so it was nothing for a while. I just called it *AV* because that was what was written over all the boxes of throwaway pages, *AV* for *Angel Visits*. When I finished it my husband read it and said you should call it *Democracy*. I thought that was a terrific idea because there was a line from the original *Democracy* that I always think about, in which one of the characters says to another, 'Democracy is shaking my world to pieces.' That just seemed a good title. It didn't start out to be about Washington.

Bigsby: It does turn into a kind of double crack-up, doesn't it: the crack-up of an individual and the crack-up of a society?

Didion: When I started writing the novel, years and years ago, it was about a family in Honolulu. Many generations were going to be involved and it was all going to take place at some kind of family reunion. I even thought it would all be in dialogue; that was going to be the technical problem. It was all going to have a very light surface but I couldn't get too interested in any of it so then I thought maybe somebody's been killed. It just sort of built from there, so the whole Washington part of it came later.

Bigsby: The book begins with the atomic tests in the 1950s. Were they the beginning of some process in America for you?

Didion: It didn't mean that to me when I wrote it. The reason I did this specifically was that I wanted to hear Jack Lovett talking and I wanted him to be talking about something relatively technical. It so happened that I had been up to Livermore, one of the big labs that the University of California runs for the government, and at Livermore I had been lent a book called *Twenty-Five Years at Livermore*, a kind of twenty-fifth anniversary book. It had pictures of all the early tests in it and it had people standing around where they had the tests, at Charleston. There was one that just stuck in my mind. I had it pinned up in my office at one point. It was of one of the physicists wearing a bathing suit and bathing trunks. He is barefoot and he is holding a fish. He has a crew-cut and is just somebody holding a fish, except he's got this AEC badge on. That whole thing interested me, so I just wanted to do something with it.

Bigsby: There is a blend of fact and fiction in the novel. Every now and then it roots itself in the historical moment. Does that blend imply that the line between fact and fiction is not a clear one to you, that it is by its nature blurred?

Didion: It's hard to know. For some reason I always thought this novel took place in real time. It had to do with real people. Real events would be involved. I specifically wanted the Fall of Saigon because it was such an intense time in this country. I was in fact, as the Joan Didion in the book was, teaching at Berkeley then and it was a very peculiar time on the campus. In my last novel, *A Book of Common Prayer*, there were no real events. It took place in an imaginary country. There were no references to real people that I can think of, except perhaps to Chicago in the late 1960s.

Bigsby: Why in *Democracy* do you keep interrupting to remind us that it is in fact only a fiction?

Didion: Every time you do something you set yourself a different sort of technical problem, and the technical problem here was to tell the reader that it wasn't true and yet make him believe that it was: to tell the reader that it was just something that I was making up and yet make him go along with it. That was the challenge.

Bigsby: So it is like the conjurer who shows you how the trick is done and then does it anyway?

Didion: Yes, that was the technical trick.

Bigsby: *Democracy* is told in a very fragmented, dislocated grammar. It is as though language itself had some kind of pressure on it. What is the source of that pressure?

Didion: For every novel you find a different voice or a slightly different tone. It is hard to hit on it and by the time you have hit on it you don't know exactly where it comes from. I actually wanted to make the tone in this one quite rich. I wanted to have a lot of allusion in it, a sense of richness and fullness in it.

Bigsby: But that richness is contrasted with paragraphs that last for two words, a kind of brittleness of language.

Didion: Yes, that is what is so nice. You have just got to change the rhythm, change the tape.

Bigsby: Those characters that are most sympathetic – and I suppose

that would be Inez Christian Victor herself, and the espionage agent –
are mysterious people. It is almost as though you have a distrust of
people or characters who define themselves too clearly, too precisely.

Didion: In real life it always seems to me that all you know of people
is what you see. You only know them externally and that is really the
only way that I can know a character in fiction, externally, by the way
they appear in a series of perhaps revealing and perhaps not revealing
scenes. Sometimes when you know a person they do seem out of
character quite often.

Bigsby: If they are the sympathetic characters, I suppose the one who
one dislikes most is the liberal senator. Do you think there is a risk
there of moving towards parody, caricature?

Didion: If you say there is, then there is. It hadn't occurred to me. He
is not a very filled-in character because he didn't interest me a whole
lot. I never even thought, for example, where Harry Victor came from,
where he was born. Are his parents alive? We don't know that; I don't
even know that myself. It never even crossed my mind.

Bigsby: There is a curious sense, both in this novel and I think in some
of the essays, that political commitment is either seen as self-serving
or evidence of a private guilt or neurosis. Do you believe that there is
such a thing as genuine political commitment?

Didion: Of course I think there is, but I don't see a great deal of it in
the United States right now. I don't see what passes for politics in this
country as being anything that approaches political commitment. I
see it as a form of careerism. It doesn't have anything to do with
political ideas.

Bigsby: You had a kind of antagonistic response to the 1960s. It is as
though you have a long-running battle with that decade. Is that going
on here, both in the figure of the senator and in the self-concern of
some of the characters?

Didion: The 1960s were an interesting time here. I have never quite
figured them out and that is probably why my relationship to the
decade is antagonistic, or may seem antagonistic, because it remains
mysterious to me. That is why it is still alive in my mind. Something

really interesting was going on. I don't know what yet, or I still haven't got to the bottom of what it was. It was either the beginning or the end of some long-term social change in America. We tend to think it was the beginning of a post-industrial society. It may have been, I don't know. I would say we had probably had a post-industrial society before that, so whether it is the beginning or end of something it is hard for me to say.

Bigsby: Did your book on El Salvador imply that you have moved towards a political position that is different from the one you once had. I think you once described yourself as a registered Republican.

Didion: I was a registered Republican; I am a registered Democrat now. I just registered as a Democrat so I could vote for Jerry Brown in California. Political parties don't seem to have any relationship to political ideas, so I don't think my ideas have changed that much actually.

Bigsby: There seems almost an accusation in this book, which is levelled at some of your characters, but also at America, and that is that America has a disregard for history.

Didion: America does have no sense of history, no regard for history, and no sense that history matters or is serious, no sense that events matter or are serious, no sense of responsibility in a certain way.

Bigsby: Exactly, the characters don't want any consequences from their actions. They want to live in a perpetual present.

Didion: Yes, and they do.

Bigsby: Apart from anything else, you are addressing the situation in Vietnam in *Democracy*. When you dealt with the situation in El Salvador you wrote a non-fiction book. Here you have chosen fiction. What determines your decision as to which form you are going to use?

Didion: Salvador was a very specific, very straightforward thing. I wanted to go down and see what was going on, see what it felt like and tell somebody else what it felt like and what seemed to be going on. My feelings about the end of the Vietnam War were very much more complicated and had to do with a whole range of other things. Also, had I been able to go out to Saigon during the war, which I never did, I might have written something in a non-fiction form, but after the fact it was overlaid with a lot of other stuff. It was part of a historical experience.

Bigsby: You say at the end of *Democracy* that it wasn't the book you set out to write and you were no longer the same person who set out to write it. In what sense were you a different person by the end of the novel?

Didion: I ended up a lot older. A lot of things happened. We had different kinds of personal and public disasters. I started this book seven years before it was published.

Bigsby: I have noticed that in this novel, and in your other work, you seem to be drawn to extreme situations, particularly to violence, more particularly to murder. It is there in some of your essays. Why is that?

Didion: I have a very short attention span. I can't write a scene in which two people are talking to each other about their relationship. I can't do it, so I tend to draw them into a situation where something is happening. So things keep happening in my books because that is the only way I can keep awake at the typewriter.

Bigsby: But isn't it also a part of what is a prevailing tone of anxiety in your work?

Didion: If there is a tone of anxiety, I can't tell. I have always been an anxious person. Some children are born anxious, some children aren't. They know now that within twelve hours of birth they can poke babies with pins and some of them flinch and some of them don't. The ones that flinch turn out to be anxious people when they grow up. Apparently you are born that way.

Bigsby: I think the anxiety is there, but out of the anxiety there comes another preoccupation which is with survival – getting through. The anxiety comes both from within and without; internally, because people are in a state of neurotic collapse and externally, because they are threatened with violence. It seems to me that that leads you to a concern with survival.

Didion: I think I grew up with a concern for survival because I grew up in Sacramento in California in a family that placed a great deal of emphasis on family history and the family history had been to cross the country and come to California in a period when that represented great hardship. We are talking about covered wagons and abandoning stuff on the way and bearing babies on the way. All of those stories had a lesson and the lesson was that the highest good was to have gotten here, was to survive, and that people who were successful survived. My concern with survival came naturally out of that background. It was just part of growing up in that particular part of America.

Bigsby: You seem to me to have a strong sense of place. You were brought up in California but lived in New York. Part of *Democracy* is set in Hawaii. Are you the same person in each one of those places?

Didion: No, actually I feel a lot different. I suppose I am the same person, but I feel quite different in different places and where I am matters a lot to me. The weather matters to me, though I notice that a lot of people seem not to register it.

Bigsby: Do you feel more secure in one place rather than another?

Didion: The place I feel most comfortable in the whole world is Honolulu. There is absolutely a benign atmosphere there in which I don't think anything can hurt me.

Bigsby: Is that because it is on the margin, because it is outside of it all?

Didion: It is absolutely outside, or so it seems to me. It is a tropic without rot. It doesn't have any of the problems that in a benign climate usually get you down. It has no typhoid that I know of. You can swim in the river; the trade winds keep it clean.

Bigsby: In *Democracy* and, for that matter, in your other novels, the characters have a very unhappy family life. I am haunted by something you once said in an essay, which was that you had a very happy family situation – you didn't actually call it life, but family situation – and yet you were thirty before you could talk to your family on the phone without crying.

Didion: Because I felt guilty at not being there. My husband and I took my daughter to college yesterday and I realized that this is the great moment of separation. She has not lived away from home for any length of time before and I had never gone through that separation from my parents. I went down to Berkeley to school and that was just going down to Berkeley. I could drive home at weekends if I wanted to. And then I moved to New York, but again during the entire time I was living in New York I maintained a California driver's licence and I was registered to vote in Sacramento, so I probably didn't make a clean separation.

Bigsby: But when you wrote about not being able to speak to your family without crying, it was almost as though that were a normal behaviour pattern. That strikes me as absolutely astonishing.

Didion: Really? Maybe it's more common in girls. I think maybe girls feel that way more than boys do.

IN CONVERSATION
WITH
JOHN FOWLES

When John Fowles published his first novel, *The Collector*, in 1963, he was thirty-seven years old. Unsurprisingly, perhaps, it turned out that he had been writing for some time; the origins of his second novel, *The Magus* (1966, revised edition 1977), went back a good decade. Both books were extremely successful; *The Magus* achieved cult status on American campuses. *The French Lieutenant's Woman* (1969) merely served to confirm his position. Later filmed, with a screenplay by Harold Pinter, it traced the moral education of a nineteenth-century Darwinian amateur scientist by a young woman previously abandoned by her lover. Partly a pastiche nineteenth-century novel, partly a self-conscious fiction into which the modern narrator felt free to intrude, the book offers the reader several possible endings. There followed *The Ebony Tower* (1974), *Daniel Martin* (1977), *Mantissa* (1982), and in 1985 *A Maggot*, another novel set in the past, this time in the eighteenth century. Since then John Fowles has suffered a stroke and then the death of his wife from cancer. In 1999 he remarried. This interview was recorded in his house in Lyme Regis in February 1992.

Bigsby: How have you managed to get through these last few years?

Fowles: I think I can only answer by saying that I am here, so apparently I have got through. If I knew how I had got through I would be a priest or a philosopher, I suppose. You just have to live with it.

Bigsby: Did you turn to writing, to books?

Fowles: No, I didn't, because I have not really been able to write since Elizabeth, my wife, died. I was slightly surprised by realizing how much of me had actually depended on her, not only in domestic ways, but in the imagination, in the making of fiction. I had always known she had been behind every female character I ever wrote, so I knew that side of it, but I had not realized how deeply we were intertwined or interwoven. I just haven't killed myself. That is the only way you get through, by not killing yourself.

Bigsby: Is solitariness something that you fear or that you embrace?

Fowles: I think I have had to embrace it most of my life and, yes, I do fear it. I think solitude is really rather nasty and I wouldn't live as a solitary. I realize that Elizabeth used to supply me in the old days with a necessary company and an amused knowledge of what was going on in literature. But solitude, no. I really would not like to be on a desert island.

Bigsby: On the other hand, the natural world has always been important to you.

Fowles: I never feel alone in nature, but of course nowadays it is becoming more and more difficult to find nature to be in. Here in Lyme Regis, certainly, it is all around one, so I suppose I am lucky in that. But always in the past, if I felt desperately lonely, I have discovered a loophole, an exit from that in nature, and I still feel it now when I go into my own garden. If I feel depressed indoors I know that if I go out of doors pretty soon it will start being distractive. It is a kind of distraction that you can find in nature.

Bigsby: What kind of a resource is it?

Fowles: Basically, I would say how mysterious and marvellous nature is and how, in spite of all the science and all the rest of it today, it does remain mysterious. Why does the spider build its web in this particular way? Why is that insect like that? Why does this plant grow? We don't really know, and I find that very pleasing. I have often said I know what hell would be. Hell would be a world in which we know everything.

Bigsby: You have reissued a book, which first came out in 1979, called *The Tree*. In that book you relate the natural world to the processes of writing. What is the nature of that connection?

Fowles: For me, there is certainly a strong parallel with walking through a wood you have not been in before, an unknown wood, which is something I have always loved in nature. You go into an unknown wood and you don't know where you are going. You may have a rough sense of direction, but certainly not a particular route you must follow. Because that was an experience I had before I began writing, that has always been to my mind a strong analogy with the fiction-writing process.

Bigsby: But by definition fiction is artifice, isn't it?

Fowles: It is. You are making up your wood. But most writers would challenge the idea that it is just artifice. A lot of fiction is my own past history. I am not saying I write highly autobiographical novels but you incorporate your own past history into your fiction.

Bigsby: Does it also mean that you don't plan your fiction as an architect would plan a house, but that it is organic in some way?

Fowles: Thank you for using that word 'organic', which can be a slightly dirty word nowadays. Yes, I would say that. It is like growing a tree. It is like planting a tree and it is a weak, little two-inch thing to begin with and then it grows and sometimes you prune it. In fiction you do have to prune it, and it suddenly begins to overshadow you and dominate your life, like a real tree might. 'Organic' is a word I like, certainly in connection with the writing of fiction.

Bigsby: Another word which recurs in your work, and in your descriptions of nature, is 'wild'. How do you reconcile the wild element with the controlled element within fiction? How do you get that balance?

Fowles: A writer has to function as two kinds of man. One is a wild man. He is the Green Man in the wood. And the other is a professor of literature: you have to be your own professor. For me there are two stages. First of all, what I call the draft stage, which is where the wild man needs to be in control. Then you come to the professor of literature phase, which is revision and correction. This is when you begin pruning what has grown. It is very important, I think, that you distinguish between these two selves. You have to admit they are both there.

Bigsby: Which do you feel happier with?

Fowles: I think probably the wild phase. Yes, definitely the wild phase. You see, before I became a novelist I wanted to be a poet and I still have a secret deep veneration and admiration for good poets.

Bigsby: The Romantics, by the sound of it?

Fowles: Not the Romantics, though I do enjoy them. But in this century two men I did not like as human beings or as men – T.S. Eliot and Philip Larkin – I think are quite clearly the two poets of this age. It is really their great skill with words, I suppose, and the ability to create phrases you never forget – or I have never forgotten in my life – which is so compelling. That is something I think every novelist secretly hankers after: the memorable phrase. Poets, lucky devils, are the only ones capable of that, I'm afraid.

Bigsby: When was your love of nature born?

Fowles: I think from boyhood. I had an uncle, now dead, who was a keen entomologist. He used to collect rare moths and butterflies. I had another cousin who was by way of being the great English expert on ants. He used to collect them, not only in England, but all over the world. He is dead now, and a slight horror of my life was that he was going to leave me his ants. I saw hundreds of little bottles of pickled ants suddenly appearing on the doorstep. But that didn't happen. They were given to some Australian university. But he certainly was very valuable, because that was somebody deeply involved with nature and a very good all-round natural historian. It was really the old natural historian image which obsessed my childhood. There was one kind of human being who was rather boring, and there was another who knew natural history well.

Bigsby: Did the kind of person you describe as being rather boring resemble your father? I ask because in *The Tree* there are various comments about your father, particularly in the context of nature, and you use rather curious expressions: you talk about 'trampling on your father's soul', and you speak of 'murdering him'. The language is odd.

Fowles: I do feel a certain guilt towards my father, in the sense that I realize I developed in ways he would not really have approved of. He would have liked to have been an officer and a gentleman, and he would like to have been richer than he was, but I think he never really understood who I was or what I am now. Therefore, it must have seemed to him that I didn't want to communicate with him. That was not the case. I did want to communicate with him, but what I realize is that he never shared my love of nature. He loved cultivating trees and he loved many things I still love, which I have inherited from him, but certainly my sort of adoration of nature, my need for nature, I don't think he ever understood. When I was still in my early twenties, he left Devon, something I never forgave him for, because Devon for me was a wonderful natural experience as well as being a natural landscape.

Bigsby: You were evacuated there during the war?

Fowles: Yes, and he was the one who decided we must move back to Leigh-on-Sea, where I was born. I know he loved county cricket and he liked to fiddle about with what was left of his business, but I still felt – and then I was old enough, I think, to judge to a degree – that he didn't need to go back. That really was like saying to a child, "OK, you have had your months in paradise, now back to reality."

Bigsby: Your first published novel, *The Collector*, raises the question of how free we are, particularly how free we are of our own background and our own upbringing. How far do you think you are a product of your upbringing, background and education?

Fowles: I think very heavily so, although most of my life I have tried to escape from it. Perhaps the very fact that you do want to escape from your background just shows that it does have this extraordinary influence on you still. I am sure that is why I have been a sort of socialist all my life, because the ambience of our home was really rather towards the other side, towards the Right. I have been violently anti-conservative all my life. Background and education leave their mark in countless ways, I cannot deny it. Even the way I speak is probably symptomatic.

Bigsby: You went on to a public school.

Fowles: I won an exhibition to Bedford, then I went on to Oxford.

Bigsby: Before I let you go to Oxford, there is something about the public school that interests me: you became head boy. You have written in a number of your novels about power and its abuses, its seductiveness. You must, given the time that you were head boy at a public school, have had power. How did you react to it?

Fowles: I am very grateful that I did become head boy, because that made me realize that I hate the head boys of existence and that I really dislike Fascism or anything tending towards Fascism. I have hated authority all my life and it can put you in a difficult situation sometimes because you know you ought to admire or perhaps agree with authority. But people who like to lay down the law don't please me.

Bigsby: Did you discover anything of that in yourself when you were in that position?

Fowles: I discovered I did quite like the feeling of power, which at that school at that time was quite considerable. Every morning I was excused lessons because I had a queue of delinquents outside the monitors' room, where the prefects of the school were, waiting to be judged. I would give them detentions or I would cane them, and that was the worst part of that system. The head boys were allowed to cane the younger pupils. Very bad, very evil.

Bigsby: But isn't writing another way of getting power?

Fowles: Yes, it is. That I can't defend. I think a writer has a kind of duty, to himself certainly, to say what he feels about life. And if you say what you feel about life, you are really demanding attention. It brings you some kind of fame if you are lucky, some kind of survival value, and in our world that is a kind of power. I know that if I am on television people begin to speak to me with something approaching a

Stone Age veneration for the supposed deities. You are godlike because you have been on some well-known medium.

Bigsby: You have said something more than that – that literature is a way of purveying your own philosophy.

Fowles: I have a very strong feeling that, first of all, behind every novelist today is the shaman, the witch-doctor in its vulgar sense, the man who is in touch with other knowledges, with other truths and with other powers, which every Stone Age tribe used to have and which every primitive tribe still has in some parts of the world. There is something slightly shamanic about all writers. In that sense, what we have inherited is what the priests used to inherit, say, up to the eighteenth or nineteenth centuries. That is, we do have this mysterious power, if the situation is right, to communicate to great masses of people. And if that is power, yes, we have that kind of power.

Bigsby: Has literature assumed some of the functions of religion in the sense that it shapes and orders things?

Fowles: Yes, very much so. Not only literature, but all the arts. The dominant art today is obviously the visual. It is the cinema or, in slightly more plebian terms, it is the television.

Bigsby: Then that is power, isn't it?

Fowles: I think so. It is the power to put your ideas or your feelings across into other minds. That is power.

Bigsby: And it shapes the world that we inhabit.

Fowles: Yes, sure. And the Fascists are certainly on that same line. But politically, I think, there is a great division. I don't think most writers really are Fascists in the political sense. I hope not.

Bigsby: From Bedford school you went on to Oxford where you read French and German, of which the French seems to have been particularly significant.

Fowles: Very much so, yes. Again, I am deeply grateful. I did a year of German. Then we were allowed to take one language only, and I thankfully took French. I am a strong believer in the value of the Romance languages – Spanish, French, Italian and so on – because I think they give you a totally different view of life. With German we are too close to gain much. In England we laugh a lot at the Germans, but that is because they are very close to us, I think, racially and culturally.

Bigsby: You have said you feel more European than British. Why is that?

Fowles: Because I deeply admire what I think of as the Mediterranean or the French side of life. I don't know Spain particularly well, but what I know of Spain I admire. Italy, I admire. I think the novelist I admire most at the moment is Calvino, who is Italian of course. And Greece. One is either Roman or Greek, and I am definitely Greek and not Roman.

Bigsby: You were thirty-seven when your first novel, *The Collector*, was published but you had been writing for some time. Why quite so long before you came into print?

Fowles: I think I knew that I just wasn't writing well enough. You must remember that my first novel was really *The Magus* and I had spent, God knows, ten, twelve years of my life trying to get that brute into some kind of shape; and all the time I knew I was failing, failing, failing. Luckily for me, I had had the idea of *The Collector*, which I wrote in six weeks or two months to begin with. I had to revise it afterwards, of course, but I was lucky that book made money so I could then take up *The Magus* and try to get it together. It was still a failure in my view. The result was that I had to write it yet another time around. Novels are like that, you see. In a perfect world you would be given forty years at least for every novel. In fact, you are given far less even than four years. If you are lucky, you are given four months in this miserable world we live in, and so all novels are under-written in my view.

Bigsby: What drew you to the subject of *The Collector*, which is about a young man from a somewhat deprived background who kidnaps someone from a rather better-off background?

Fowles: That aspect of it, the better and not-so-good background, came in part from an opera by Béla Bartók, *Bluebeard's Castle*, which I remember always obsessed me. And probably, if you went into my own subconscious history, there was some attraction to this idea of capturing a woman. I have never met any man who does not admit it is a faintly attractive idea. Of course, it is not kidnapping or locking in a room that I am talking about, but the method of courtship of most males is to find themselves alone with some woman they love. A fantasy I can remember from my own boyhood was being shut in a lift with a woman whom you knew would normally never speak to you. It didn't lead to anything violently physical, nothing like rape or anything like that. It would allow her to know who you were because you could explain yourself to her. It was really a place where you had an opportunity to explain what you were to someone who, you suspected, would normally never want to listen.

Bigsby: And yet, the educator in that book is really the woman, isn't it?

Fowles: I think so. But when *The Collector* first came out I got some nice bouquets about how good the monster was, the clerk, and what a bore the woman was and how right it was that he had kidnapped her and killed her off. I can realize what was behind all that now. But that was an effect I had never calculated.

Bigsby: You followed that book not with *The Magus* but with *The Aristos*, which is a curiously non-British book, a series of thoughts on just about every subject under the sun. It is like two students at three o'clock in the morning with cups of coffee. That must have taken some gall. There was something foolhardy about that, wasn't there?

Fowles: Certainly, foolhardy in terms of my career as a well-brought-up young novelist. I was just very determined I wouldn't be trapped in this pigeonhole marked 'novelist'. I knew that life somehow was more complicated for me. And you are quite right, it was very French. I was under the influence of Pascal and all the French makers of apophthegms. And La Rochefoucauld I used to love, too. What I realize is that you cannot bring a typically French way of writing and thinking across to England and expect any success. I duly didn't get it.

Bigsby: The original edition of that book had a subtitle: 'A Self-Portrait in Ideas'. That subtitle subsequently vanished. Insofar as it was a portrait, how do you imagine you emerged from it for someone reading the book?

Fowles: I can't tell you that. I meant to give people some notion of the ideas that obsessed me. I regard it as philosophically almost certainly a non-starter. I just suppose I wanted to give an impression of what I thought I was. Not a good answer, but I don't think I can answer more precisely than that.

Bigsby: It is something you didn't want to let go of, because you came back to it later.

Fowles: I never want to let any book go. The agony for me is finishing a novel, because when you have corrected the final edited proof some guillotine comes down. It is dead from then on and if you keep writing it, if you think 'it is not finished, I have got to do a bit more work on it', it does still have a marvellous living sense for you.

Bigsby: Is that why virtually all of your novels have a kind of implied ellipsis? There is a sense in which they often feel incomplete.

Fowles: They never are complete, I suppose, as far as I am concerned. It is the feeling that, if you had the time, you could write more, you could develop it in a different way, perhaps. *The French Lieutenant's Woman*, where I gave two very different endings, really expressed a wish that I could write another novel: *The Son of the French Lieutenant's Woman*, *The Grandson of the French Lieutenant's Woman*. I get this with *The Collector*: 'Please give us *The Son of the Collector*.'

Bigsby: With *The Magus* you did go on to write another version of it. What is it about that book especially which makes you not want to let go?

Fowles: *The Magus* was to be the great novel of my life and I really had struggled over it and not brought it off. I was very influenced by Henry James's *The Turn of the Screw*. I always knew it ought to be my great novel, my most important one, and I always knew it wasn't and I felt 'if I go at it again, I will get it better'. I didn't really alter it very substantially. I changed certain aspects of it, but not basically. I also tried to make the end clearer, but I still get letters from people who can't see what it could have been, although I think it is fairly clear how I meant it to end. You see, I was not Nicholas, but in a way he was my substitute, and the girl, Alison, in that novel, was my wife, Elizabeth.

Bigsby: Who you met in Greece, where the novel is set.

Fowles: Yes. She was married to somebody else, and so in a sense the biographical part of that book was describing my realization that I was falling in love with this woman, who was married to somebody else and who was unhappy. There is more of a biographical element than most people realize.

Bigsby: So the trickery and the deceptions have a co-relative in terms of actuality?

Fowles: I wouldn't call it trickery as I have presented it in *The Magus*. I simply mean a man being torn between two different women. In my case, it was between Elizabeth and the endless imaginable women that a young man gives himself.

Bigsby: In *The French Lieutenant's Woman*, as you have implied, there is a resistance to an ending of a different kind. We do have alternative endings. At what stage in the writing of that novel did it become apparent to you that that was how you would conclude it?

Fowles: I think about halfway through. If we go back to the analogy of the wood: you go to it and you see two paths forking off. About half way through I asked myself, am I going to bring these two together or am I going to force them apart? That is when I had the idea that I would show both possible ways it might have gone. Years ago I read a detective novel, American I think, where it did show endless forks. The forks become a very important element in my own theory of writing fiction. You are constantly faced with forks or alternatives, even in the choice of individual words. In narrative it becomes really quite formidable: you might go one way or you might go the other. Therefore, I tried to put those forks into the experience of reading *The French Lieutenant's Woman*. Most people much preferred the bad ending, the unhappy ending, where they never come together.

Bigsby: But in a novel in which the male protagonist is a Darwinian who has a very deterministic view of the world, presumably these alternative endings represent the other possibility, that is to say, a world full of endless choices?

Fowles: I think that is so. In a way Darwin made that impossible with his theory. But in another way I am a great admirer of Darwin and I think Darwin is essential for non-conscious life. You can only understand it in his terms.

Bigsby: And yet you have got the paradox that in the novel you determine those alternative possibilities.

Fowles: Yes, that is true. But I would say that in that case I am only really a representative of the general system; that is, the system by which I think we live.

Bigsby: The key figure here is a woman, Sarah. In a way, she becomes a kind of moral, philosophical teacher. That was equally true, I think, of *The Collector*, and to a larger degree of *The Magus* and *Mantissa*. Why? Why is it the woman who becomes the educator?

Fowles: I am reading a very interesting book by two Jungians at the moment, *The Myth of the Goddess*, which deals with the time when man really did venerate woman as the source of most wisdom. I have always shared that view, and I realize this is partly because there is a strong feminine component in my own personality. I think that would be true of most male novelists. I suspect that with female novelists it is probably the reverse. In other words, the animus and the anima have to be well balanced if the person is to become a good creative artist.

Bigsby: Isn't there a risk of a kind of sentimentality, though, in the suggestion you have made that men represent artifice and women reality; that one is rational and the other warm and spontaneous and intuitive?

Fowles: I think this is true, but for me it is because man has taken the wrong track for at least the last two millennia, possibly longer still. I would like to re-establish the balance between the sexes. I don't suppose most feminists would count me as a fully paid-up feminist, but I do have great sympathy for that general view of life.

Bigsby: You have said that it is very useful for a novelist to be clear as to what a novel can do that the cinema can't. *The French Lieutenant's Woman* was made into a film. In your mind what was it that the film couldn't hope to do, simply because it was a film?

Fowles: You can give quite a great degree of particularity in a novel, which you can't in a film because of the obvious compression of the medium. Also, it is difficult in a film to analyze character properly – what really makes people work, why they are what they are and what that means in general. You can only give images or hints about what you are getting at in good cinema. The cinema cannot, I think, get at the truth about what people are, because you can't do it all visually. If you could do it all by a look or gesture that would be fine, but you can't.

Bigsby: Does the film have an effect on how the novel is read? Can you read *The French Lieutenant's Woman* now without seeing it through Meryl Streep and Jeremy Irons?

Fowles: I can, personally, but whether ordinary readers can, I don't really know. This does worry me that the film will stamp out all the imagery you get from the reading experience, that the concrete visual experience becomes very overbearing towards the verbal imagery you get from the novel.

Bigsby: Particularly in a novel which is partly trying to talk about imaginative freedom.

Fowles: Exactly. If in the novel it says 'the old man crosses the road' everyone will invent their own old man, they will invent the crossing, they will invent the road. But, of course, in the cinema you're given no choice. That is Fascism, pure and simple, I'm afraid. You have to just accept the way it is done. I happen to know this very well at the moment, because I am doing a script of a novel which has deeply influenced me: *Le grand Meaulnes*, by Alain-Fournier. I have always admired that novel precisely because it does evoke verbally some of the images in the mind and I find that trying to write it so a director can make it is very difficult.

Bigsby: I am interested that you mention that novel, because you have suggested in the past that you cannot really write novels until you are in your thirties. But Fournier was not in his thirties. It is a young man's novel.

Fowles: It is an adolescent's novel. That is one of the great difficulties about the novel. It is really to be read by adolescents. Hollywood has commissioned it, and it is very difficult to suggest to them that putting a slightly older star in it, and incorporating glamour and all that, is a total travesty of the book. I am doing it because I adored the novel and I just hope that I can keep it fairly closely written. But I don't think that the cinema is really equipped to present it.

Bigsby: Why does it still haunt you in your sixties? It was partly behind *The Magus* as well, wasn't it?

Fowles: I think it's simply an old man's thing: it is remembering what it was like to be young. I still think it is one of the most marvellous evocations of what it is to be young.

Bigsby: *The French Lieutenant's Woman* took us back into the nineteenth century. *A Maggot* takes us into the eighteenth century. Why the past?

Fowles: It is partly because I have always been interested in history. I still read a lot of history. In the case of *A Maggot*, I have always been attracted by the Shaker religion, which is mainly American, although it started in Liverpool. I wanted to try to present to a modern audience what that was about. I can't believe in it theologically or metaphysically at all, but I find it deeply attractive in some ways.

Bigsby: Is there any sense in which going back is a way of not talking about now, as though now were actually difficult to address?

Fowles: I certainly hoped that *A Maggot* could be taken as partly about now. I think all historical novels are really concealed criticisms of today and so, too, are all novels of the future, of course. They always refer to the present, when they were written. I didn't want to suggest that *A Maggot* was just a sort of cobwebby account of what was happening in the eighteenth century.

Bigsby: There comes a curious moment in *A Maggot* when we seem to verge on science fiction.

Fowles: Yes, we do. I probably didn't do it terribly well, but I wanted to suggest that there was great mystery in the past and that there is actually a kind of mystery in the future.

Bigsby: You are interested in mystery. Are you interested in mysticism?

Fowles: Not terribly, no. I am not very fond of all the alternative theology that floats about nowadays. Somebody wrote me a letter only this morning saying that I had said in some newspaper article that I had no belief in God or an afterlife. He insisted that I must believe in reincarnation or I would not be a full human being. That, I am afraid, I have no time for.

Bigsby: Surely the whole point of mystery in your books is that it leads us back to the real? You are interested in Zen, but Zen less, I presume, as a religion or as mysticism, than as something which is concerned with the immediate, the tactile, the real.

Fowles: I think so, yes. I am definitely a realist, I'm afraid. I do enjoy fantasy, as long as there are walls around it. No, that is not the right way to say it. As long as there is always a gateway through to realism in the fantasy.

Bigsby: The sense of the real seems to me strongest in *Daniel Martin*, not least perhaps because it seems closest to your own experience. It may not be strictly autobiographical, but there are elements there.

Fowles: It is certainly not strictly autobiographical but it is, I suppose, closer to my real life, to my practical daily life.

Bigsby: There is a kind of *mea culpa* on behalf of a generation in that book, a sense that your generation has failed in some significant way. What is the nature of that failure?

Fowles: It is fairly clear to me that we have failed by not having something the Victorians did have, possibly to excess, and that is seriousness. This seems to me to be an intensely superficial generation, obsessed by success. In a strange way it is technology which has done this. It is so obsessed by the transmission of information that this allows one not to be serious. There is so much information that you don't really absorb it all, you don't take it seriously. The other way I would say we have failed is by not passing on the lessons that we ought to have learned from all the discoveries in the social sciences in the first fifty years of this century. I think we are politically backward. We have shut our eyes to possible political progress, and in effect we have slowed the whole of human evolution down by being as we are. That is how it seems to me. I don't mean only political progress, although I am a socialist. The worst thing for me is the way we have abused nature. That is our principal failure. We have absolutely mucked up nature.

Bigsby: There is another anxiety in *Daniel Martin*: an anxiety which is specifically about writers. The narrator describes writers as 'vampires who sleep with a slaked smile while men and women are tortured, children starve'. In other words, it is an anxiety that the process of writing is a process of evasion. Because you are writing, you are not out there in the world acting and changing.

Fowles: I think I would accuse all artists of this. Art is a form of evasion. I don't see how we can deny it. Of course, countless artists have witnessed or acted against all that is wrong in the world, and that is a part, I think, of any decent artist. But I feel also that in our society, especially our Western society, that art can be a form of evasion.

Bigsby: You are a democratic socialist, which presumably means you wish to see society transformed. Meanwhile, you sit here in Lyme with a pen or a typewriter and you spin inventions.

Fowles: I do, yes. It is a paradox. I know I am a paradox.

Bigsby: You collect books because, as you have said, they give a sharp feel of the age in which they were written. What view of the age do you think readers who collect your books are likely to get?

Fowles: Very confused, I think. They will sense in me that there are people from different historical periods in my books.

Bigsby: You have said that nine-tenths of all artistic creation comes from the energy produced by the engines of repression and sublimation. Is it an impossible question to ask but, what is the nature of those repressions and sublimations that have generated your books? There is a strong erotic element in your work, isn't there?

Fowles: Yes, of course. In a 'perfect' world I probably would like it to be slightly more erotic. I do think the erotic is very important. There is some connection between the imagination and the erotic. I am sure that for a novelist it is valuable to be erotic as a person, not because you can then transfer it into your novels but because it stimulates your imagination.

Bigsby: When you started your career you said your aims were: first, to be a good poet; second, a philosopher; third, a good novelist. Are those still your priorities?

Fowles: I am too old now to talk about things like that as a 'priority'. Yes, I would have liked to be a good poet and I would have liked to have been a great or good philosopher, but I realize now that I have got to make do with being a middling novelist, or whatever I am.

Bigsby: Does your grasp – or interest in retaining a grasp – on reality and the real connect with your interest in receiving letters from readers? I should think many authors just don't want to know, but you don't feel that way, do you?

Fowles: First of all I would disagree with the 'many authors just don't want to know'. I should think many of them would be so bloody grateful if somebody would actually write to them. I find letters from readers almost continuously interesting, even when you know they are absurd and they have misunderstood you. They are revealing. I don't perhaps meet enough people here, but the way I meet them is through letters. I feel it is really an interest in humanity which attaches me to those letters.

Bigsby: Many of your characters are teachers, and the processes of the novels are to do with a kind of moral education. Do you see that as a function that attaches to you as the writer of those novels?

Fowles: I think it is a duty to try to educate readers, morally and ethically, in a way that must mean getting them to share the same point of view as yourself. I certainly think that is something I try to do, that I am happy to do. Very occasionally I get letters which more or less tell me I have done it. I don't really like giving examples, but I remember a monk, who had left his monastery, writing to me and saying, 'Thank you for *The Magus* because that persuaded me I must leave.' Obviously I am rather glad for people to leave monasteries. I felt I had probably affected him in a good way. Over the years I have had quite a number of letters like that.

IN CONVERSATION
WITH
URSULA LE GUIN

Ursula Le Guin was born in 1929, the daughter of A.L. Kroeber, an anthropologist, and Theodora Kracaw Kroeber, an author. She is perhaps best known for her novels *The Left Hand of Darkness* (1969) and *Always Coming Home* (1985), and for the *Earthsea* saga, which has been compared with Tolkien's *The Lord of the Rings*. Her first book, *A Wizard of Earthsea*, appeared in 1968, and the fourth, *Tehanu*, in 1990. In 2000 she published *The Telling*.She has received a number of awards for her writing, including the National Book Award for Children's Literature and Hugo and Nebula awards for science fiction. Ursula Le Guin is also the author of short stories, essays and poetry. This interview was recorded in Portland, Oregon, in 1990.

Bigsby: You were born into a fairly remarkable family, were you not? Your father was an anthropologist and you met people who were professionally interested in other cultures while you were growing up. Do you think that may have influenced your own interest, as a writer, in creating other worlds and other cultures?

Le Guin: Yes, I think it was inevitable. It was not only that my father had many American friends who visited, but this was the late 1930s and refugees were coming through Berkeley all the time from German universities, from other worlds as it were. As a kid I saw this happening. It wasn't a little closed university-town universe as it might have been; it was open, the doors were open.

Bigsby: Both your father and your mother had, at different times, a special interest in native Americans. Though, for the most part, you don't write about them I get the feeling that they represent some kind of an ideal for you.

Le Guin: Well, not exactly an ideal but a reality. I came to grips with it when I returned from a year in England in 1975. I came all the way back from England to the West Coast of the United States and looked around and thought that while I had enjoyed England enormously and had read up on the Celts, visited stone circles and so on, this is where I am, this is my dirt. And who lived here? It was the Indians, of course, and it became important to me to acknowledge that. What I did was simply to discover a little more history than I knew about the West Coast Indians, but I investigated their literature, the old oral literature which was recorded by anthropologists and linguists, and the present-day writing which is, I think, some of the most exciting that is being done by some of our native American writers. It is a non-European world and it became important to me to be able to uncentre from Europe in that way.

Bigsby: Is that concern also something to do with the relationship between the individual and the natural world, and the individual and the group?

Le Guin: Definitely the individual and the group; the consensual politics of the small to medium American nations and units is fascinating because it worked. As for the relationship between the individual and the universe, the person and the cosmos, the Native

American religions are extremely appealing to me in that sense. On the other hand, there is a lot of sentimentality about that. If they had the equipment we have they might have done the same kind of land-rape we have done. But they do see themselves as being part of the land and this goes very deep and is very spiritual. It is curious how, with so many different peoples, Native American spirituality does come down to the same few things and one of them is that: belonging to the land.

Bigsby: What did you read when you were growing up?

Le Guin: I read everything. I have always read everything, particularly novels and poetry, and science for idiots.

Bigsby: Were you particularly interested in fantasy or science fiction?

Le Guin: If it was a novel I would read it.

Bigsby: You wanted to be a biologist at one stage. How far is the science-fiction writer in you partly the disappointed scientist?

Le Guin: There must be some relationship there. It was largely a matter of not being able to handle mathematics. You can't do science if you can't do maths and I either can't or was somehow led to believe that I couldn't. Also, you really cannot have two full-time careers; one of them had to go. I could support myself as a French teacher or professor and write. I don't think I could support myself as a working biologist and write.

Bigsby: Does the writing of science fiction satisfy some of those elements in you that otherwise you might have satisfied by becoming a scientist?

Le Guin: Probably. In particular, I think I inherited from my father a great fascination and respect for detail and for concrete, small facts. I love them and, though I know it sounds rather odd because I write so much that is fantasy, the stories tend to be built up out of small hard things, facts. I do like facts and artefacts.

Bigsby: You started writing science fiction very early did you not?

Le Guin: When I was about ten or twelve my brother and I were reading the old pulp science-fiction magazines. We had been doing that for a couple of years, and the first story that I ever submitted to a magazine was a science-fiction story. I think I was twelve and of course it came back. Then I stopped reading those magazines for nearly twenty years, so I missed what is called the golden age of science fiction. I was reading everything else. I was getting towards thirty when I picked it up again. A friend introduced me to some other writers who were just beginning to write and who were using science fiction quite differently, much more literarily. I had been sending out my stories to all the magazines for getting on for eight or ten years and without any sales at all. I was getting fairly desperate and I thought, well, some of my things which are sort of odd, which have this fantastic element, maybe they are science fiction. And, sure enough, my first sale was to a science-fiction magazine. Oddly enough, in the same month I had my first publication in a literary magazine, one of the small literary quarterlies. It was one of the Orsinian stories, which take place in an invented central European country. They are completely realistic, except that the country doesn't exist.

All my work tends to have this slight off-centredness – or one can be fancy and call it a magical realist quality – and my problem in getting published was apparently that they didn't know how to label me. It so happened that the label that first stuck was the science-fiction label. It fits some of my stories, maybe a quarter to a third of them. I do write science fiction and for a while I read a lot of it. I like being in a science-fiction community, but it was never all that I do. There was perhaps an element of calculation in that as soon as I had published fantasy or science fiction and had some reputation – especially when *Left Hand of Darkness* became a well-known book and I won some prizes – then I could use that clout to spread back out and publish other kinds of writing. I don't like to be locked into any genre.

Bigsby: How did you handle that business of having rejections? It wasn't only a matter of stories, but four or five novels had been rejected. What motivated you to keep going in the face of all these rejections?

Le Guin: Obduracy. Stupidity. An arrogant conviction that I knew what I was doing and that it was worth doing, which any artist obviously has to have somewhere in them. But it was getting a bit tough. I was publishing poetry all along and that helped. At least my poetry was getting published in the little poetry magazines.

Bigsby: So you had a self-image of being a writer?

Le Guin: Absolutely, always. I didn't *want* to be a writer, I felt I *was* a writer – and by God they were going to notice it, finally.

Bigsby: But there was an additional irony to this, wasn't there? While you were not being published your mother, quite late in life, was.

Le Guin: Yes. She beat me to it, although she started in her fifties.

Bigsby: Was that particularly awkward?

Le Guin: No, basically it was lovely. I had fits of jealousy and she had a fit of tears once and said that she wanted me to be published and not her, but it wasn't true. The fact is we had a lot of fun talking shop together. She was a lovely woman, a very good-natured woman. It was kind of nice when Ma got published. And then when Ma became a bestseller to her own total surprise and the surprise of the University of California Press, who didn't know what to do, that was great fun. *Ishi* just soared, just took off, and was on the *New York Times* bestseller list for weeks. University press books in those days never did that.

Bigsby: Did that fire you still more?

Le Guin: No, I just plodded along.

Bigsby: After your first few science-fiction novels – *Planet of Exiles*, *Rocannon's World*, *City of Illusions* – you wrote the first of what was going to turn out to be the *Earthsea* books, *A Wizard of Earthsea*. How would you describe the world of Earthsea to somebody who had not yet encountered it?

Le Guin: By now there have been so many imitations of Tolkien and me, and other fantasists, that you can say that in some senses it is a fairly standard fantasy world: it is pre-industrial and vaguely medieval. It has a strong class structure, with nobles and kings on top and the peasantry going about their business unnoticed, obviously keeping the economy going, only my peasants seem more to be fishermen and boat people. All that is quite unquestioned, stock European fairytale stuff. The people of power in the *Earthsea* books are wizards, and of course one can easily make a parallel between wizardry and science or wizardry and art, except art in our world doesn't confer power. Call it knowledge, then, but those people, the wizards, are the source of power. There are no kings until the third book; there is an absence of political power at the top until, in the third book, the balance begins to change from wizardry towards politics. In the last book, the fourth book, this world is reperceived from underneath, from the point of view of one of the people not in power, that is to say a woman who is simply a farmer's wife. Unsurprisingly, it all looks a bit different from underneath.

Bigsby: When you wrote *A Wizard of Earthsea* did you know that the other books would follow?

Le Guin: No, I honestly didn't. For one thing we weren't into this feast of trilogies that is a publishing device now. I was asked for the book by a publisher, a small press called Parnasus in Berkeley, which is my home town. My mother had published a couple of children's books with him. He was doing beautiful children's books and wanted to expand into the adolescent market, the young adult market. He asked me if I would like to write a science-fiction or fantasy book, something for young adults. At first I was intimidated by the idea, but it is one of those things – every now and again an editor asks you for a story or a book that is just waiting to be written. I went home and wrote what became *Earthsea*. But I left clues to myself for the next books, which then came off fairly promptly.

Bigsby: Why was there an eighteen-year gap between the third and fourth books in the series?

Le Guin: Believe me, I was extremely nervous about it. After I had finished the third book within a year or two of the previous one, I knew there was another book there. I had got a three-legged chair. I started that book about 1974 or 1975, I suppose. I got a chapter or two into it and it was simply going nowhere. I knew what Tenar had done, that she had given up power and wizardry, married a farmer and had kids, but I had no idea why she had done that. I didn't know the story and so after working at it for a couple more years I gave it up and thought, that's it, I can't write this book; I wish I could, it ought to be written but I can't do it. Then a couple of years ago I was practising my Spanish by reading a Spanish translation of the *Earthsea* books – my Spanish is self-taught and very poor so that I can really only read

Borges and myself – and I got back into Earthsea. This other book began growing in my mind and I thought, 'My God, I can't do this after sixteen years, I can't go back.' But the book wanted very much to be written. It was imperative that I write it and, to my immense joy, I was able to write it.

Bigsby: In some ways this fourth volume seems to answer some of those feminist reactions against the early *Earthsea* books, which protested that you had created a world dominated by men.

Le Guin: Sure it does. There are a lot of hidden questions in the first three books, and part of the reason I could not write the fourth one was that I did not know how to pose the questions back in 1974–75. Some people, of course, look upon *Tehanu* as a sort of deconstruction of Earthsea. I don't see it as that at all. I see it as finally answering some of those questions. For instance, why do only men do wizardry and why do they live as they do? Why are they celibate? You know what happens to Merlin when he is not celibate. What are the hidden balances – the books are all about a balance of forces? In *Tehanu* I was trying to look at wizardry from a different angle. My hope was that it would pull the whole thing together, although it does leave a lot of questions open.

Bigsby: It takes us to the point at which power seems about to shift and shift towards women.

Le Guin: I don't know if power is shifting towards women. There is a king in Earthsea and he is obviously going to try to rule well. Political power has been reborn and it is in the hands of a man. But one gets the impression that there has been a fatal blow struck against wizardry. Both women and dragons seem to be more closely involved. Power is going to be opened out.

Bigsby: However different the worlds of fantasy or science fiction are, aren't they in some way bound to be rooted in your sense of what is going on in your own culture?

Le Guin: I hope so. What I always assumed I was doing was describing the world that I live in. That is what all fiction does, whether it is realistic or whether it is realistic at five or six removes.

Bigsby: Reading all of the *Earthsea* quartet it strikes me as not being that remote from a kind of anthropology. You create this world and then you document all the phases of development within it, particularly on the sexual front.

Le Guin: The sexual front and the hidden world of politics, yes. This seemed to be the way my mind worked. Give me a world and I start doing this to it.

Bigsby: This time you have announced that this will be the last *Earthsea* book.

Le Guin: That was a kind of tactical thing. I didn't want people to think I was cashing in on the success of the trilogy. There are too many series now. It is purely a publisher's device and it has been pretty much the bane of imaginative writing. Fantasy is in a terrible state at the moment because all this mechanical sausage is being produced by the boloney factory in little sections: section one, section two, section three. I just did not want people to think that I was going to go on and on with Earthsea. This is the last book. I can't go back now. It is done. Finally, I got it where I wanted it after eighteen years, and I left the door wide open again, which is what I wanted. There you are with a child and the dragon and the couple. What next? God knows.

Bigsby: Let me take you back again to what I suppose was your major breakthrough, *The Left Hand of Darkness*. Did you have a sense of how important to you that book was going to prove at the time?

Le Guin: I knew it was important to me. I knew I had finally got one right. I wasn't sure, though, that I could sell it. I thought it would be extremely ill received. It is long, it is slow, it is not the way science fiction was then or is now. It isn't snappy and fast and there isn't a lot of blood and action in it and I thought men might hate it. I thought they might be unnerved by being, as it were, unsexed. I was quite wrong.

Bigsby: This is because you are dealing with a world of androgyny.

Le Guin: I thought men would resist getting into the androgynous persona. Not at all. I see no difference in male and female reactions to androgyny. Everybody seems to enjoy being an androgyne for a while.

Bigsby: But you have accused yourself of lacking the courage of your own invention in that book by not looking at androgyny from a woman's perspective.

Le Guin: I wrote the book as well as I or anyone else could have done in 1968. There are aspects of the book which, with hindsight, I would like to do again from scratch. I cannot, for example, imagine why androgynous people would have the highly hierarchical societies I gave them – why would they have kings and so on? I don't think it would happen that way. I was a bit mechanical about the politics and just took what came to hand. I wish there was something I could do about the pronouns, which at the time didn't bother me or hardly anyone else, but now, after fifteen years of consciousness-raising, they are very much in the way. I keep saying 'he' and it isn't 'he'. There is no solution, though. You cannot switch pronouns. You cannot make them up. In a long novel that would drive the reader mad. A few years ago, in writing the screenplay of the book, I was able to use an invented pronoun because in speech you don't use the third person very much and I could make up a simple neutral pronoun. I could also show Estraven in roles that we think of as women's roles, though in the book you seldom see Estraven doing anything that we think of as feminine. Estraven is almost always perceived as doing male things, being a prime minister and pulling sledges, stuff like that, and my joy in that was that I got out of the woman's hide into this sort of androgynous hide. But to believe in Estraven as a genuinely androgynous person we need to see him/her maybe nursing a baby, something as simple as that. I didn't think to do that in the book and I wish I had.

Bigsby: The book did not begin with the idea of androgyny, did it? You did not initially set out to write a book about an androgynous society.

Le Guin: No. It began partly with a vision, a scene – two people pulling a sledge, and the landscape – which is often how books begin. I had a notion I wanted to write a book about a culture that had never had war and the vision gave me this snow landscape. I thought it would be fun to write a book about a world deep in its ice age. So a lot of things came together and the androgyny grew upon me. It was as if, watching these people, I realized that they were neither men nor women except that on a given day they could become very forcibly either one or the other.

Bigsby: You have a tactic in a number of your books which is to place a stranger in a strange land. How far is that person partly you, partly the reader?

Le Guin: It is an old device in utopias, in fantasies: you get someone who can mediate between your reality and theirs. It helps the reader to have someone from our world to be a stranger with them in the book. And, of course, this device justifies a lot of explanations. That is why, in utopias, there is always this poor person standing around being explained to. It can get awfully boring but it is a pretty common thing in science fiction.

Bigsby: Why is it that until the last couple of decades science fiction has been such a male preserve?

Le Guin: I have no idea. I suppose it began as engineering fiction. It was extrapolation from invention. The Jules Verne kind of thing. But why women didn't pick it up as this lovely sort of speculative thing that it is, I don't know. Anybody who is dissatisfied with the way things are is likely to find science fiction a wonderful form. You can say, well, what if it were this way? And then you can do a thought experiment: you can change society, you can change psychology, you can follow a frightening trend to its awful end, or you can follow a hopeful trend. It seems to me that since women started writing it in any numbers – which is about my generation, the people who came into it in the 1960s – there has been a lot of playing around with sociological and political ideas and so on. It is a lovely playground for the imagination.

Bigsby: There is something almost illicit about it, isn't there? And it tends not to have a critical response.

Le Guin: This issue is much on my mind for several reasons. One is because I write in many genres. I write science fiction, fantasy, young adult fiction, children's fiction, historical fiction, and then so-called mainstream fiction, that is to say realistic fiction, which is really no broader a category than most of the others. For some reason that last category is the only one defined as literature by the critics and the academics. Everything else is called a 'genre' and is looked upon as inherently inferior, which is awful nonsense and very destructive of the wealth of our literature. Some people, mostly not English, sneak through. Magic realism is pretty respectable. For a long while, though, they swept Borges under the carpet. They managed to sweep Calvino under the carpet for decades. None of those people ever got a Nobel Prize or any of the big prizes. There is a great unwillingness to consider anything but the kind of stuff Philip Roth writes as literature. I find this simply incredible.

Twenty years ago I thought naïvely that everything was changing, that the doors were really opening and the barriers coming down, and that, by 1990, there would be no difference between science fiction and non-science fiction, between romantic fiction or Western fiction and what now passes as literature. After all, there are many mansions in the house of literature. But we are worse off now than we were twenty years ago. I think the mainstream apologists are more dug in than ever. If you teach science fiction in a course in college it has to be segregated as science fiction. You can't put Tolkien in a course on twentieth-century English literature, though, of course, this is exactly where he ought to be. Whether you like him or not, he is a great writer. He is one of the great English writers of the twentieth century. Mervyn Peake ought to be studied. Why aren't the professors mad over Mervyn Peake? Because they don't know where to put him. I am very sad about all this and rather cross as you can see.

Bigsby: An increasing number of writers are turning to science fiction. Both Doris Lessing and Margaret Atwood have written futuristic novels.

Le Guin: I particularly admire Lessing for just coming out in the introduction to *Shikasta* and saying 'This is space fiction', whatever she wants to call it. Atwood has been a little cagier. I have heard her say that *The Handmaid's Tale* was science fiction and she has also said that it wasn't. It is pretty thin on science, but I am sure it is science fiction. It is interesting that these crossover people seem largely to be women. Women are apparently tired of these boundaries set up by the academic establishment, which is 95 per cent male, and the critical establishment, which must be about 99 per cent male. There is a lot of white male lawgiving going on here. Lessing's science-fiction books are discussed with considerable discomfort, I notice. The funny thing – the heartbreaking thing – is that within the little science-fiction community, the self-ghettoized science-fiction community that doesn't want anything to do with the outside world, they don't ever talk about Lessing and Atwood. And these days they are rather uncomfortable with me because I have 'betrayed' them. I have refused to stay only in the ghetto. I want to have the freedom of the city. So it is a bit of a mess on both sides. There is a lot of territoriality; people spraying and marking their boundaries.

Bigsby: In *The Left Hand of Darkness*, and certainly in *The Dispossessed* and the *Earthsea* books, there is a sense of longing for a lost unity. These are books about people who were once one, then became divided and separated. What are the roots of that feeling?

Le Guin: A sort of nostalgia, which must be almost the root feeling of modern fantasy. It is very strong in Tolkien, of course, and is incredibly powerful. It is in Peake too. You must be talking about something very deep in human beings, some sense of going back to childhood, to some golden security.

Bigsby: That suggests that you have a model of utopia somewhere in your mind, but it is a utopia that exists more in the past than the future.

Le Guin: I certainly don't want to turn back. I have always been intensely aware that if we turned back the clock more than about twenty years before my birth I would have died aged six because I had acute appendicitis and they wouldn't have been able to operate. No, I don't harp back. But you are right, I don't harp forward either. The fact is that I don't believe in the future. It doesn't exist. All we have got is 'now' and it is what we make of now that matters. That is where the imagination comes in. With the imagination you can make now into anything you please and that may lead you towards a different future than the one you would have if you simply projected the present forward. One of the things that fiction does is offer endless options, different ways of being that would not occur to one otherwise. That is why I will read novels till the day I die. I want to know about other ways of being that I never would have thought of.

Bigsby: In that sense, fiction resists the authoritarian and, therefore, isn't it also in a way utopian?

Le Guin: Yes. Utopian fiction is always at war with itself. Of course, that can be very interesting. That tension can create a fascinating book. And utopia is also always at war with character because it wants to be theoretical and political. So, having done a fairly classic utopia in *The Dispossessed*, I wanted to deconstruct utopia. I think that is the proper word to use. *The Dispossessed* goes in two directions, but I wanted a book that went in about twenty directions at the same time, which I did in *Always Coming Home*.

Bigsby: Doesn't the writer always want to put some grit in the machinery?

Le Guin: Absolutely, a spanner in the works.

Bigsby: Speaking of *The Dispossessed*, you said once that Taoism and anarchism coincide. What exactly has Taoism meant to you in your work?

Le Guin: It is very hard to say, it is so inward and underground. I read the *I Ching* when I was fourteen, I suppose because I saw my father reading it and it was around the house. I thought, 'What is that funny Chinese book?' Even then it appealed to me enormously, it got into me. Taoism is so hard to talk about; it is so evanescent. As soon as you say what it is then it isn't: the name that can be named is not the name, the way that can be gone is not the way, and so on. I find this whole way of looking at life endlessly fruitful and nourishing to me as an artist.

Bigsby: Can you explain it by reference to a metaphor?

Le Guin: Perhaps the best thing to say is that central to Taoism is the concept of balance. This sneaks through my books, feebly disguised in one form or another. The Chinese idea that if you go too far in one direction you just find yourself all of a sudden right around on the other side of things appeals to me temperamentally. It satisfies me.

Bigsby: We are having this conversation in your home city of Portland, in the state of Oregon, which is a place that crops up from time to time in your fiction and in your poems. Has living here in the Pacific northwest influenced your values?

Le Guin: Oh, enormously. I am a Californian and I lived my first seventeen years never going further than sixty miles from home, one in the Napa Valley and one in Berkeley. I am deeply centred in northern

California and increasingly, as I have got older, I have realized that I am a westerner, although I went to college in the east and had my education in French and Italian Renaissance literature. I had a nice European-centred, eastern-centred education, but we came back to live in the west and I am a West Coast writer fairly consciously and with great pleasure. In fact, my writings are becoming increasingly regional. This is quite hard to explain, particularly in English terms. What is important to have in mind is the size of the United States. It is three thousand miles between New York and my city, Portland. New York keeps insisting that it is the centre but there is no way that it can be. It is the centre of publishing but it is not the centre intellectually or emotionally. There is no centre to this country. There is an East Coast literary establishment which hands out most of the prizes and plays most of the games, but that is increasingly less important to what is really going on in writing. The United States is decentring, and this is fine. I think it is a wonderful process. I really hope to see publishing spread out so that some of the small West Coast publishers get a little more clout.

Bigsby: What interests me is the qualities that come out of this part of the country. Is it to do with the relationship with the natural world? Is it a sense of the quality of living that is highlighted here?

Le Guin: I don't know what it is. I can't tell you. I am an urban person. I grew up in a city in the Bay area, and I live in a city and I wanted always to live in a city, but the western cities are very different from the eastern cities. We are more aware of the landscape and also of the vulnerability of human occupation of this country.

Bigsby: We are certainly close to Mount St Helens here!

Le Guin: There is that. For a Californian it always comes down to water. Is there going to be enough water? We are in the fourth year of drought and there isn't enough water. It is not metaphorical. It is quite literal and it is scary. I think there is a sense of vulnerability which has been lost in the east. People in the east think that the cities are just going to go on in one way or another because they are there. I think there is a different sensibility at play here, a western sensibility which has to do with deserts and large spaces between people.

Bigsby: That is certainly reflected in a book such as *Always Coming Home*.

Le Guin: I was trying very much to get the sense of the fragility of our tenure of the earth. You have got to use it right or it all goes wrong. I don't know how many times we will have to prove that to ourselves.

Bigsby: As a writer, do you feel the need for the space and room for manoeuvre that science fiction gives you?

Le Guin: Oh, yes, I like the imaginative freedom. Evidently this is the way my mind works. I have written an increasing amount of realistic fiction but I do also keep returning to these forms of fiction where you are allowed to make things up.

Bigsby: But you also have a suspicion of science fiction. You have said that it is not yet a great art form and that you rather think it never will be. Why do you feel that?

Le Guin: I said that about twenty-five years ago.

Bigsby: And have you radically revised your opinion?

Le Guin: Yes, I have, because I have radically revised all my thinking about what genre is. What is science fiction? I don't think anybody has a right to say that it is or is not a great form because I don't think it is a form. Nobody has ever satisfactorily defined it.

Bigsby: How is it that so many of your stories, whether they are science fiction or fantasy, involve journeys?

Le Guin: Perhaps because I didn't make any until I was eighteen. There is a lot of snow, too, and I didn't see that until I was eighteen. I have no idea, really. Of course, a journey is a good, classic fictional device. And it is a good solid metaphor. There are fewer journeys now. There is one in *Always Coming Home* but it is not really central. They walk thirty miles across the mountain and that is it.

Bigsby: Not all your novels are set in the future. Is visiting the past any different from visiting the future?

Le Guin: Yes, you have to know some history. In the future you can make it up. You have to know the history of your future, but at least you get to make it up.

Bigsby: You also invent the past, don't you?

Le Guin: I invented a little country, Orsinia, which has strong similarities to Czechoslovakia. But I had to fit it into European history and to know exactly what was happening elsewhere in Europe at that time.

Bigsby: One curious thing is that in some way the past doesn't date but the future does.

Le Guin: The future dates terrifically, yes. But then I write about the present, too. I never seem to be given credit for this fact. Most of my *New Yorker* stories are simply about here and now. Anyway, the future is just another word for the imagination. I certainly have no desire to prophesy. I don't want to be a prophet. I am not writing about the future. In science fiction the future is a metaphor for the imagination. We just call it the future.

Bigsby: Can the future be anything but a displaced today?

Le Guin: No, I don't think so.

Bigsby: How far do your political views come into your work? I am thinking of, for example, *The Word for World is Forest*. Was that a response to what was then going on in Vietnam?

Le Guin: It was indeed. I wrote that book in England. Here, I had been demonstrating furiously against the war, and there I was in England, as a foreigner, and demos going on and I felt a little odd demonstrating against my country. I got a little itchy about that because the anti-American feeling was so strong in those demonstrations. I felt, well, I am against the war but I am not totally against my own country, so I was trapped. But I was very angry and very frustrated and so the book came out of that. It is certainly the most overt political statement I have made in fiction. It is an anti-war book.

Bigsby: Do you feel nervous about that? Is there a sense of violation going on there?

Le Guin: Yes, I am a good Virginia Woolfian, you know. She was extremely uneasy about openly preaching, getting on a soapbox and using art in that way. So I was a little uneasy that that was a preachy book and also that it would die with the cause. But I looked at it again a year or so ago and was pleased to see that it is, in effect, an anti-war book, an anti-violence book. It was hitting enough permanent injustices that I think it has a certain permanence and ethical relevance. I also like some of the things I did in it. I like the small green people I invented. My original title for the book was *The Little Green Men*, but I was not allowed to call it that.

Bigsby: Your novels have grown structurally more complex with time. On the table in front of us, among the other books, is *Always Coming Home*, which came out in the mid-1980s. It includes drawings, notes, poems, music. It has a cassette which accompanies it. Why that interest in a mixture of forms?

Le Guin: I was trying to create a total world, to draw the reader into a whole society and landscape and surround him or her with it. The book is not a straightforward narrative; it is all bits and pieces. There is a novel-length story in it but that is cut into three pieces. My hope was that instead of a linear drive from beginning to end I could build a house and invite the readers in to wander about and choose whichever room they liked. And the rooms are decorated with drawings. There is music, too, if they respond to that, the music of these people. I simply wanted to involve the reader in this small valley and the lives of the people who lived in the valley. I tried to make it seductive, attractive, a nice place to go and be. I was grinding many political axes at the same time – about the uses of technology, for example – but my main purpose was to put the Napa Valley of my childhood into the book with the same passion that Hardy put Dorset into his writing. I have no idea why writers want to do this, but there are many readers who respond to it. I love books about places, and readers want to go somewhere and be there as fully as possible.

Bigsby: Why do we need stories at all?

Le Guin: I think they are absolutely essential to human living. All human beings tell stories. You watch children beginning to tell stories. That is when children begin to be people. They are telling their life stories.

Bigsby: You have been both a strong supporter of feminism and a critic of some aspects of it, particularly the assumption that writing and family responsibilities are incompatible. You wrote books while raising a family, but did that change the kind of books that you wrote, do you think?

Le Guin: Oh, absolutely. I have no idea in what way because I don't know what I would have written had I not had children. Who knows, my imagination won't reach that far. But it is only some feminists who have beaten that drum. But the weeding out from the canon of writers who were mothers has been so methodical as to be quite terrifying. Apparently the only way you can be a mother and a writer is to kill yourself, like Sylvia Plath. That makes her respectable. That is too high a price to ask for the privilege of being allowed to have children and write books. I think we ought to be allowed to stay alive.

Bigsby: Having children creates an awareness of vulnerability, doesn't it?

Le Guin: Amen. Yes, and complication, endless complication. You realize that life isn't ever going to be simple, not ever again.

Bigsby: There is a character in *The Lathe of Heaven* who dreams worlds into existence, which is what you do as well. In his case they never quite turn out to be what he expected. Is that true of you, too?

Le Guin: Yes, I would say that that describes the process of imagining. But I am also a conscious artist and I do see some intellectual control.

Bigsby: You have finally closed the covers of the last book of the *Earthsea* quartet. Where to now?

Le Guin: The Oregon coast, I think. I have been writing a series of stories about a small town on the Oregon coast and the people who live there. The Oregon coast is almost as strange a place as Earthsea. It is very beautiful and rather similar, actually, in a physical sense.

Bigsby: This is not the end of fantasy from Ursula Le Guin, though.

Le Guin: I never know what is coming next. All I know is that I have no idea what book I might write next and I have no wish to know.

IN CONVERSATION
WITH
ARTHUR MILLER

Arthur Miller was born in Harlem in 1915. He was educated at the University of Michigan where he began writing plays. He briefly worked for the Federal Theatre, and wrote a number of radio plays during the Second World War. His first Broadway play, *The Man Who Had All the Luck* (1944), was a disaster and closed in four days, but he followed this with *All My Sons* (1947), which was highly successful. His next play, *Death of a Salesman* (1949), won him a Pulitzer Prize, while *The Crucible* (1953) responded to the growing conservatism in America and especially to the anti-communist witch-hunts. Miller's audience began to slip away, though, despite the considerable achievement of *A View From the Bridge* (1955). After a nine-year gap he returned to the theatre in 1964 with *After the Fall* and *Incident at Vichy* (1965), followed by *The Price* (1968), which proved to be one of his most popular works. Other plays include *The Archbishop's Ceiling* (1977), *The American Clock* (1980), *The Ride Down Mount Morgan* (1991), *Broken Glass* (1994), which won Britain's Laurence Olivier Award for best play, and *Mr. Peter's Connections* (1998). The interview was conducted in Roxbury, Connecticut in 1991 and 1994.

Bigsby: Can you explain the somewhat gnomic title of *The Ride Down Mount Morgan*?

Miller: Mount Morgan is a non-existent mountain in upper New York State down which the main character of the play comes in a heavy blizzard and crashes his car. He ends up in a hospital and, in effect, falls into his life. He is married to two women at the same time, one unbeknown to the other. The point of the exercise is to investigate some of the qualities and meanings of truthfulness and deception. He is a man of high integrity but no values. I think he is a very typical figure in our present world. He was probably always there, but he is especially evident now. It is a play in many scenes, set in different places, but it is very fluid; it moves in and out of his memory, a little bit like *Death of a Salesman*. Some of it is in the present, some of it is in his past. It involves a very fluid use of the stage, so that scenes pop up whenever they need to, wherever they need to. It is quite exciting, for me anyway.

Bigsby: It is comic but there is also a sense of the tragic.

Miller: When it is funny I let it be as funny as I feel it is. When it is tragic it is as tragic as I think it needs to be. There is no attempt to create a tragic tone. It is very idiotic at times and almost farcical. But this is riding all the time over a tragic tide. I hope it all comes together in the end.

Bigsby: The central character is almost two people: one rather conservative, an uptight individual who embraces American values; the other one not at all like that. One doesn't like driving his car above sixty miles an hour and is afraid of flying. The other is a pilot. Part of what the play seems to be concerned with is the fact that people contain different things within their own personalities and sensibilities.

Miller: It is an attempt to investigate the immense contradictions of the human animal. It is also an attempt to look at man's limitless capacity for self-deception and for integrity. This character is terrible, he is ghastly, but he does create, for example, a very socially responsible corporation. He works himself up from nothing to being chief executive of an immense insurance company, which has very progressive liberal policies towards minorities. He has a lot of terrific qualities. He has also got an immense appetite for life, for women, for everything. So he is a kind of Faustian character and, like our civilization, he is capable of enormous construction and destruction. I have just let it fall as it is. The play does not condemn him particularly; it simply leaves him standing to one side of himself, trying to find himself.

Bigsby: He is divided in another interesting way: he starts out as a poet, as a writer, and then becomes a businessman, a salesman. We have seen that division before, haven't we, in the figures of Biff and Happy Loman? One is the poet, the other is rather more prosaic. The two brothers in *The Price*, likewise, seem to represent two sides of the same sensibility.

Miller: I would never have thought of that!

Bigsby: Why did you open *The Ride Down Mount Morgan* in London?

Miller: Initially I was going to give it to the National Theatre, but their schedule was such that they couldn't do it for about seven months and I didn't want to wait that long. I love the National Theatre; I think it's terrific. That led me gradually towards London. Then the director who I particularly admire, Michael Blakemore, is himself British. He had just spent many months in New York, directing two plays, and he preferred not to be away from his home again after such a long time away. The other thing, though, is that in New York, on Broadway anyway, it is very difficult now to find actors who will stay with a play for more than a few months. You are lucky to get two months. That means the director is constantly having to put in replacements because actors are off to the movies and television. This play requires mature actors. It can't be done by neophytes or young actors who would be more likely to want to stay with a play. There is still a tradition in England – which I hope remains, but I think will probably be weakened in the future – of people who are basically theatre actors. They will do movies because the money and the fame are there, but they are excited by the theatre. We don't really have that any more. Our theatre is basically a stepping stone to the movies. Period.

On Broadway now there is one play. That is in a city of eleven million people. The rest are mostly musicals. It is a desperate condition. There is a great pessimism there and I just didn't want to throw my play into that kind of environment. Finally, we have one newspaper in New York, the *New York Times*. In Britain there are at least a dozen whose reviews mean something. The fact is that one doesn't like to think that one reviewer can kill or make a play. It just seems undemocratic and cruel and stupid, which it is. So, for all those reasons I decided not to do that play first in New York. New York, London, Paris, these are all provinces of one great human empire. No one of them is more central than the others any more. That is one thing that has happened since the Second World War. So, I opened it in London.

Bigsby: How is it that Lyman can have high integrity and low or no morals?

Miller: It is a paradox. He is intent on not suppressing his instinctual life, on living fully in every way possible. That is his integrity. He will confront the worst about himself and proceed from there. The question is, what about other people? As he says in the play, 'What we all know is that a man can be faithful to himself or to other people, but not both.' This is the dilemma of the play. He manages to convince himself, and I believe some part of the audience, that there is a higher value than other people and that value is the psychic survival of the individual. That is the dilemma. The play has no solution to it. If it did I could probably cure a lot of people. But it is laid out in front of us.

Bigsby: Let's turn to your new play. How was the idea for *Broken Glass* born?

Miller: It actually goes back fifty years or more. I've known about that woman who lost the use of her legs and nobody could diagnose the reason for many years, since, I would say, 1940. I thought about writing it many times, but I could never find a way in. And there is another image that is as old as that, that of her husband, who was a very curious fellow. He was curious because he always dressed in black. The first title of this play was *Man in Black*, but it didn't mean anything, except to me.

Bigsby: What were the circumstances of the real person whom you knew fifty years ago?

Miller: A lot like those of the character in the play. But of course I have had to invent a character, create a character, because all I really had was a visual image. I could have made a movie out of it without going any further, but on stage there has to be some depth and so it became part of my own psyche.

Bigsby: Was this just an image or was this a woman who had reacted to the same events as the woman in this play?

Miller: This is my conflation of two things. I only found out the other day, in January 1994, that there was, in the 1930s especially, an unusual amount of physical paralysis among some Jews in America. The weirdest thing. I never knew that. Just the other day there was an article in the paper about Cambodian women. After the Khmer Rouge got finished with them – and they supposedly murdered several million Cambodians in the most brutal fashion – there is a lot of hysterical blindness among them. They can see but they seem not to register what they are seeing. All this came up after I had written my play. Then, again, my daughter was telling me about a woman she knows – a concert pianist, divorced with one child – who sat down to play one day and couldn't feel her hands. That was five, six years ago and she was never again able to play the piano. They cannot find any physical reason for this. I don't know much about the circumstances, but it is fascinating. It seems to be a matter of the brain or the spirit controlling the physiological function of the body. In my play this process is associated with the terror which reached the United States in relation to the rise of Fascism in Europe, though in truth this was felt by very few people.

Bigsby: It is set at the time of Kristallnacht, when Nazi thugs went around smashing up synagogues and shops.

Miller: But there was remarkable little reaction to it here.

Bigsby: Can you remember your own reactions? You were in your early twenties.

Miller: I remember very clearly because neither I nor anybody else knew where this was going to end. It just seemed to be alarming, like a society going crazy. Of course, in 1938 we were in the last year of a deep depression in this country. Despite later mythology, the country was in a state of deep spiritual disorganization. There was a real struggle going on between people who were spiritually alive with fascism and those who were not. I am convinced that the largest part of the Mid-west was on the wrong side. It was a combination of isolationism and the feeling that they knew nothing about Europe. They couldn't see why we should ever get involved. Furthermore, nobody was making the point that this was not just about Jews: it was about France, it was about England, it was about Europe, it was, indeed, about the world. But, at that moment, it appeared to be some argument with Jews in Europe. I knew better even at that time. It seemed perfectly clear to me what it was about. It was a new imperialism that was going to crush everything around it.

Bigsby: So you weren't like one of the characters in the play, the doctor, who is confident it will go away?

Miller: No, but I would say that his was the most common attitude on the part of people who knew anything about Germany at all. He studied medicine in Germany, spent four years there. People who did that had a high opinion of the Germans, which I never had. But I was just a kid then.

Bigsby: One point that the play makes is that anti-Semitism was scarcely a function of Europe. It was already there in America.

Miller: Yes. Oh God, it was there in America. In my experience it was dense here in America, especially in New York.

Bigsby: This idea or image has been in your mind for fifty years. Why has it coalesced now into a play?

Miller: Those people come alive and it becomes possible to write about them. It is fundamentally that. You feel them, begin to hear them, and for one reason or another I hadn't heard them before. I think that is basically the reason.

Bigsby: The characters in the play are virtually all Jewish. This is the first play, maybe since the first one you wrote back at university, of which that is true, except for *Playing for Time*. What is the nature of your own relationship to your Jewish background? Has it become more important to you or less important?

Miller: Both. It has become more important in the sense that I see that a lot of my own attitudes come out of that tradition, which I wasn't really aware of for most of my life because there are other traditions that contain the same attitudes. I am speaking mainly of American democracy which, to me, is the political experience of Judaism.

Bigsby: That would come as news to the Founding Fathers.

Miller: Yes, but let's face it, when they opened the Bible they opened it at the Old Testament. When I wrote a play called *The Crucible*, about the antecedents of the Founding Fathers, any reference to the Bible was an Old Testament reference. It always struck me that these were a lot of Jews running around going crazy about things. I only later realized my connection with that. It was far from political; it was ethnic, among other things. But what are you saying when you say that? You are not saying very much. Another person had the same feeling from a totally different vantage point, a completely Christian point of view, or even a Muslim one.

Bigsby: Philip Gellberg, who is the centre of this play, resents his Jewish identity almost as though it were a kind of unfair burden that has been put on him. As he says, 'Why is it so hard to be a Jew? Why must we be different? Being Jewish is a full-time job.' Were you ever made to feel guilty for not making it a full-time job?

Miller: I didn't know how to do that. My father, who was an uneducated man who never read a book in his entire life, had travelled the United States many times for his business, so he had experience with all kinds of people. From the earliest times that I can remember, when people referred to some character as particularly Jewish or some trait as particularly Jewish, he would say, 'Oh, no, no, no. They are that way in Milwaukee,' or Texas or Chicago or somewhere. From the very beginning I was weaned away from the idea that certain things were particularly Jewish. I knew a woman in Ohio, who was Catholic and of German and French background. She was my first mother-in-law. We were having breakfast and the paper arrived and there had been a vile bank robbery the night before during which somebody had got beaten up. She saw the headline and said, as she handed me the paper, 'Oh, I hope he is not a Catholic,' meaning the robber. This is exactly what the Jews would say. I am sure anybody who feels a minority status would. You would hardly think the Catholics would, because they were running the state of Ohio, along with Illinois and Michigan, but they still had that feeling that they were on the edge of the abyss for historical reasons. The blacks feel it when an African-American is caught doing something bad. I am sure in certain circumstances, God help us, even the English would. This is an anxiety that comes with feeling that you are not running the place, that you are there on the sufferance of others.

Bigsby: There have been critics over the years who have said that you really write about Jewish characters but don't admit to their Jewishness.

Miller: That isn't really true. The characters in *All My Sons* are not Jewish, they are out of Ohio. The people in *A View from the Bridge* are not Jewish, they are as Italian as you can get.

Bigsby: *Death of a Salesman*?

Miller: In *Salesman* they could be, but they needn't be. That's my point. If I make them walk around with a 'Jewish' sign on it is utterly pointless, any more than if I said the people in *All My Sons* are Catholics, which to me they were. I don't know why these labels mean anything.

Bigsby: Whereas in *Broken Glass* the Jewishness is central.

Miller: It is central because you can't tell the story otherwise. It is impossible to imagine this story without the Jews, because they are the ones who were being attacked at the time in Germany and very few people, including the Jews in America, had very much feeling about that.

Bigsby: Yet 1938 is not only the time of Kristallnacht it is also the time of the Depression, and the Depression is in this play too.

Miller: Sure it is. It is in the atmosphere of the play. It is said of the protagonist that he never knew any Depression. He worked for a big bank and his position seemed very secure and always had been.

Bigsby: Yet his job is foreclosing on other people.

Miller: He gives loans, but he also forecloses; he giveth and he receiveth.

Bigsby: In fact there is a relationship, is there not, between some of the lessons that came out of the Depression and some of the lessons that came out of the events in Europe? There is more than glass being broken; there are human contracts and promises.

Miller: Civilization is being broken. The social contract is being torn up. To me, one of the basic threats posed by the Fascists was that here was a movement that was going to literally tear up all the underlying web of obligations that keeps society in place. A key image, for me, of that whole period was the time one Nazi bomber flew over Guernica, an undefended town in Spain. Picasso later did a painting about this. In broad daylight it sailed above that town and dropped a bomb right in the middle of the square where all the people were shopping, sitting on benches in the sun and so on. I can't tell you what an effect that had on me. I could understand artillery bombardments from a distance during the First World War which destroyed one village and town after another, but that guy doesn't see where the missile goes so he can snuggle into his irresponsibility by saying, 'Well, I'm just a soldier. I'm in danger myself.' But this was something else. This was a guy looking down at this peaceful square and dropping high explosives on it and I can't tell you what a concatenation that made in my head.

Bigsby: We are talking about this play as though it were purely about the 1930s but isn't it a very 1990s play too, not merely because of the revival of fascism in Germany, but also because of places such as Sarajevo?

Miller: They are bombing the hell out of that town and we are all sitting here saying, 'Tut, tut, isn't that terrible.' They blew up sixteen or more schoolchildren today and did you see anybody pause on his way to lunch? I didn't.

Bigsby: Isn't that in part what *Broken Glass* is about?

Miller: That's what it's about.

Bigsby: Buried in the play seems to be yet another question, which is why we behave as though we can't do anything in the face of these events. We let them disable us in the same way that the character in *Broken Glass* allows it to disable her.

Miller: You know, I think that we are so helpless about it because in each of us, whether recognized or not, and it usually isn't recognized, is this same bloody ethnic nationalism. This is not coming from the moon. This is coming from us and we haven't even come close to confronting this thing. All the patriotism, the ethnic nationalism and the rest of it is at the door, knocking on the door, and it is as dangerous as it ever was.

Right after the Second World War I happened to meet Jean Monnet, the French originator of the Common Market, and he said, 'We are never going to have another war in Europe because there is no such thing as a German coalmine or a French railroad any more. The capital is so mixed. International co-operation is so alarmingly powerful now. Ford has plants in every country, including Germany, France and England. General Motors, likewise. So they are not likely to bomb themselves.' I took that very seriously for quite a while, although emotionally I found it hard to accept. I thought, maybe we are at the end of something here. I don't know about that any more. I don't know if that is strong enough to withstand the rush of emotion that comes with these ethnic feelings.

Bigsby: That is because these things are not external to us. In this play the reason that Sylvia has become momentarily disabled, unable to walk, is partly to do with an external public event, a betrayal on a social scale, but it is in part to do with a betrayal on a private level.

Miller: They are both the same thing. That paralysis could destroy the world now.

Bigsby: There is a sense in which this play seems almost a companion piece to *The Last Yankee*. Certainly some of the same concerns are there. In *The Last Yankee* there are two women who have retreated into mental instability in the face of distrust, horror, broken relationships. They have to work their way back to the possibility of reconstructing their lives, and the possibility of reconstruction is as important in *Broken Glass* as the analysis of the sickness, is it not?

Miller: It certainly is. The two plays are related. I guess I had never thought of it that way. Well, why wouldn't they be? I am the same writer, more or less. But what intrigued me in *Broken Glass* is the human animal's capacity to create a fantasy – based on reality to be sure – so powerful as to paralyze an otherwise physically sound woman. She has made war against herself, and the trigger is what she reads in a newspaper, something she can't possibly believe. She says, 'You mean I'm sick because I read a newspaper?' Well, yes, in a way. I don't propose to solve that dilemma in the play, of course. In real life it would probably be impossible to solve.

Bigsby: But apart from anything else it is concerned with something I find elsewhere in your work, namely a concern with survival, with finding some way of going on which involves more than mere resignation.

Miller: Oh, certainly. In this play they are struggling with resignation all the time. Everybody in the play, including Gellburg. Gellburg is trying to find the way out of it, too.

Bigsby: Could you tell me how you see Philip Gellburg?

Miller: He is a very conservative man, conservative in every sense of the word. He believes in the system as it was then and as it still is, in most places, now. He believes that the banks open in the morning and you take your money out. And most of the time that is how it is. Most of the time. He is a material person. He is also a snob, a snob not only about non-Jews but also about Jews, about everybody, to tell the truth. That is his defence against the feeling of emptiness that he has.

Bigsby: Doesn't that emptiness come in part because he lives a life based on denial?

Miller: He is denying everything. He is denying his ethnicity, his Jewishness, and he is denying his wife's love as well. As the doctor's wife describes him, he is a miserable little pisser. He is also a pathetic one. But I think he is a significant one.

Bigsby: Why does his wife stay with him?

Miller: He adores her, for one thing, and she knows that. He is also a good provider. He knows how to make money and has a good job for that period, that time when people often didn't have jobs.

Bigsby: But he has sexually withdrawn from her for over a quarter of a century.

Miller: That is right, but people didn't rush to the divorce courts in those days. You got married for better or worse, especially in this class of people. They were not about to renounce this marriage. They might not be all that religious, but the customs were more important than the people. The custom was that you stayed married unless there was some extreme problem, which in this case there is, but she is not about to appeal to it. Why? Because her mother would collapse and, though people did get divorces for just such a reason, her character is not such that she will do it.

Bigsby: In fact, she has put her life on hold, hasn't she?

Miller: She just stopped and, let me tell you, the Brooklyn neighbourhoods were full of them. I suspect the London ones were likewise. Just stop the organism. Psychologically speaking, it goes into a state of arrest. It is just pulsing, not moving any more.

Bigsby: So she is also a denier.

Miller: Everybody in the play is. Including the doctor.

Bigsby: Who you describe as a scientific idealist.

Miller: He is a great idealist. He is also a womanizer, when he can manage it, but not for some years now. He is telling the truth when he says he hasn't been with anybody for a number of years. He can't remember the last one.

Bigsby: But he must have been with quite a few before, because his wife instantly assumes that it is going to happen again.

Miller: Yes. But that is partly because it amuses her. The idea attracts her.

Bigsby: Although the doctor's wife, Margaret, is in a way a minor player, along with Sylvia Gellburg's sister, she plays a significant role.

Miller: I don't regard those characters as minor at all. They bring the neighbourhood into the play, for one thing. They are the neighbourhood, a kind of secret chorus in the drama. They are carefully placed in the play so that they offer us a sense of normality, the average man's attitude towards this incredible set of events.

Bigsby: There have been a series of drafts of the play. After the first read-through you have already been typing new parts of the play. When does that process stop?

Miller: I think it is going to stop right now. I can't think of anything more now. This is not unusual for me, of course. I have done this before. But these changes are minor, a few words here, a sentence there. I might cut an exchange simply because it does not add sufficiently to warrant its presence in the play. The scene I wrote today was one I had had in mind for weeks. I simply couldn't latch onto it until the read-through when I suddenly saw where it belonged.

Bigsby: Do you learn in rehearsals or is it simply a case of watching actors work their way towards something you already know exists?

Miller: You do learn, of course, but I try not to learn too much because you begin scribbling when you shouldn't. In this case, what is being bonded together is a public concern and a private neurosis. In my opinion this is always the case, but to try to find the juncture where it meets is not so easy. I knew it was central to this play but I hadn't quite realized it. I was quite aware of that before we ever had the reading, but I thought, I'll wait until I hear it before I attempt to make the concrete juncture. I think I have now; that is what was bringing my director to tears a little while ago.

Bigsby: What is the ideal relationship for you between writer and director?

Miller: First of all, the director should be the servant of the play. He should not conceive of himself as being co-author. There are some authors who want a co-author, perfectly legitimately. Hundreds of plays have been written by two or more people, but my concepts are mine and I don't want them to be messed with. So, for me, the best director is somebody who will plumb what I have done, perhaps come up with contradictions, say, 'You can't say this if you are going to say that.' I want someone who will objectify what to me is still subjective. Then I will have to defend it, but I like to do that. But I do not like someone trying to use the play as something that reminds him of something else. You see a lot of directors who think they should use the play at hand as a skeleton for some other play that they have got in their minds. Maybe they could get some poor play that hasn't got any life of its own and make something interesting of it. That is possible, but I don't want to be involved with that because I think I would rather see my own stuff on the stage, and sink or swim with it. In other words, the director should try to interpret the play, not create his own.

Bigsby: One of the problems, it seems to me, is the desire to see everything in terms of realism, to allow all meaning to bubble to the surface.

Miller: Right. They can't stand a metaphor. Metaphor is dangerous, ambiguous; it leaves people slightly mystified and the conscience of the American theatre is that of an intelligent businessman. He is a realistic, intelligent, even sensitive person, but he ain't interested in metaphors. He wants to know who's on first and this has made for a very strong realistic tradition, not just in the theatre but in the novel, the movies and so on. But as soon as you begin to stretch that into a metaphoric area, they get uneasy.

Bigsby: Have you found problems of that kind?

Miller: Oh, sure. They are always trying to push you back into the old bucket. To them, this isn't a play about America, like, let's say, *The American Yankee*, it is a play about a neurotic woman and her stupid husband. It is remarkable, the absence of that kind of sensitivity. I suppose it is a part of the cultural strength of the country as well as a weakness but, to me, it is destructive. They make allowances for it in other arts, like painting or the ballet, which, of course, can't be realistic. But to make a juncture of some kind between a concept and an action is very difficult for some of them. I find the audiences are better than the critics in that respect. Critics are always trying to get to the bottom of things, while they are already at the bottom of things if they only knew.

Bigsby: The cast in this American production is almost entirely Jewish. I can see how this is going to help with the rhythms of language, but it is scarcely a requirement of the play, is it?

Miller: No. As a matter of fact, in the course of trying to cast this play, I would say that 90 per cent of the actors we talked to were not Jewish at all. But we have real problems in America because when actors get any good they are taken by the movies. Let an actor, God forbid, give an especially striking performance in a play and he has immediate offers to go to the movies where he is going to make a lot of money. He can't make any money to speak of in the theatre. So, when they get good, they go. What you are left with is people nobody happens to want at the moment. They may be perfectly good actors but your choice is much more limited than it used to be and this makes it tough. We get an actor who is perfect for the part and he says, 'Gee, I would love to do it but I have got a TV thing that they want me for or they may want me for and I have got to keep myself free.' It is the difference between making a few thousand dollars a week and making a hundred thousand dollars for half an hour's work. It is tough.

Bigsby: If you were in any other profession, virtually any other profession, you would have retired fifteen years ago. Can you retire or is writing the same as getting up each day?

Miller: I can't imagine what I would do with myself if I wasn't writing. I don't write that much. I haven't got thirty plays or so by me. It takes me a long time to get a play from start to finish, several years usually. But I couldn't retire. I wouldn't know what to do. It would be like cutting my heart out. Why would you do that?

IN CONVERSATION WITH ALICE MUNRO

Alice Munro was born Alice Laidlaw in Wingham, Ontario, in 1931. Her first book of stories, *Dance of the Happy Shades*, appeared in 1968 and won the Governor General's Award. This collection was followed by a series of others including *Lives of Girls and Women* (1971), *Something I've been Meaning to Tell You* (1974), *Who Do You Think You Are?* (1978), *The Moons of Jupiter* (1982), *The Progress of Love* (1987), *Friend of My Youth* (1990) and *Open Secrets* (1992). This interview was conducted in October, 1990.

Bigsby: You were born in the small town of Wingham, Ontario. Now you live in Clinton, which is just a few miles down the road. What sort of place was Wingham?

Munro: I think if you were driving through Wingham you would probably think it was a very typical Ontario small town. It got started in the 1850s. Most of the big buildings are still Victorian, ugly but old and so interesting to us. Then a bit of modern building went on after the Second World War. These towns all rose to a peak before the turn of the century when they were really booming industrial centres. We outsold the Western provinces which were just opening up and had to buy from Ontario and so Ontario towns got rich. The West has never forgotten. So it is that sort of town: big Victorian buildings, big churches, big trees, rather nice looking, I think.

Bigsby: What sort of population?

Munro: The population now is about three thousand, nearly all of British descent. Nearly all are Protestant, with a small Catholic minority that has been there since the beginning. These are not very liberal-minded places. They are generally neighbourly, though, and not too uncomfortable to live in, depending on who you are.

Bigsby: Is the life that you examine not changed by the fact that you have already fictionalized it, so that in a sense you return not to origins but to a fictionalized version?

Munro: No, that is not true. The fiction that I do, I cast off. I can hardly remember it. I can remember the stories now that are in *Friend of My Youth* because I am going around talking about them. Two years from now I would have to be reminded of them. My earlier books I tend to almost completely forget. It is like a snake's skin: you shed each one and you start growing another and you shed that one. The fiction that I have made of my life is out there, accessible to everybody else, but I carry on as if I had forgotten about it.

Bigsby: When you began writing there was a sense, was there not, that Canadian writers were in some way parochial. Indeed, they themselves used to feel that reality lay elsewhere. So Margaret Laurence took herself off to Europe, so did Robertson Davis and eventually so did Margaret Atwood. Is that an impulse that you felt?

Munro: Never, because I was too poor. I was living at such a distance from the places where people thought this way that I did not understand that the fact that I was Canadian made it unlikely that I could be a writer. I did not realize that this was a problem, or that it was a problem that I was a woman. Both these things were apparently huge problems in the 1950s, together with the fact that I wrote short stories. I did not know that short stories were dead and that they were just terribly unfashionable. Because I did not know any of these things it never occurred to me to go to any other country to become a writer. I would have loved to be able to travel. The idea excited me, but it was not a possibility in my life. I married when I was twenty and had two kids before I was twenty-five. My husband got two weeks' vacation a year. So we were going to go to Europe so I could write? Not likely! I didn't know other writers, and I didn't know how they talked about Canada or any of this. It was not until much later on that I heard that I should have been thinking about going to France to write a novel. None of these things occurred to me as problems.

I did have another problem, though, for a while when I was not writing about my own material. I went through that young writer's thing of imitating the books I was reading. I was reading very great books at this time. I was reading Thomas Mann or Proust, or something like that, and so, though the stories were set in Canada, my people behaved as if they lived somewhere else. It probably took me until I was twenty-five to really start writing about the kind of people I had grown up with.

Bigsby: I half expected you to pick out American models because although you live in Canada you are a very short distance away from the United States and must have been exposed to the American media.

Munro: Yes, but I think the Canada I grew up in had its sights very much set on Britain. This would have lasted probably until about 1960 when I began reading American writers. They were not taught in our universities and they were not particularly well thought of. It was not the anti-Americanism that is fashionable now, but there was a feeling that they were a little rough and unfinished, indelicate. But I began to read American writers, the writers of the American South, short story writers, and I thought they were wonderful. It was probably from American writers that I got the idea that you could write about places like Wingham, places like Heron County.

Bigsby: This is Eudora Welty?

Munro: Yes, yes. And who ever was writing short stories in the *New Yorker* then: Jean Stafford, the early John Updike. These were writers whom I felt close to.

Bigsby: What is the pace at which you would like people to read your work? Would you like them to read stories as they appear in the magazines or in a book in which you have no sooner finished one story than you go on to the next one?

Munro: I do not at all like the idea that you finish one story and go on to the next one. I think people should take as long to read a story as it takes me to write one. That would be a couple of months! That may be a bit unrealistic, but I definitely think you should read one story and put the book away and then read another story some time later. Of course, I do not follow this advice myself. I have been reading two or three books of short stories recently and I do read them all at one gulp and then go back and read favourite ones. All the books I love I read over and over again. When I read them again I read them more slowly.

Bigsby: Your stories seem to have grown longer. If a novel were a baby, some of these stories seem foetuses close to term.

Munro: You mean if I could just hold on a little longer I would give birth to a full-blown novel! Don't think it hasn't crossed my mind. I look at novels. I go into bookstores and I look at very short novels and I think, 'Hmm, Muriel Spark, 118 pages, now if I . . .' but somehow I think it is not as simple as that.

Bigsby: You recently spent time in Scotland, again in a very small community. Is that a case of returning to your roots?

Munro: Oh, yes. When I finished this book, and was waiting for it to come out, I thought, I am going to write a non-fiction book next time. I went to Scotland and I did this thing of looking for the place my family came from. I knew a lot of stories about my family and I didn't know what I really wanted to write. I still don't, and I am not at all sure that anything is going to come of this because when I was in Scotland what I did was go around getting all this information, unconscientiously researching. That had always impressed me, people researching books, and I thought, here I am, I am researching a book. But really I was getting up early in the morning and writing a story set in an Ontario small town. So I am not sure what is going to come out of this. But it was great fun, the going around and looking things up. It beats writing. It's a lot easier. Then, of course, you have to go home with all these things, with all this information, and make something of it. I haven't figured out how to do that yet.

Bigsby: Which do you think will come first, the non-fiction book or the novel?

Munro: Probably neither. Probably more stories.

Bigsby: When you started writing, the fact that you were a woman was not, you felt, an issue. The culture hadn't made it an issue. In the 1990s the culture has made it an issue. Do you feel that pressure bearing on you at all?

Munro: I would if I let it. I try very hard to remain unaware of pressures like this. Occasionally I have had to become aware because of some review in the feminist press. Usually the pressure on me is a fairly crude notion of one's duty as a woman writer to be presenting reality in certain ways, to be giving women what they should have according to a certain point of view. Of course, if I was going to give in to pressure like that I would have listened to what they told me in the United Church Sunday School in Wingham long ago. So I have never felt it as anything very serious, no. It is a fact that as a woman writer right now one has a certain simple advantage. I think most fiction buyers are women, most buyers of serious as well as popular fiction, and they tend to buy books by other women. So you have a sympathetic audience. This is not the audience which is telling you what you should write. I felt when I was a very small child that I lived in a totally different reality from everybody else and that it would be very hard to protect it. I always thought that it was under threat. There always seemed to be people who wanted to destroy that and make it a more acceptable reality. I think this is probably the way most writers feel. Maybe it is not a normal way to feel.

Bigsby: Perhaps you are right about the difference between men and women in that regard. I once suggested to Margaret Atwood that the telephone call which rehearses the day seems to me much more a female thing than a male thing.

Munro: I think it is. But what do men talk about when you say, 'How was your day?' Do they even say, 'How was your day?'

Bigsby: 'Fine' is probably as elaborate as they get.

Munro: Yes, I know, and they come home and that is what they say to their wives. Women never do that. If a woman says 'fine' that means I don't really want to talk to you. More often women cement their friendships by telling each other the awful things that happen. This doesn't mean that they are depressed, really. It is just, 'Oh, my God, you know what . . .' and this is a very bonding thing in a way. Don't all of us find our lives are reflected by the people who know about us? They are reflected back to us in strange ways. I think we construct villages wherever we go.

Bigsby: That is true, except that in the city or in suburbia there can be a clear separation from those around you. You can lead a very private existence. The people next door don't know who you are or what you do.

Munro: That is true, and I love this when I come to the city. I love walking along the street and being anonymous. When I first left my small town when I was eighteen I was intoxicated with the idea that no-one knew who I was and I didn't intend, at that time, ever to go back.

Bigsby: There is a story of yours in which a man exposes himself to a young girl. The surprising thing is that it is described not as a provoking shock, but with a kind of detached interest.

Munro: I guess that is the same thing as watching the horse being shot. It is just the kind of writing I like. It doesn't gloss this over with any sort of preconceived opinion that this is either bad or not nice or whatever. If you were a writer intent on showing the way children are sexually abused you might want to show the young girl as feeling immediate horror, disgust and fear, which she might well feel if the man then went on to make certain threats. But, at that moment, I think it is correct for her to feel surprised, interested. This also goes along with the kind of character she is. I don't know what the psychologists' explanation for this is. If you don't accept the parent of your own sex you may have trouble accepting yourself, or something like that. I seem to have come closer to it, but that doesn't mean that I write for therapy. I write to investigate whatever it is that I am feeling.

Bigsby: Is there nevertheless a therapeutic element?

Munro: No, I am not sure that there is. I think that you can reconcile yourself to something through writing but I am not sure that you solve your personal problems that way. I think maybe you help other people by writing. I am not sure it has that much to do with the personality of the writer.

Bigsby: Did you find it difficult to recapture that kind of sensibility of childhood?

Munro: I might now but I didn't when I was doing my earlier books. I feel now that I have finished with it. But as soon as I say that it turns out not to be true. No, I think I can very easily find in myself pretty well all the people that I have been. They are all still there.

Bigsby: A number of those stories do plunder the early years when you were growing up. One of your characters accuses herself of a cowardly, tender nostalgia, of trying to get back to a gentler past. Is that an accusation you would ever level at yourself: the desire to reach back to a world where things were simpler?

Munro: I don't think so. The world I remember was not particularly gentle, though it may have been simpler in some ways. No, it wasn't even simple; it was full of very bewildering, puzzling and sometimes brutal things. I don't think that the way I use the past is in any way an evasion.

Bigsby: Do you ever consider writing a novel?

Munro: Of course I do! I not only think them up, I try to write them. I try to write them and they break down. Many of my stories have started out as novels, even some of the stories in *Friend of My Youth*. Then I realize that the thing that excites me in this is something that really makes a story and that if I stretch it into a novel I lose whatever it is that is important about it.

Bigsby: Yet those stories are very often full of enough material to make a novel in their own right. They are full of detail, multiple characters; they stretch across time.

Munro: That is the kind of story I like. I like to do lots of layers and intertwinings, but I like blanks, too, which you don't get away with in a conventional novel at least. I like to make jumps and bring in unexpected things.

Bigsby: You have to date produced seven books of short stories. I know two of them are officially described as novels by your publisher, but really there are seven books of short stories. How different are the short stories you are writing now from those that you wrote all those years ago when you began?

Munro: I don't have a very good descriptive vocabulary about writing but they feel completely different to me. I know that I now find it very difficult to read one of the earlier stories because I wouldn't write it now. I suppose the stories I write now are much more complex and maybe less pointed, in a way. One always feels that the work you are doing now is the real work, that you have finally discovered what you were meant to do and that the work that you did ten years ago was perhaps a bit of a blind alley. Yet I know that this opinion is not at all reliable. It may well be that one did one's best work in the very first book, or something like that. A writer is simply no judge of this kind of thing. It is just that you make changes in your way of writing and your way of approaching your material which have something to do with changes in yourself. You can't really analyze or describe it; you just know it. There is one story – that I have never published in a book and was going to put in this last book – that was only written about ten years ago and it just didn't fit at all. It wasn't right because of some change in the way I look at things.

Bigsby: Given that you have mined your own life to some degree in your stories, does that mean that whatever non-fiction work you produce it won't be an autobiography?

Munro: I have never thought of writing an autobiography. I can't bear the idea. So, no, I don't think I will ever do that. I suppose what you say is true. You get used to the satisfactory fictionalizing of things that you are interested in about your life and then to stick to facts would be very difficult. Also the part I don't like about it is that you have to deal with other people. Would you like being in anybody's autobiography? I wouldn't, and I don't quite like the idea of doing this to people – of saying, 'This is what they were like.' In a story you change them, you can investigate, you can jump to conclusions. But in an autobiography, no. I also hate the idea of anybody else ever writing about me, and they say autobiographies are a defense against this. However, I don't think this will happen because not much happens to me.

Bigsby: You seem to have a particular fascination with time. I am reminded of Virginia Woolf's *To The Lighthouse* where we learn about the details of people's lives and then suddenly they disappear only to reappear much later. You do that.

Munro: I love that. I love that dreamlike kind of feeling. It is what I actually feel about reality, what I feel about the world, so it isn't something artificial in my work. I never decided to do it; it just started happening. Maybe it was something I got on to as I became older, too, because we all have that experience of people vanishing and reappearing with the same names and completely new faces and ideas. It is just one of the strange things in life.

Bigsby: One thing that does is give you a new sense of perspective. We have been looking at an affair, at a relationship, and suddenly it disappears and we return later and see it in a different perspective. Its significance has changed simply because of the passage of time. Also you come back into a different world, a different sociological world.

Munro: I think all that is the kind of writer I have become because I have lived to be this old. It is particularly part of the world we are living in now. The popular press is always talking about the 1970s, the 1950s and the 1980s as if these were different worlds. We are all trained to see the world this way, and to a certain extent it is this way because of the changes in what everybody thinks about, the kind of houses they live in, the kind of food they eat and everything. I suppose a writer is naturally going to pick up on this in an impressionistic way.

Bigsby: Your stories don't strike me as the kind that have twists at the end of them, but very often the final sentence is absolutely crucial. I get the impression that you work very hard to get that last sentence right.

Munro: I want the ending to do something important. It is not to be a twist. It is more as if I sometimes want it to be a drop, like a shift of the surface on which we are standing, or a change in some fundamental way. But it has to be justified by everything that came before. It can never be a trick. So, what happens at the end should be very simple, but it should somehow make you see what you have been reading about.

Bigsby: There is a classic example of that in *Friend of My Youth*. One story ends with the words 'they are fairly happy'. Very Hemingwayesque. What it means, however, is that you have to reread that story through that final sentence.

Munro: Yes. That final sentence is very important to me. But it is just very hard for me to say why. That really is a fairly straightforward story of two different women and their lives. They come together and talk about things when they are well into middle age. I very much like the picture of them sitting there, on that deck, looking out at the lake, saying things and not really understanding each other's point of view about the world. They are thoroughly happy with their lives, but they are also very happy in that they are more than fairly happy in that moment. That is one of the moments that may redeem other moments that aren't happy at all. So that is the way it had to end. I didn't have to work with that ending. I knew that ending long before I got to it.

IN CONVERSATION WITH MORDECAI RICHLER

M ordecai Richler was born in Montreal's Jewish quarter in 1931, the son of a scrap merchant. He dropped out of university and travelled to London where he worked as a journalist before returning to Canada in 1972. His books include: *The Acrobats* (1954), *Son of a Smaller Hero* (1955), *The Apprenticeship of Duddy Kravitz* (1959), *Cocksure* (1967), *St Urbain's Horseman* (1971), *Joshua Then and Now* (1980), *Solomon Gursky Was Here* (1990), *Barney's Version* (1997), and *Belling the Cat* (1998). Mordecai Richler is also a short story writer, a television and film scriptwriter, an essayist and the author of children's books. This interview was conducted in 1989 on the occasion of the publication of *Solomon Gursky Was Here*.

Bigsby: This is your first novel for ten years. Why is that?

Richler: I am getting older and slower, but it was a novel that gave me a great deal of trouble. I made a couple of false starts, got to a certain point – let us say 130 or 140 pages – and came up against a blank wall. I hit that wall again and again, so I put it aside and got on with other things. Then, about five years ago, I went back to our place in the country and I was resolved to stay out there until I finished the novel. It was a novel which involved me in a certain number of risks. I found myself grudgingly doing a lot of research about life in the Arctic in the nineteenth century, about the Franklin Expedition, and indeed about life in England in the nineteenth century. Suddenly I was writing dialogue for people who lived a hundred or a hundred and twenty years ago and I was feeling very shaky about that. It is not a music I knew so I went through many drafts before I felt confident enough to let it go.

Bigsby: At the beginning of your career, the fact that you were a Canadian Jewish writer was the source of some anxiety to you. It is an anxiety you plainly got over fairly quickly because those elements of your identity became your subjects. Certainly *Solomon Gursky Was Here* is about Canada and about being Jewish, isn't it?

Richler: Yes, you could say that. I was very taken with the generation of Jews who came over to North America around 1900. It seemed to me that they were a very heroic generation: men of great appetite, hooligans of great appetite, if you like. They founded Hollywood and they created great real estate fortunes and, in the case of this novel, an enormous liquor fortune built on the rock of bootlegging during the Prohibition years. I was concerned with how these families diminished over succeeding generations as there was a compromise between Jewish tradition and the need to be North American. So that is one of the things in the novel, but the original impulse was to write a novel about Solomon Gursky, a man who was not satisfied to live within the confines of one life and invented others for himself.

Bigsby: Something very strange happens with this character because, starting as a solid, three-dimensional, tangible, larger-than-life figure, he slowly begins to dissolve and change into a kind of myth. Why that second stage when he transmutes?

Richler: I don't start a novel with any kind of route map. I really don't know where I am going and in this case I had no idea. I was terrified of taking wrong turns but that is where the novel took me and that seemed like the right highway.

Bigsby: Solomon's grandfather was an amazing figure, almost the stuff out of which myths are made. He is certainly a conscious creator of myths, is he not, a man associated with the figure of a raven.

Richler: Yes, that is true. The image of the raven snuck up on me, really. What happened was this: we lived here in Britain for twenty years and when I returned to Canada with my family in 1972, I had only been there a short time when an old friend confronted me and said, 'You have read a lot about Canada but you have never been to the North. How could this be?' I said, 'You are absolutely right.' Shortly after I was invited on a trip by the Commissioner of the Northwest Territories, who is very much like a nineteenth-century Russian Inspector General. He flies around in a plane and lands in an Eskimo community and says, 'What would you like?' and they say 'A fire engine' and he says 'What colour?' and they say 'Yellow' and he says, 'You've got it.' I had a wonderful time and it was an immediate fascination to me. So I went back again and again and began to read deeply about the history of the North, really out of curiosity, with no ulterior motives. But then it surfaced in this novel. And there were the ravens, out on the telephone wires, at sixty below zero. I have never played with that kind of imagery before but having read about the raven in mythology it seemed to be a perfect metaphor for Solomon, because he was both the creator and the destroyer. Also the raven is a mischievous creature. That is how that happened.

Bigsby: It also eats flesh, and cannibalism seems to be another theme that runs through the book.

Richler: Cannibalism is central to the history of the North, so it is not seen as so great an outrage.

Bigsby: But the characters themselves have elements of cannibalism about them, that is to say, they do consume one another and other people.

Richler: The Franklin Expedition ended in cannibalism. Franklin himself was a very intrepid man, but a rather foolish one and he did not know anything about native life. Had he addressed himself to the natives, all those people – 144 of them – could have survived, but they had their dress naval uniforms and all kinds of silly clothes which were of no use in the North and they did not know how to hunt seal or caribou and, driven to the final extremity, they resorted to cannibalism. Dickens, among others, couldn't accept this and said it was a dreadful lie by thieving natives, because it was the Eskimos who first reported this. He thought it was a calumny and this just could not be true of British naval people. But of course it was absolutely true.

Bigsby: *Solomon Gursky* is a novel that bounces around a good deal in time. Stories are picked up and broken off as you move to another story. For the first hundred pages I found myself checking back to the family tree that you give at the beginning. Why have you opted for that particular structure?

Richler: I started playing around with time and that kind of structure in my last novel *Joshua Then and Now*. Mind you, that was comparatively easy. It only covered about forty years. This covers 150 years and so it does wind its way in and out. Some readers have found it rather difficult. Others just go with the flow and get on with it. There was no other way I could go about it. I tried all kinds of constructions but dealing with so many societies and groups of people in different places I saw no other way out. I did try a linear construction once and I just felt that dying on the vine. I didn't think it worked. It would have made it easier to read, I guess, but why should I go to that trouble?

Bigsby: There is a moment in the novel when Solomon tackles anti-Semitism head on. He buys up a hotel that has restrictions and won't allow Jews in. If I can take you back to your own early years in Montreal, when did you become aware of anti-Semitism?

Richler: I became aware of it as a child, but it was not peculiar to Quebec. It was part of urban society at that time. I can remember things being painted on the highway but that was the experience of that generation.

Bigsby: Did it ever reach out and touch you in a personal way?

Richler: Yes and no. The Jewish community was very much self-contained and as a kid I hardly wandered out of that world. It was only when I did that I came across it to some extent. We went to the Protestant schools. We were thirteen years old when we entered high school and the first thing we were told, when we were lined up in the gymnasium, was, 'If any of you want to go to McGill University, admission is 65 per cent in your matriculation exam. But if you are Jewish you have to have 75 per cent in order to get in. And, furthermore, if you want to go to Madison there is a much more rigorous quota.' So this was laid out on the table and when you are thirteen it is a bit of a shock to hear that. Of course, all this has changed. It is no longer the case.

Bigsby: You were brought up in Montreal in an English-speaking community, though your parents spoke Yiddish. In a country with divided loyalties, which looks to France and to Britain, and with America just across the border, as a young man what did your loyalties consist of?

Richler: Now we are going to do Canadian problems! And there is such a problem with Canada. The fact is that there is a very fragile sense of nationhood and our loyalties are largely regional. This is what is threatening the country with fracture at the moment. As to ourselves, the French resented the Jewish community because we identified with the English and the children were brought up to speak English but, of course, that was inevitable because the language of achievement in North America was English and not French. Also, it must be said, the French Catholic community was not very welcoming to immigrant Jews. Far from welcoming. So we identified with the English Canadian community. What was peculiar to the Jewish community was that we looked on New York as our cultural capital, not Toronto or whatever. We took the New York newspapers. Even my father, who was not a reader or a literate man, always took the *New York Daily News* or the *Daily Mirror*. And heaven was New York, where Jews were really integrated into the city and had a role to play. The Jewish community of Montreal still looks to New York. The *New York Times* has a huge circulation in Montreal.

Bigsby: Why did you finally decide at the age of nineteen to leave, to pack it all up and go elsewhere?

Richler: Well, we are going back to 1950 or 1951. Canada was a country of about twelve to fifteen million people. It was very parochial, very boring, and I could not wait to get out. I wanted to be a writer and I felt, at that time, that to be published in Canada would be more of a stigma than anything else. This is not true today but it was at the time. The publishing scene there was rather pathetic and so I thought, 'OK, if I am going to be a writer I have to prove I can publish in New York or London.' I chose Europe because it appealed to me more than New York.

Bigsby: Was there a sense, almost, that reality was what existed elsewhere?

Richler: Yes, because we seemed to have no more than a window on reality in Canada. Very little was happening there. I was brought up on Hemingway and Fitzgerald, and I just longed to go to Paris. It was very romantic. It was not a very original idea, but 1950–51 was a wonderful period in Paris. There were a lot of Americans there on the GI Bill and there was a community of writers and painters. We were broke but we had a splendid time. I certainly don't regret it.

Bigsby: Your first novel, *The Acrobats*, seems almost an attempt to write from as far away from your own experience as is possible.

Richler: It was an appallingly derivative novel. I have very cunningly kept it out of print ever since. It was very exhilarating. It was delightful to be twenty-one or twenty-two and have a novel published in England. But, yes, I was imitating writers I admired: Malraux and Hemingway. At that time I thought, 'Who in the hell would want to read a novel about Montreal or St Urbain Street?' I was a very arrogant and pompous boy, but when you are twenty-one you are armed with that kind of arrogance.

Bigsby: One review in Canada said, 'You have never heard of Mordecai Richler, but look out, she is a name to watch for.' You have had some very strange responses over the years from Jewish and Canadian critics, have you not? Is that because they want you to be on your best cultural behaviour, to produce a literature fit for Canada?

Richler: Yes. Both the Jewish community and the Canadian are self-conscious. My troubles with the Jewish community in Canada stem from *The Apprenticeship of Duddy Kravitz*, which was a novel about a young hustler on the streets of Montreal. *Duddy Kravitz* was never meant to be a metaphor for the Jewish people but it created certain problems for me in Montreal. I am not a Canadian nationalist, a cultural nationalist, and I ridiculed them and poked a lot of fun at them. So I made a number of enemies. I became fair game, having attacked them.

Bigsby: You do take some real risks at times. In your novel *Cocksure* you have a scene to do with the burning of the millionth Jew in the gas chambers of Treblinka, which is staged like the millionth person coming into a supermarket. In *St Urbain's Horsemen* you have a scene with Himmler where someone comes in and says, 'Hello, Heinrich, what's cooking?' and the answer is, 'The Jews.' That is a very dangerous game.

Richler: Yes, it is. But these are rather satirical notions.

Bigsby: What leads you to do that?

Richler: I guess anger or outrage. And you could point to *Solomon Gursky Was Here*, which is probably the same.

Bigsby: But who is this directed against?

Richler: Against people who accepted these things, people who corrupted the past by using the Holocaust as the background for meretricious thrillers or glamorous novels and just vulgarized the experience. The fact is I have won the Jewish Book Prize twice, and my books do very well in Hebrew translation in Israel.

Bigsby: When you got to England, did you feel more Canadian than you had done in Canada?

Richler: I was never confused about not being a Canadian. I never thought I was an Englishman and I realized that some time I would have to go home. But it did enable me to see Canada more clearly, from a different perspective. Maybe I would have been a better writer if I had never left Canada, but that is conjecture. I don't know. I enjoyed it here in England enormously. It is still my other home. But what I felt, after I wrote *St Urbain's Horsemen*, was that I just could not write any more novels set in England. I had not been brought up here. Naipaul put it very well. He said, 'I don't know what an Englishman does when he goes home at night.' My problem was, not having been brought up here, I wasn't familiar with the banalities a novelist has to be armed with. I didn't know who the football players were, what a haircut cost, what comic books you read, what movies you saw, and if you have not got that at the tips of your fingers, if you start worrying about those things, then the real writing does not come through.

Also, life here was very pleasant but most of the people I knew were other writers, directors, journalists or playwrights and, although life was fun, it was limiting and not what I wanted to write about. By going home I suddenly had a much wider community available to me: of plumbers, house painters, doctors, lawyers and politicians. And by meeting with them, talking to them and going out with them, I could reconstruct their childhoods, or a plausible childhood, because I was a native of that country. What also worried me in 1972 is that I saw other novelists, Commonwealth novelists, whose work I admired and still admire, suddenly writing novels set in the biblical past or in imaginary countries or even on other planets, and I got pretty scared. I thought, 'It is time to go home.' Which is what I did.

Bigsby: Although you lived here for twenty years, somehow Montreal and a particular part of Montreal seemed to continue to exert a powerful influence on your imagination. Why was that?

Richler: Because it is my home. It is a cherished place for me, where I was brought up. I would rather have been brought up in a place with a better climate, but I am stuck with it and Canada is stuck with me, I guess.

Bigsby: There is a part of you which seems to want to document places and people and cultural moods.

Richler: Well, you know, Canadian writers are very fortunate in many ways. Because nineteenth-century Canadian writing is not worth a damn, we are mapping the territory. There was no Dickens or Henry James or Mark Twain. The tradition does not exist, so we are mapping the territory ourselves, which is an enormous advantage. It gives you a lot of freedom.

Bigsby: But hasn't Canada changed significantly since you originally left it?

Richler: Yes, it has. While this political quarrel has been going on between the so-called two founding nations, the English and the French, the fact is that, at the moment 40 per cent of Canadians are neither English nor French. There has been enormous immigration from Italy, Portugal, Greece, Central America and Asia. And I welcome it. About ten or twenty years down the road the majority of Canadians will be neither English nor French, and you will have Sikhs and Chinese and Greeks and Italians sitting in Parliament. They are going to look at this quarrel between the English and French and say, 'This is ridiculous.' So the solution to that problem may be immigration.

Bigsby: You once said that you were looking for the values by which in this time a man can live with honour; you say that any serious writer is bound to be a moralist and an entertainer only incidentally. I am not sure that people reading your work would think of it that way round. The entertainment quotient is so high in your works, which are full of life, which have a satirical view and which are performances.

Richler: Yes, but even 'cocksures' are quite moral when indignant. I think they are informed by a search for values but what I really set out to be was a witness to my time and place, and to one day write, I hope, a book that will last. Each time you start off with this dream of perfection. You are really going to write a novel that is absolutely right and, of course, it never really is, because there are always compromises down the road. Some things work and some things don't. In a sense each novel is a failure. Then you begin again by going back to the drawing board.

Bigsby: Will it be another ten years before we have another book?

Richler: I haven't got that much time any more. No, I hope it will only be two or three years. I am very much aware of time now.

IN CONVERSATION
WITH
W.G. SEBALD

W.G. Sebald was born in Wertach im Allgäu, Germany, in 1944. He studied German language and literature in Freiburg in Switzerland and in Manchester, where he became an assistant lecturer at the University of Manchester in 1970.

Sebald then worked at the University of East Anglia in Norwich as Professor of Modern German Literature and subsequently as Professor of Creative Writing. In addition his academic publications, Sebald is the author of *The Emigrants* (1996), *The Rings of Saturn* (1998) and *Vertigo* (1999). His fourth novel *Austerlitz* appears in 2001, all originally published in German.

Sebald has won numerous writing prizes, including the Berlin Literature Prize, the Literature Nord Prize and the Johannes Bobrowski Medal. This interview was recorded at the University of East Anglia in January 2001.

Bigsby: You were born in a village in the Bavarian Alps, Wertach im Allgäu. What sort of a place was it?

Sebald: It was a rather cut-off place on the Austrian border, about three thousand feet above sea level. In the 1940s and 1950s, when the winters were generally quite severe, this meant that there was snow for something like five months every year. The main village had about one thousand inhabitants, and then there were some outlying hamlets. I think the most characteristic feature of that village in those years was the fact that there weren't any machines: there weren't any cars, nobody had a fridge. There were ice boxes but not electric ones and the only machine was, I think, a circular saw that our neighbour had. The first tractors came in in 1948 or thereabouts. I grew up in an environment which was pretty much noiseless, except for natural sounds, and that is something which today, fifty years later, is scarcely imaginable and which must have had quite a considerable influence on me.

Bigsby: In what way?

Sebald: In the sense that to this day I have something like a noise phobia. Being surrounded by machines makes me panic. All day long the fridge goes on and off and the central heating goes on and off. Only when it finally stops at half past eleven at night do I feel reassured that quieter environments are actually possible.

Bigsby: So you are not one of those people who writes to music, then?

Sebald: Certainly not. I couldn't possibly work with any sort of background noise. The constant grinding is also something which irritates me about computers – they tend to mutter under their breath in a demanding sort of way.

Bigsby: Did those five months of snow mean that you read a lot.

Sebald: Oh no. There was scarcely any reading material about. There was a local paper which came out once a fortnight and had two pages. If you visited an old aunt or some other acquaintance you might find one or two things lying about – a book of cartoons, turn-of-the-century cartoons, that sort of thing – but there wasn't really any reading matter as such. There was no bookshop; there wasn't even a local lending library or anything of the kind: you grew up without reading. And you grew up without listening to music – there wasn't any music. Nobody had a gramophone; there was scarcely a radio. Local groups of yodellers would meet occasionally on festive days to perform something or other, but otherwise there wasn't any music.

Bigsby: So what did you do in the evening?

Sebald: You pottered about. You had odds and ends and bits of string, and there were the animals of course. You went out into the stable and looked after the cows and threw the hay down from the loft. In the summer the pastimes consisted of going out in the open, going down to the river, that sort of thing. In the winter, if the weather was fine, you would be out skiing or tobogganing or else, if it was foul, you would be indoors and you would fiddle about with odds and ends. I think that, too, still determines my working method to this day: I always begin by scratching around for bits and pieces and then seeing what I can do with them.

Bigsby: In one of your books you describe the village only by its initial letter. Why is that?

Sebald: Yes, 'W', and the small town to which we moved subsequently is called 'S'. These two places have more of a symbolic significance than anything. I wanted to avoid the trap of them being identified and the text being seen as a realistic and faithful portrayal of these places, when in the texts they are in fact imaginary locations.

Bigsby: It sounds almost like another century, another time, that you grew up in.

Sebald: Perhaps I ought to describe my early experience as one determined by the inequality or the unevenness of time. Time reached further back in certain locations than in others. Clearly, Detroit in the 1930s was much more advanced in terms of social and economic evolution than this place was thirty years later. By now everything has been levelled out. Certainly, in the Federal Republic there is no unevenness of time any more. You can go to what were once remote regions, such as the Bavarian Forest on the Czech border – which was very, very backward in the 1950s – and find that consistent and continued investment have brought these places to the same level of social and economic development as the rest of the country.

Bigsby: What did your parents do?

Sebald: My father was a trained locksmith and came from a working-class family in the Bavarian Forest. He was unemployed for several years in the 1920s and then, just a year or two before the Nazis seized power, he joined the so-called 100, 000 men army which Germany was entitled to keep under the Versailles Treaty. So, for the first time, he had a regular income of sorts and could afford to buy a suit and have certain aspirations. Pretty quickly after that, of course, came the Nazi takeover. My father remained in the army, which was one of those instruments – in terms of social evolution – which allowed people to advance themselves. There was no hermetic seal between NCOs and officers. Rising through the ranks was part of the general scheme. My father was a prisoner of war in France for about two and a half years and then came out of the war as a major. He returned in the summer of 1947, I think, and then worked again as a locksmith for several years until he joined the new German army, the Bundeswehr, in the mid-1950s, and he served with them for another twenty years or so before he retired. That particular story also indicates that I wasn't brought up by my father. I was born in 1944. My father returned home in 1947/48, found employment in the nearest small town and only came home at weekends for the next three years. So I spent the first five or six years of my life under the tutelage of my grandfather who was born in 1872 in the 'deep south'.

Bigsby: As you grew up, did you talk to your father about his service during the war and the events of the war?

Sebald: No. In most German families this kind of topic was taboo. As a very young person you wouldn't really be aware of what had happened. I had considered, for instance, for a very long time that the destruction which was wrought on German cities and which, in the form of huge piles of rubbish, was still much in evidence in the 1950s when you went to cities such as Munich or Augsburg, was a quasi-natural condition of city life. It did not occur to me that this was a consequence of war. In primary school you wouldn't ever talk about the war. It was only some ten years later – at the age of sixteen or seventeen and during history lessons in grammar school – that one gradually became aware of these things. Then, of course, you tried to talk to your parents about it. But these attempts inevitably ended in family drama and arguments, so you left it after a while. I think there was certainly what has often been described as a conspiracy of silence. I don't even think that couples talked to each other much about that sort of thing. One had tacitly agreed to leave this behind and developed an attitude which was entirely forward-looking, which was bent on *not* remembering.

Bigsby: Is that because you felt that there was a secret back there that they didn't want to divulge or that your father had been involved in something that he didn't want to talk about?

Sebald: No, it wasn't so much that. You just didn't quite know ever, and I still don't know to this day, exactly what my father did or did not do.

Bigsby: You have never had that conversation?

Sebald: We have never had that conversation. You didn't know what your parents had done but, perhaps more decisively, you didn't even know what they had seen or not seen. And the question, to my mind now, is: What did they witness? What did they see? We should recall also, in this context, that the horrendous occurrences and atrocities that are now recorded happened not only in the latter part of the war, they happened as soon as the Germans marched into Poland in September 1939.

Bigsby: In *Vertigo* you refer to your father as being assigned to Poland.

Sebald: Yes. He was among the troops who were in the so-called Polish campaign. He was stationed behind the Slovakian border for four months before the 'outbreak' of war. It is clear from that that the whole thing had been prepared, though I am sure that the troops at the time didn't exactly know what was in store for them. But you could certainly not ask any detailed questions about any of this. The first line of defence was always, 'I can't really remember exactly what happened.' If you pressed harder then the atmosphere would become increasingly uncomfortable and arguments would set in.

Bigsby: Do you think this is the source of your interest in the problematic nature of the past?

Sebald: Yes, because it is extremely difficult to determine what the past contained in terms of the personal experience of others. The accepted version of the past is largely of a fictional nature, or large tracts of it are. As regards the lives of your immediate relations – parents, for instance – there are stock memories which are constantly or repeatedly reeled out when people start talking about the past. Between these 'stories' there are enormous lacunae of non-memory, of a past that somehow seems to have had no existence at all.

Bigsby: And it is constantly being re-edited in the present, is it not?

Sebald: It is always being re-edited in the interest of what one attempts to do at a certain point of time. People make up myths about themselves and they stick very closely to those stories that they have once 'written' about themselves in their own minds. I believe that any form of historiography, whether it is personal or professional, is largely based on figments, on stories, that we make up about the past.

Bigsby: You once said that you felt oppressed by your country's history, that you felt it was a terrible burden. Yet you were born in 1944. Why would you feel that history as a burden?

Sebald: In one sense because I grew up in this rather peripheral place where no bombs had fallen and where you scarcely noticed that there was a war, except for the fact that many young men never returned. There was a farmhouse in our vicinity where out of six boys not one came back. They had all perished in Russia. But otherwise there was no material evidence of damage in the village of W. There were food shortages in the postwar years but we probably had more to eat than people in Sheffield, for instance. Now, however, I have a sense that while I grew up in what was, after all, quite an idyllic environment, at the same time the most horrendous things had happened in other parts of Europe. While I was sitting in my pushchair and being wheeled through the flowering meadows by my mother, the Jews of Corfu were being deported on a four-week trek to Poland. It is the simultaneity of a blissful childhood and these horrific events that now strikes me as quite incomprehensible. I know now that these things cast a very long shadow over my life.

Bigsby: A shadow, yes, but do you feel any responsibility?

Sebald: No, I don't feel any responsibility, but there are other emotional facets: a sense of shame, for example. While I don't feel any responsibility, I do feel a sense of shame.

Bigsby: But why does someone born in 1944 feel a sense of shame?

Sebald: Because this is where I come from. This is my identity. Although I was born 'late' and consequently was spared direct responsibility, I naturally feel at the same time that this is where my origins lie. My parents were involved in it and my grandparents' lives led up to it. The mistakes made go a long, long way back.

Bigsby: In *Vertigo* you describe going back to your home village – though every time I talk about you in relation to this I feel there perhaps ought to be quotation marks around 'you' – and coming across the photograph of a gypsy behind barbed wire. Is that what you mean when you talk about your sensitivity about the past: that, being German, at any moment a door could open and there could be an image or a fact waiting to come out and confront you?

Sebald: This particular picture that you refer to is a photograph from an album that my father put together for my mother for Christmas 1939. The war, while horrendous from the beginning, still had those leisurely moments when you could saunter out with your camera and take pictures. It seems to me quite eye-opening, however, that as early as late-summer 1939 there was a German NCO who took pictures of gypsies behind barbed wire somewhere in Slovakia. It shows that before the war actually started gypsies were being rounded up and interned in open-air camps in this puppet-state. That, I think, is an indication that these things were accepted as part of the operation right from the beginning. I looked through this album as a thirteen-year-old, blindly, as one does at that age, without noticing it; only much later did it strike me that there was a whole tale in that one image.

Bigsby: But you can't alter the past, or maybe you can. Is the act of writing a way of altering the past or of giving some sort of different shape to it? Is there anything in the act of writing that gets this out of your system, or that confronts it or deals with it?

Sebald: People who tend to have rather blithe views of life often consider that writing is a form of self-therapy. I don't particularly think so. Rather, I believe the more you turn your mind towards things the more difficult it gets. From book to book it gets harder to look at the determinants of your life yet again. And there is no way in which you can say, 'Well, I have done this now and I have put it in a shoebox on the shelf.' These things, once you have seen them, have a habit of returning, and they want attention. I don't think that writing helps to exorcise the ghosts.

Bigsby: Involved in the act of writing there is, or there can be, a kind of appropriation of experience, other people's experience, and that can have a suspect morality at times. Would you ever go through the gates of a concentration camp?

Sebald: No, I don't think so. I have been to certain places associated with this horror history. For my last book, *Austerlitz*, I went to one of those forts that the Belgians built before the First World War. It is outside Antwerp and in the 1940s it was a sort of reception camp where members of the Belgian Resistance were tortured. I visited this place for the first time, quite inadvertently, in the 1960s and then I went back to it about two summers ago. But that is as close as I dare to go because, of course, most of these places, whether you talk of Belsen or Auschwitz, are tourist places. If you were to look into the wastepaper baskets to see what people consume while they walked through these museum camps, then you would realize that visiting these places, in the way we do, is not the answer.

Bigsby: There are, then, certain doors you wouldn't open?

Sebald: Yes, there are. I would never attempt to describe a scene of violence in a realistic fashion because in doing this one invariably falls into the trap of action writing. The only way to write about persecution and its consequences is to approach the subject obliquely.

Bigsby: And, indeed, that is the way you work: by a kind of peripheral vision.

Sebald: A peripheral vision, yes. The sense that it is always there. Even if you concentrate very hard on what is good and promising in life somehow this is always there at the edges.

Bigsby: You left the village and went to university in Freiburg. A very different world, presumably.

Sebald: German universities in the 1960s were vastly overcrowded places. More than a thousand students used to sit in the big lecture rooms and listen to professors who had, as it occurred to me only later on, made their grade in the Nazi years. Everybody who had a chair in the humanities in Germany in the 1950s and 1960s had come up through the system in the 1930s and 1940s and hence had certain 'qualifications' which he didn't care to be reminded of. There was an atmosphere of falseness, I think, in higher education at the time. It was also quite impossible for other reasons to seriously pursue one's subject. The libraries were still in a rather dysfunctional state and so eventually I decided to go to Switzerland where conditions were much better.

At this time (1964/65) the Auschwitz trials took place in Frankfurt. This was the first *public* acknowledgement that there was such a thing as an unresolved German past. There were daily one-page reports about that trial in the *Frankfurter Allgemeine Zeitung* for many months. I read these reports every day and they suddenly shifted my vision. I realized that there were subjects of much greater urgency than the writings of the German Romantics. I understood that I had to find my own way through that maze of the German past and not be guided by those in teaching positions at that time.

Bigsby: So you went to Switzerland and then to England.

Sebald: I went to the French part of Switzerland when I was twenty-one, which means that I was outside my 'natural' language environment from very early on and that I haven't really ever returned to it, although I still write in that language.

Bigsby: But that is odd, isn't it, that you continue to write in German when, as you say, you are so far distant from it? Most of your life has not been conducted with German as your first language, yet you write in German. Why is that?

Sebald: One of the obvious reasons is that my career was in German studies. Most of my reading was always in German and the kind of writing that I later embarked on had its source in written materials to a very large extent, whether these were in book form or more peripheral material, amateur memoirs, letters, et cetera. Most of it came to me in a written form.

Bigsby: But English is scarcely your second language any more.

Sebald: Oh, yes it is. I don't in the least feel at home in it. I use it but it sounds quite alien to me.

Bigsby: After all this time?

Sebald: After all this time it sounds alien to me and there are days when I try to write a letter and I come up against some hurdle. I wonder, 'How do you say this?' It would be easy for you to write a letter of this sort, to just dash it off, whereas I agonize over it.

Bigsby: So, you are not going to become a Joseph Conrad. You don't see yourself moving to writing in English.

Sebald: I think it is very unlikely. I had a lot of trouble with my last book, which isn't out yet. I reached a point where I thought I can't string together another German sentence at all and I wondered whether I was now faced with this notorious problem of having to change my coat, my linguistic coat, as happened to some other writers. But it is too late for that in my estimation. I don't quite know how old Nabokov was when he had to make that fateful decision but even he, who was a superb linguist, which I am not, wrote about how awful an experience it was for many months and years and that he despaired and feared that he would never be able to write a decent English sentence.

Bigsby: But is it just a matter of words, usages, or do you think differently in the different languages?

Sebald: I don't even know what thinking is. There is something that goes on in one's head but I always have this notion that it is pretty much like these tentacles which some creatures have, organisms halfway between plants and animals that exist in the sea. They just float these tentacles out in the hope that something will drift by that they can catch and ingest. Certainly in my case, I think that is how thinking seems to work. It is a completely random process. I cannot imagine anything like systematic thought. Even when I try to follow someone else's systematic reflections – say, Wittgenstein's musings on pure logic – it becomes something completely unfathomable for me.

Bigsby: What about the non-rational world? What about the world of dream, because in some ways your prose has a kind of associational logic in the way that a dream does? Are you aware of dreaming in a language or is language not relevant to dream?

Sebald: I think hardly anyone knows. Most of my dreams are of a non-linguistic kind. They are dominated by images and it is the images that are associated with each other. Dream images are extremely articulate, detailed. They speak for themselves, quite literally. There is the occasional dream in which you are able to give a speech in Hungarian before a gathering of learned Hungarian chaps, but generally I think dreams are of a non-linguistic nature, certainly mine are. I am not at all aware of dreams being either English or German.

Bigsby: Let me take you back to when you first came to England. I know you talk about this in part in *Vertigo*, but how much of a shock was it, or did you find what you had expected to find?

Sebald: No, I didn't expect anything. I was completely unprepared for it. I decided to go to Manchester because in Freiburg I had come across an English guest professor for whom I did some quite decent work. He was my only contact in this country and it was through him that I found my first teaching post in Manchester. I knew very little about England. I had practically no English – at school I had done Latin and Greek. English wasn't on the curriculum for me. And I certainly had no idea of the history or the culture of this country, or of its topography. I knew nothing about the north/south divide or any of the other great English myths. Nor had I ever lived in a large city before. In Germany and Switzerland I had lived in idyllic, beautiful towns. I had no concept of what an industrial wasteland was because I hadn't seen that kind of degradation before.

I arrived at Ringway airport and as I drove into town in a taxi I could not believe my eyes. I thought I had arrived on another planet and it took me a long time to get used to it. The experience cast me into a considerable depression which lasted until Christmas.

Bigsby: But why on earth did you subsequently decide to stay in England?

Sebald: Because England had much to offer in those days to aspiring young scholars, things which to me were quite out of the ordinary. I had a heated office. I could go to the library at any time and pretty much all the books that I wanted were there. I didn't have to wait for weeks before discovering they were not available. I had a salary which was paid in what were then quite valuable pounds sterling and I could, for the first time, buy an aeroplane ticket and even put money aside. Assistant lecturers at the time earned the equivalent of one thousand marks per month; as a student I had had one hundred and fifty, so this was nearly six times what I was used to.

Bigsby: Was it material things that you wanted?

Sebald: Yes, it was material things and then also, of course, you gradually got to know the people and you found out that these British were a strange race but extremely nice. They left you alone most of the time but if you needed them they would be there in a very generous way. At the university there wasn't anything that resembled an authoritarian structure. For someone who had grown up in a system of this sort and who, by nature, has perhaps something of an anarchist streak, this really felt like freedom. The freedom to follow my own designs was an extremely positive aspect, something that I felt was lacking when later on I attempted to go back to Germany.

Bigsby: One of those attempts to go back wasn't that long ago; surely Germany has changed a lot.

Sebald: Well, it has changed a lot but some of the old attitudes are still in place. The hierarchies in German universities are still very pronounced. It matters whether you are a C3 or C4 professor. It is reflected in the way you dress, in the way you sit on a chair or the sort of car you drive. In German institutions there is a great deal of intrigue and oneupmanship, a vice which is now beginning to grow in British universities also.

Bigsby: It must have struck you that coming from Germany, where the war was to be forgotten, you found yourself in a country that seems to love remembering it.

Sebald: That is true both for the First World War, the Great War, and the Second World War. The literature being written about the First World War in this country is absolutely endless. Whenever you go into a bookshop you find new books written about this aspect or another. Very little is published in Germany about the world wars. As I mentioned some time ago in an essay I did about 'air war and literature' there isn't even a historiographic account of the destruction of German cities, written by German historians. You would have thought that, Dresden quite apart, Hamburg quite apart, this would have been an obvious topic for research.

Bigsby: Doesn't it strike you as odd that the British can't let go of the Second World War? It is as though it were about a triumph of the spirit.

Sebald: Well, that is how you have to see it. It is more difficult to explain about the First World War because the British got into it in almost as muddle-headed a way as the Austrians did.

Bigsby: But we even celebrate our defeats in this country.

Sebald: Yes, and that is one of the really endearing things.

Bigsby: What brought you to the University of East Anglia? Was it just that there happened to be a job?

Sebald: It was a new university and jobs were advertised on a fairly regular basis. It is unbelievable now but on the day I was appointed here, in the autumn of 1970, three people were appointed to posts in the German department all at once. Of course one can't imagine that sort of thing now. The colleagues I met at interview were extremely nice, the atmosphere was very good and so I thought, well, yes, that looks like a rather pleasant place and I decided to stay when I was offered a job.

Bigsby: And you settled in and became an academic and for twenty years, literally for twenty years, you wrote academic books, articles and so on. Then in 1990, suddenly, you started publishing a different kind of book. How long had you been working on that and why that change of direction?

Sebald: I think it must have several roots. The first reason probably was that I always felt somewhat hemmed in by the discipline of academic writing. I was always intent on developing hypothetical notions to suggest that there is circumstantial evidence for a certain case. In Germany, where my books were published, I frequently got into hot water because of this. Increasingly I felt drawn to write in a much more tentative sort of way and I moved from the straight monograph to essayistic exploration, dealing with my subjects in an elliptical sort of way. But even so I constantly came up against a borderline where I felt, well, if I could go a little bit further it might get very interesting, that is, if I were allowed to make things up.

That temptation to work with very fragmentary pieces of evidence, to fill in the gaps and blank spaces and create out of this a meaning which is greater than that which you can prove, led me to work in a way which wasn't determined by any discipline. It wasn't history, it wasn't literary criticism, it wasn't sociology, but it was all of these things together.

Then, of course, the other reason was that once you have been in an academic career for twenty years certain chores are given you and your range of freedom becomes restricted. Demands of all kinds are made at the same time as family pressures begin to mount and you feel that at that midway point in life your personality is being eroded and you must think of measures of self-defence. One of the best means of self-defence, as one knows, is to go into the potting shed and build something that no one understands or no one knows what it is meant to be.

This is how the writing of literary texts began for me. It was an eccentric pastime that no one knew about; not even people in my own house knew what I was doing exactly. I just pottered away and produced these bits. I initially had no idea that I would publish them. I was just setting things down. Eventually, of course, it grew into something that was an organized whole and could be published. When I published it, it very quickly became very successful, successful not in financial terms, initially, but in terms of the public response. All the reviews in Germany were very positive and then, of course, one somehow feels obliged to go on. Once you have put your arm into the literary machine you easily get pulled into it altogether.

Bigsby: I notice how British you have become. You refer to the potting shed. I can't see you having done that in Germany, although it does go back to what you were saying about childhood and bits and pieces around the house and making things up and improvising things. As you say, this is about the blurring of boundaries. In fact, your own publisher doesn't quite know how to describe your work on the fly leaf, the category in which this is going to be placed in the bookstores. One of those boundaries you blur, however, is that between fact and fiction. Is that blurring partly because you think each of them already contains the other?

Sebald: Yes, I certainly do. It isn't anything new. If you read a novel by Thomas Mann, the vast majority of his characters are based on people he knew and observed closely, or he collated a character out of two people he knew. For those who knew the Mann family and their social surroundings, these novels were romans-à-clef.

The people in the village where I grew up were scandalized when *Vertigo* appeared because this wasn't at all how it was. He wasn't called that, he didn't have that particular illness – the closer you are to your home territory in your writing the more you get accused of having made mistakes of this kind. Whereas, of course, for the people in London or Paris this is neither here nor there. They read the tale for other reasons. I fully agree with you that fact and fiction are, as it were, both hybrids. They are not alternatives. They are both hybrids with the constituent parts in different measure.

Bigsby: But there is potentially a problem in dissolving history, dissolving the self. If you think of Paul De Mann, for example, who wanted to deconstruct history and deconstruct the self, it turned out that he had a very good reason for wishing to do so because he didn't want to confront that history and he didn't want to confront that former self. So it is not quite a value-free mechanism, or device is it?

Sebald: No, it isn't. Anything one does in the form of writing, and especially prose fiction, is not an innocent enterprise. It is a morally questionable enterprise because one is, of course, in the business – however honest one attempts to be as a writer – of arranging things in such a way that the role of the narrator is not an entirely despicable one. There is no way around this. There are very few writers who publicly declare 'Je suis un salaud.' Writing is by definition a morally dubious occupation, I think, because one appropriates and manipulates the lives of others for certain ends. When it is a question of the lives of those who have survived persecution the process of appropriation can be very invasive.

Bigsby: And part of your mind is already thinking of the uses to which you could put such information.

Sebald: Yes. A writer's attitude is utilitarian. I think Graham Greene said somewhere that most writers have a splinter of ice in their heart. This seems to me a very perceptive remark because writers have to look upon things in a certain way. There is this horrible moment when you discover, almost with a sense of glee, something that, although in itself horrid, will fit in exactly with your scheme of things.

Bigsby: Your books are scattered with photographs. I take it that there is a level of irony in some of them in that photographs appear to be authenticating devices and yet yours, forgive me for saying it, are not terribly good. Are they working in a double way? They appear to be offering to authenticate at the same time they are undermining the authenticity they seem to offer.

Sebald: I think they have several functions. The main device is certainly one in which, I think, every writer of fiction has to have an interest: the narrator wants to tell the reader that he has been there and that he has seen this with his own eyes and what better proof than a photograph. All nineteenth-century writers of fiction have this problem, certainly the German ones whom I know best. They always tell you a tale about how they found this manuscript, which they are going to pass on to us in a minute, on top of a stove in some small town in Holstein or something. They are insisting that theirs is a bona fide account. A photograph attempts to do something very similar.

As it happens, the vast majority of pictures in my books are in fact authentic, that is, they come out of the albums or boxes of people like the ones whom I am trying to describe, whose life I am trying to relate. Sometimes these pictures contain very dense information which it would take you a long time to get across in writing. There is, for instance, in *The Emigrants*, a picture of a large Jewish family who were resident in Munich. They stand in a meadow, about two dozen of them, and are all in traditional Bavarian costume, the full works, lederhosen, Tyrolean hats and so on. That early twentieth-century photograph of a Jewish family assimilated in this particular, almost farcical way to the Bavarian folk tradition says more than you could tell in a whole essay about the processes of assimilation and acculturation.

A photograph can be something like a very condensed account or a shorthand cipher. It can also put a different angle on things and it can have that ironic quality that you refer to, that is, that the writer says this is me on the seashore of New Jersey and you can't see anything on the photograph except some dark blot in a scarcely visible landscape.

Bigsby: Do you ever work to degrade the pictures?

Sebald: Yes, I do. A very small proportion of the pictures are retouched. I change things in them, brush things in or cut things out or make them more gloomy or lighter, depending on what I need to do. I write up to these pictures and I write out of them also, so they are really part of the text and not illustrations and hence, if they were produced in a much better form, which would be technically very easy to do nowadays, then they would ruin the text. They must not stand out; they must be of the same leaden grain as the rest.

Bigsby: Would it be a good rule of thumb in your work to say that the more unlikely, the more absurd something is, the more likely it is to be true?

Sebald: Yes. Sometimes I make up one out of two or three stories but, in essence, what I write is how it happened. Naturally there are moments where it is necessary to abbreviate or to condense or where one needs to extend or extrapolate from an element of information that is capable of development. On the whole, though, you are quite right in saying that the most shocking, the most hair-raising, the most coincidentally absurd moments are precisely how things did happen. The fictional changes are on the margins, are largely of a stylistic nature, adding a touch here and there.

I can give you one example. The story of the schoolteacher in *The Emigrants* is completely authentic, including the ghastly way in which this man ended his own life. The photographs are photographs from his album. What is added to the story is the parallel with Wittgenstein's time as a primary schoolteacher in upper Austria. There are some moments in that text which I borrowed from Wittgenstein's biography. For instance, when the schoolteacher is boiling a dead fox in a great pot in order to clean up the skeleton for his pupils. That is what Wittgenstein did.

Bigsby: Stylistically, why do you resist paragraphs? They are there but they are there in sparing numbers.

Sebald: I don't generally need them. If you don't have much dialogue, if all your speech is reported and hence forms part of a longer sentence, then you don't particularly need paragraphs until the point where your narrative really changes direction. If you write crime fiction you need to change direction quite frequently since you have something like a plot to negotiate. I haven't, and I always dwell on things at length. The whole concept is based on patterns of association, and so one moves fairly easily from one thing to another. The book I have just finished hasn't really got a paragraph at all, in four hundred pages.

Bigsby: One thing that does is increase the pressure on the reader, doesn't it?

Sebald: It does, but at the same time I think the reader senses that there are two sets of dynamics. On the one hand, there is a pull, which there ought always to be in fiction, towards the finish. Kermode described that 'gradient' very beautifully in *The Sense of an Ending*. That is almost inevitable, and as a writer one senses that from the mid-point onwards. There is, though, another function. A picture, being visual information, can be contemplated, it does not have to be decoded in time. You can just sit and see it, and the ideal reader for me would be a reader who doesn't read the text but sees it, who lifts it out of the perennial wasting which occurs in time.

Bigsby: You referred to it then as fiction.

Sebald: Yes, it is prose fiction.

Bigsby: Is that how you think of your books?

Sebald: Yes. They reinvent a life almost lost or something that perhaps nobody thought might be recovered. And it is that reinvention, that attempt to answer the question 'who was this man or this woman?', which necessarily draws you into all kinds of fictional strategies because you have to make things up. Why did he become like this? Why did he do this? What drove him to do that? Yes, it is certainly fiction. I don't know what else it could be.

At the same time, I think it is fair to say that *Vertigo*, for instance, has elements of pretty much all literary genres in it – crime fiction, autobiography, travelogue, it is all there – and I don't think it is illegitimate to make use of the various forms which are, after all, there for us. We have them in our heads. If your profession is that of a teacher who talks about this kind of thing a good deal in class then it is part of the furnishings of your head and you always have it at your disposal. If your text reaches a certain point where it might be useful to change into a different mode, then there is, in my view, no reason to hesitate.

Bigsby: You mentioned *Vertigo*. Is something lost in the translation from German into English?

Sebald: Yes, there is, because the German title, Schwindelgefuhle, does mean vertigo, but Schwindel on its own also means legerdemain, conjuring or confidence trick. The text is a sort of confidence trick by the writer who is able to pull the wool over the reader's eyes and who is, and that is the point we talked about before, engaged in a morally dubious exercise, particularly perhaps when that exercise is executed with a great deal of virtuosity.

Bigsby: Is part of the legerdemain in that book the fact that you give a portrait of a Napoleonic soldier but don't tell us who he is? He is Stendhal.

Sebald: Yes, it is Stendhal. Most people who are reasonably well read would recognize this. You can also read the text without that information. Beyle could equally well be an anonymous young lieutenant who then goes on to write books. It happens to be Stendhal and most of this comes from Stendhal's own autobiography, or autobiographical sketch I think it ought to be called, which is full of false memories. Almost nothing in it could have been as he describes it. Obviously there are terrible flaws in all these constructions and you very easily fall through trapdoors, several storeys down.

Bigsby: There is a moment in the book when you, or the person representing you, loses your passport, or somebody loses your passport for you. Would you like that to be true metaphorically; in other words, not to be a writer of a given society, a German writer, an English writer, or whatever?

Sebald: In one sense it would be much better if one didn't have to constantly walk around with a particular package that one has inherited, but it is also true to say that the quality of the writing is to do not least with the degree of faithfulness to one's origins, that is, one mustn't attempt to be anything else or anything better than one actually is. To a certain extent I think the quality of fiction is determined by the opposite of *mauvaise fois*. There has to be something like veracity, something that is 'made' as honestly and as truthfully as possible, even if it employs devious means.

Bigsby: So there is an integrity of the text behind the conjuring that goes on.

Sebald: The integrity of the text is the *sine qua non*. Flaubert said at one point that in order to be able to write you need clean hands, but then, he said, you make one concession and then you make another and then nothing matters any more. I think there is a lot of truth in this. The process of writing is a constant battle against the temptation of saying, 'This will do and I will hurry on to the next scene because this one will do.' Nothing ever does do.

Bigsby: For those reading your work in English, people came across *Vertigo* as though it was your third book because it was published in German in 1990 and English in 1999, by which time *The Rings of Saturn* and *The Emigrants* had already appeared. Does it make any difference, do you think, in what order people come at your work?

Sebald: Not particularly. Although I don't like to look back at my own work, I do sometimes feel that even the first one can still hold its own. It isn't just a trial run, it is just of a different nature. At the same time the three books do belong together somehow because of the autobiographical thread that runs through all three of them.

Bigsby: Not the fourth?

Sebald: Scarcely. The narrator does figure in a very abstract sort of way, which is one of the difficulties I had with it.

Bigsby: *The Rings of Saturn* almost begins with you in hospital. It has been said that you were in a state of nervous collapse.

Sebald: That is what some people have inferred. There have even been reviews which have said that I had been interned for a long period of time in a mental institution.

Bigsby: What were you doing there?

Sebald: The journey which is described in that book was down the east coast of Suffolk. If you walk along the seashore for several days in the same direction your frame gets lopsided. I never had any back problems before, but after that journey, and perhaps also occasioned by other things that crashed onto me, I suddenly developed quite severe back pain. The condition eventually led to a fractured disc, the bits of which had to be dug out of the nerves that run down the spinal column. Before I went into hospital I was pretty much immobile for about a fortnight, which was quite frightening. The operation was reasonably successful but I was for a while in a state where I could imagine what life must be like if you are, as it were, stuck somewhere without much hope of recovery. Obviously that concentrates the mind in certain directions.

Bigsby: But if it almost began with you in hospital it also almost begins with Sir Thomas Browne who is a good Norwich figure. What drew you to him?

Sebald: As you can gather from the things I have said, when I first came to this country I was almost wholly unfamiliar with English culture. I knew the odd play by Shakespeare in German translation: but that was about it. So, when I came to Norwich and saw Thomas Browne sitting outside the C&A store on a chair I had no inkling of who he was. I can't quite remember how I got to read Thomas Browne but it can't have been before 1985. From the first page, I was absolutely mesmerized by the quality of his writing and this very, very curious mixture of scientific enquiry carried out by someone still half held by medieval magic.

Certainly, one of the things that has always interested me most is the much-despised discipline of metaphysics, which was relegated from philosophy proper generations ago. I always thought that metaphysics was by far the most interesting branch of philosophy and anything to do with it always held my attention. And in Browne there is no end of it. It doesn't matter whether he writes about a bittern or a stone or indeed about the angels, he always has that very pronounced metaphysical bent.

Bigsby: You have often been described as melancholy. One American review was headed 'Germanic Depressive'. The *Guardian* called you the 'Eyore of the East'. Do you recognize any of that Eyore quality in yourself?

Sebald: Not particularly. Melancholy is a very respectable mood to be in, whether you are a philosopher or a writer or indeed a physicist. Most people who work at the frontline where you really try to find things out, whether the work is in pure mathematics or any other field, need the isolation which melancholy provides. Andrew Giles, who solved Fermat's Theorem, sat is his study for several years jotting down endless rows of figures no one could understand. What did his poor wife think of him? Obsessive work is a natural part of trying to solve difficult, intricate problems. Writing difficult, complex sentences takes that sort of attention which makes you appear to the outside world like someone who keeps staring into the same hole. It is inevitable. Even comedians, who have to pay a great deal of attention to the precision of their work, tend to be of that dark bent.

Bigsby: And I suppose another aspect of that is solitariness, is it not?

Sebald: Solitariness, yes.

Bigsby: You appear in a lot of your books walking on your own, alone in a city, and so on.

Sebald: Which I do quite a lot because what interests me, in Milan or elsewhere, is not what any 'normal' person would be interested in. So if I want to see it I need to go there by myself. It is as simple as that. I could not take my family around the back yards of Arras or other abandoned places. They don't want to do this, quite understandably, but I don't want to see the sights. I never wanted to see the sights. I always thought that sights are only for postcards. You see the Rio de Janeiro Jesus figure and the Eiffel Tower on a postcard, you don't have to go there and see it 'in reality'.

Bigsby: But you are also a private man, aren't you?

Sebald: I am fairly private, yes, which may be one of the reasons why I really like being in this country because here it is understood that you don't enquire into someone else's life until or unless they invite you to. To me this is the most positive aspect of the kind of society that has grown up here over the generations.

Bigsby: *The Emigrants* deals not only with emigrants but with Jewish life. What pulled you towards that?

Sebald: The fact that the persecution and the attempted eradication of the Jewish people by my compatriots loomed largest among the historical experiences in my life. When you first learn about these things, at the age of seventeen or eighteen, you stare at them in incomprehension. So you carry on as if nothing had happened. And then there is a gradual process of becoming aware of it, which in my case went into a quite different mode as soon as I arrived in Manchester. One of the consequences of the so-called final solution was, of course, that those who grew up in Germany after 1945 hardly ever encountered a Jewish person. Up until the 1930s they were present pretty much everywhere. Even in villages and in small towns like S, where I went to school, there were several of them: the surgeon at the local hospital, the man who owned the cinema, and so on. All that remained after 1945 were small fragmentary communities in Frankfurt and Berlin, and it was thus that you could grow up in Germany and not meet a Jewish person for thirty years.

When I got to Manchester I realized that what I had read in the papers and in history books and seen in films wasn't about anonymous victims, but that it had concerned real people. The person who rented me that rather nice room in Manchester, and who fished me out of the depressive melancholic soup into which I had got when I arrived there, had, as a boy, been skiing in the same places where I had gone skiing. These coincidences made me realize that this man's parents must have been real people, even though they are part of those unbelievable statistics. They were deported to somewhere near Riga where they perished or, more precisely, were murdered. The Manchester years were, for me, a kind of journey of discovery. There were Jewish old people's homes in Didsbury and when someone died in there the books which some of these people still owned, works of nineteenth-century German fiction mostly, would turn up in the local secondhand bookshop.

To my mind there is an acute difference between history as historiography and history as experienced history. Moreover, I knew from the work that I was doing as a young academic that most of the literary texts that had been written in Germany in the 1950s and 1960s about the Fascist years were dismal failures, marked largely by tactlessness and by very dubious moral positions, as regards the representation of Jewish lives. So I felt that it was necessary to at least attempt to write about these lives in a different sort of way.

Bigsby: But *The Emigrants* wasn't your first book. Does that mean that it took time for you to find a way into this?

Sebald: It wasn't my first book but the topic was there very early on even in a long prose poem which I wrote in 1988.

Bigsby: How far are your books made in the making? How far do you have the thing entire in your mind and how far does the process of writing generate the book?

Sebald: That is very difficult to answer. I generally have an idea of roughly where I want to go. I think it is perhaps easiest explained if I refer to *The Rings of Saturn*. I had just finished *The Emigrants* and I thought I will go and make a little excursion and then I will write something very neat and tiny about it – ten tiny little essays about these topics – an ergonomic exercise, the product of which I can then have set in large letters and sell for nearly the same price as a 400-page book. But of course things have a habit of getting the better of you and no sooner did I try to keep to that small format than I realized that there was much more to some of these topics than I had bargained for. My curiosity as a reader was awakened and the project proliferated until it reached its full-scale proportions. The book I have just finished was supposed to be ninety or one hundred pages; it has got four hundred now.

Bigsby: And is the new book, *Austerlitz*, a departure from the other three?

Sebald: No. You might almost describe it as a sequel to *The Emigrants*. It tells the life of one of those people who came over to this country on the so-called kinder-transports immediately before the outbreak of the war. That particular story is based on two and a half real-life stories that I became acquainted with. Again, there is a process of collation. What interested me particularly in it was the fact of this young man's hidden identity. He came as a four and a half-year-old boy from Prague and was brought up by a Welsh fundamentalist, Calvinist, childless couple who, for reasons of their own, resolved that the boy must be spared the knowledge of his true identity. The father ended up in a lunatic asylum and the mother died rather early. The mother's death happened first and the father could not cope. The boy was put, with a grant of some sort, into a public school in Oswestry and never really knew who he was, although the headmaster before his O Levels informed him that his name was actually not David Elias but Jacques Austerlitz. There you have a situation of someone who has been deprived, by active intervention or by default, of any knowledge of his own origins and who later resolves not to investigate his own case. He goes through life as an academic in this country without ever attempting to find out where he came from. Only when he is on the threshold of retirement does the whole thing catch up with him and is he cast into a crisis which eventually forces him to examine his hidden past.

Bigsby: That is interesting because one thing underlying so many of your books is a feeling of loss.

Sebald: That is what life is about to a very large extent. On the one hand, when you grow up promises are held up in front of you. Get your O Levels done and your A Levels and then everything will be fine. And then you do your BA and your PhD, but the more you are lured along this road, the more is taken away from you, the less the scope becomes. Day by day you leave things behind, ultimately your health, and so loss is perhaps the most common experience that we have. I think somehow this has to be accounted for and as there are few other places where it is accounted for it has to be done by writing. It is quite clear to me that many people can identify with this view of life. It is not necessarily a pessimistic one; it is just a matter of fact that somehow this whole process is one in which you get done out of what you thought was your entitlement.

Bigsby: Why do you publish under the name W.G. Sebald?

Sebald: The G is for Georg, which is my father's name, and as I never felt particularly close to him I did not want to use that one. The first one is one of those Germanic names that all those who were born before 1945 were given. There was an actual edict by the Fascists which said that those who bring children into this world have to be aware that they ought to be given proper German names. Some of the old biblical ones slipped through, but the vast majority of my generation were called Holger and Volker and Manfred and so on. Of course, the craze goes back a lot earlier: it goes back to Wagnerian opera and very ironically, in those days, it was the Jewish assimilees who endowed their children – Walter Benjamin, Siegfried Kracauer and so on – with these inappropriate Germanic handles.

Even when I was very small I thought there was something wrong with my name. How could you possibly – in an area where, up until very recently, everybody had been called Hans and Fritz and Franz – have such a preposterous polysyllabic name? I never did like it, although I lived with it for a long time. The whole thing was then precipitated when I came to this country where this particular first name is only known as a female name and I often got letters addressed to Miss Sebald or was embroiled in other confusions.

Bigsby: That first name being?

Sebald: Winfried, in German and, of course, in English there is Winifred. When I went in for my back operation in the Norwich & Norfolk hospital the consultant who came to see me the first afternoon was taken aback to find a chap lying in this bed where he had expected to see a female patient.

Bigsby: By not using that name are you refusing a particular line of descent?

Sebald: I just don't want to have this label publicly on my forehead every day, so I used my third first name, which is one of the traditional names which you find in eighteenth- and nineteenth-century Germany everywhere.

Bigsby: For quite a few years you were able to, in a sense, hide away here. That is to say you had a reputation in another country. Then the books appeared in English and suddenly the light swung onto you. Has that been an unalloyed pleasure or would you just as soon go back into the semi-darkness?

Sebald: It has both aspects. On the one hand, it was extremely gratifying because I know that it is very difficult for books written in France or Germany to come 'over the barrier' into this country and be seen or noticed. So when it happened, obviously I was very pleased but not just because they were noticed. It was the kind of reaction that I got, both from critics and also, and more so, from readers. I got many letters of a very personal kind from people in this country and in the United States, letters of the sort I had never received from my German readers who tended to be very reticent. And some of these letters, in turn, provided me with insights and lines of enquiry and bits of information that I could scarcely have hoped to come across myself. So that was extremely good. On the other hand, of course, it doubles the work load. Not only do you have to answer these letters, but the process of translation, in which I am very deeply involved, is extremely laborious, right through to the editing stage. Because of the way these books are made, at all stages, this is a labour-intensive process. It means also, of course, that your diary gets clogged rather more quickly than if you are only operating in one language and so now I am journeying about, throughout Western and Central Europe, for a week almost every month. It sometimes does get too much. I certainly often think that that very first phase, before anything was published and when I was sitting in the potting shed, was the best one.

IN CONVERSATION
WITH
ISAAC BASHEVIS SINGER

The novelist and short story writer Isaac Bashevis Singer was born in 1904. He left his native Poland to travel to America in 1935, the year he published his first novel, *Satan in Goray*. He wrote in Yiddish, which is the language of European Jewry, but which was spoken by very few people in his adopted land. Indeed, it was fifteen years before any of his books appeared in translation. Singer wrote for the most part about the world he had left behind: a world of frank sexuality and religious pieties. The body and the spirit mix sometimes incongruously and even farcically together. Singer remained virtually unknown to a wider audience until an English version of his second novel, *The Family Moskat*, appeared in 1950, and his short story 'Gimpel the Fool' was translated by Saul Bellow. Other works include *The Manor* (1967), *The Estate* (1969), *Enemies* (1972), *Shosha* (1978) and *The Penitent* (1983).

Singer divided his time between New York and Miami, where he lived in a high-rise apartment overlooking the sea, which is where this interview was conducted. He died in 1991.

Bigsby: Where were you when you learned that you had been awarded the Nobel Prize in 1987?

Singer: I was living right here, and I went down to the drugstore to have breakfast in the morning, and my wife was supposed to come also to have breakfast with me a few minutes later. I waited for ten minutes or so and she did not come. When she finally came I said to her, 'Why are you late?' She said, 'They say that you got a Nobel Prize.' I said, 'The Nobel Prize? Nonsense! Someone made a joke.' And we continued to have our breakfast as if nothing had happened. Then I came over here, which is half a block from the drugstore, and I saw the reporters and photographers so I knew that I had got it. And all the reporters asked the same questions. 'Were you surprised? Were you happy?' And since I didn't want to have discussions about happiness with them, I said, 'Yes, I was surprised and I was happy.' This went on maybe for ten minutes. And then it quietened down. Then came a new reporter and he said to me, 'Are you happy? Were you surprised?' And I said to him, 'How often can a man be happy and how often can a man be surprised? I have already been surprised. I have already been happy. And now I am in the same way as I ever was before.'

Bigsby: You were raised in a small town in Poland. What sort of a place was it?

Singer: I lived in a very Jewish community, a community which was almost all Jewish. It was an old town. The synagogue had a garret and there were many manuscripts and old books. I felt that I was living in the olden times. I went back into the seventeenth century easily because nothing really had changed between the seventeenth century and the twentieth century; not much. It did a lot for me, but like every place does for a writer.

Bigsby: Your father was an authority figure to you, but also to the community at large. Did that mean that as you began to rebel against him in one role, you necessarily rebelled against him in another role as well?

Singer: Exactly. My father wanted me to become a rabbi. He was a believer not only in God but in every rabbi who has lived from the time of Moses until today. And when I said that I didn't believe in these things it was a terrible shock to him, also to my mother. But I had a rebel before me: my older brother. So a lot of the dirty work was done by him already. He had altered the base with my father and told him that we cannot be so sure that every sacred book is really so sacred, that it was written by God and so on.

Bigsby: Your first novel, *Satan in Goray*, was published in 1934. The following year you joined your brother in America, leaving behind not only the world that you had known, but also your mother and younger brother. A few years later, in 1939, both were dead. Deported by the Russians in a cattle-truck in the middle of winter, they froze to death. But for you the signs seem to have been clear enough, and the decision to leave was straightforward.

Singer: It was difficult to leave, but the decision wasn't. The decision to go was very easy because Hitler was already in power when I left Poland, and he threatened that he would attack Poland and I knew that he would keep his word. I also knew that he and his Nazis would do all the things they threatened to do, and even more so. So my decision was made easily. But then I needed a Polish passport and a visa, and to get all these was very, very difficult. I had to work on it and many times I felt that I would not leave Poland at all; they would not let me leave Poland. This to me was as good as a death sentence. When I finally got on to the ship and I saw that I was going to America, I felt that I had saved my life, no matter how unworthy it might be.

Bigsby: But, believing that, what about the other members of your family? Do you feel any sense of guilt about not having tried to force your mother to leave?

Singer: I feel a lot of guilt although, according to the Freudians, the feeling of guilt is a very terrible thing and one should get rid of it. I feel that a man without guilt is not a man at all. I think we should all feel guilty about the things which we might have done and have not done.

Bigsby: What image did you have of America before you arrived there?

Singer: I felt that I was going not to a well-off culture, but at least to a well-off civilization. And I wanted to be there.

Bigsby: How did America compare with the images that you had of it before you got there?

Singer: I would say that when I came to this country, instead of rejoicing, instead of being very happy, I felt terribly disappointed because I wrote in Yiddish, so I wanted my Yiddish readers to exist, I wanted to continue to speak Yiddish, but I saw without any doubt that Yiddish in America will not last long. I felt that I had come to a place where everything I did would be of no value whatsoever. As a matter of fact, I stopped writing for a number of years. Then I said to myself, if I really am able to tell a story, there will be people who will listen to it, whether I write it in Yiddish or not.

Bigsby: When you did publish in Yiddish, in the *Jewish Daily Forum*, your novels appeared in serial form. Presumably that presented you with problems?

Singer: It has good qualities and bad qualities. The bad quality is that you are bound to repeat yourself. Since you don't have the whole manuscript before you, but only write four weeks at a time, you may repeat. On the other hand, it creates a discipline for the writer. He knows he is in contact with the reader. He knows that he is talking to people. I could not write a novel in continuations and write, let's say, like a Joyce, because the reader would not take such a thing. The reader who likes my novel, he is there. What I write today he is going to read next week. And I cannot just talk nonsense to him or talk in an obscure language; it has to make sense. It is being in contact with the reader. Many writers write like this in the nineteenth century, and this is the reason that nineteenth century novels don't have all this futurism and obscurity and Dadaism as the novels of today do.

Bigsby: Do you as a Jewish writer feel any special responsibility?

Singer: No, I don't feel really when I sit down to write that I have any responsibilities. I feel my responsibility is to write what I think is a good novel or a good story. If it is right, it is right. I don't think so much about literature that I would say that if I write a better book it will make any difference, it will make a better world or a more moral world. I don't have this feeling. I always denied it to myself. I said to myself, no matter how good fiction will be, it will never change the world or change human character or change human fate; because of this I don't feel that I am a man with a message or with messages. I feel that if I write a good story, I have done what I wanted to do.

Bigsby: On the other hand, you are celebrating a world which Hitler set out to eliminate totally.

Singer: I will tell you, Mr Bigsby, when you say that I am celebrating I consider it a compliment, but I never had this feeling that I celebrate anything. My feeling is that since I lived there and I know the people, and since I want to be a writer, I should write about them. On the other hand, who knows? Maybe I am really celebrating. But, like a girl who never thinks that she is a beauty, but gets many compliments and goes to the mirror and says, 'Maybe I am really good-looking', maybe it is so. But I just don't have this kind of feeling of importance.

Bigsby: If you could write your own epitaph, what would it be?

Singer: I hope that I might have contributed a few readable novels and a number of readable stories, stories which not only simple people may enjoy but even refined people. This is a maximum I wanted to reach and this is the maximum I reached. I don't think that I have made the world better or wiser; maybe I made it worse. I wouldn't debate with you much if you would say so, because people who read my stories also learn certain things which they shouldn't learn about. My father said that people who like novels are learning how to commit adultery, because they get a lesson in adultery, which is absolutely true. Today they also get lessons in how to swindle, how to cheat. In a way my father was right: novels and fiction and all these things teach people not only good but also evil things. He was right, but people – modern man, especially – need some entertainment. He cannot just live, eat, sleep and do business. And he needs literature.

IN CONVERSATION
WITH
GEORGE STEINER

George Steiner was born in Paris in 1929 to Austrian Jewish parents. In 1940 he fled with his family to the United States where he was educated at Chicago and Harvard. He studied at Oxford before teaching at Princeton. Steiner subsequently became a Fellow of Churchill College, Cambridge, a Professor at Geneva and, subsequently, Oxford. His books are hard to characterize, blending as they do literary criticism with linguistic analysis and philosophy. They are, in effect, humanist documents which contemplate history, language, translation and the shaping power of the imagination. Steiner's books include *The Death of Tragedy* (1961), *Language and Silence* (1967), *In Bluebeard's Castle* (1971), *After Babel* (1975), *Antigones* (1984), *Real Presences* (1989), *No Passion Spent* (1996), and *Errata* (1997). He is also the author of a novel, *The Portage to San Cristobal of A.H.* (1981), of a volume of stories called *Proofs and Three Parables* (1992) and *The Deeps of the Sea and Other Fiction* (1996). This interview was conducted in 1992.

Bigsby: You speak, write and, as I understand it, dream in three languages. Do your German dreams differ from your English ones?

Steiner: Very, very sharply. The rule of thumb seems to be that I dream in the language in which I have been travelling, living that day, and they are very different kinds of dreams. Dreams of childhood are in French, because the setting is that of my birth and childhood in Paris. German dreams tend to have – I wouldn't say violence, that would be silly – a curious intensity, a weight which goes back to very difficult memories, and fears, of course. But the fun of the thing is if you try and find out 'Is there a bedrock? Do we translate in dreams?' No one knows the answer to these questions. Up to now nobody has been able to think of a test whereby we could settle this curious problem. Are there translations inside the subconscious? I suspect that there are, but we have no proof.

Bigsby: Does that mean that the imagination and the mind are shaped by the language we use?

Steiner: Language seems to reach to that unknown land, that active shadow land, between the nervous system and consciousness. We make love very differently in different languages. I have put away in a safe a long chapter, not to be published perhaps for a long time, on the Don Juanism of language: that is to say, when you make love to a woman in English it is different from German, it is different from French, it is different from Italian. The levels of taboo are very different in different languages. The place at which you enter intimacy is very different in different languages. The slang of recognition between men and women which, of course, depends in part on their class, their history, their social background, their economy, is different. It looks as if sexual excitement or depression, tension or imagining, are also in large part linguistic. It reaches right to the heart of us.

Bigsby: The reason you speak three languages is that you were born in Paris of Austrian parents. They were both Jewish. How far did you have a religious upbringing?

Steiner: These were the years when, on the kitchen radio in our home – my father saw to it that we listened – Hitler's voice was coming through and my father never doubted for a moment that the man meant what he said. So they were the years of a rising panic and darkness over our lives, and my father's instinct was that we would be hunted down. That was quite clear to him and his view was that if that was so we had better know why. And so my upbringing was immersed in the history of the Jewish people, in their condition, in what had made us what we are. He was a sharp agnostic, probably very near to atheism; but not my mother. Neither was observant in any ritual sense. We kept the high holidays and Bible-reading was part of my education, right from the beginning. What proved him to be such a prophet is something which it is almost impossible to imagine.

I think there were one or two Jews in my class in the *lycée*, the school I went to in Paris, who survived; all the others perished. From what witness we have it is possible to say that though it was unimaginable to be in the sealed train, it was even worse to be in that train and say, 'Why me?' Those who had no idea what it was to be a Jew, or that they were Jews, suddenly entered a bottomless nightmare without even being able to make rudimentary sense of it. My father always said to us: 'At least you will know something about why you are being hunted, or why you have certain advantages or certain possibilities or certain duties.' So it was a historically rather than a formally religious education.

Bigsby: Because you escaped you could have said, 'Why not me?' Does that place a special kind of responsibility on you?

Steiner: You have asked the central question. In a very early book, *Language and Silence*, I describe myself as a kind of survivor totally baffled by the miracle of good luck – to be able to escape. But I am afraid the thing is more complicated than that. If one is obsessed by a great terror it is always a little bit ambiguous. You are also, of course, drawn to it and, if there was a devil's advocate here – and one must learn at all times to think and feel against oneself in one's own work – the devil's advocate would say: 'Don't you envy a little those who actually found out how they behaved when it came?' And I suppose I do. My own image of myself is that I am the most awful coward. I am almost certain of that. I don't have any idea how I would behave if the knock came at the door. But we are sitting in my privileged home in Cambridge and we have just been having some fun with my soppy, ill-behaved Old English sheepdog. I am convinced that if anybody began beating that animal I would break down in no time at all and hand over the names or whatever information they were trying to get. I just do not know. And, not to have known how one would behave at the midnight of history, not to know and yet to meet from time to time those who behaved magnificently and do not even want to talk about it – those who have been to the frontier of their own selves – leaves one with a feeling of, I would not call it envy, but a certain ache of unknowing. It is ambiguous. I feel ashamed and not ashamed of such feelings.

Bigsby: A key moment for me was meeting someone from a concentration camp and discovering that he was not a saint, that he had all the flaws of anybody else. For some reason you feel that experience ought to have produced a new man.

Steiner: But, on the other hand, they know something that we will never even be able to imagine. They have been in hell. They have been at the other end – the anti-end – of human creation and come back. They not only know themselves better but, of course, they know us better. They have seen man *in extremis*. I do not think language can cover that adequately. Sometimes there is a street corner, where something of that kind happened, and you have the feeling that the sounds of human suffering survive there. This is not mysticism at all. It is an attempt by an outsider to perceive, to imagine; and it has influenced everything I have written, right from the beginning.

Bigsby: I am very struck by that remark. For example, you place enormous stress on the importance of memory and, in particular, on the memorizing of poetry. You say that something is lost to people who do not commit to memory works of literature. But, behind that, there is another concern about memory, isn't there? Because, after all, that period was about an attempt to obliterate memory and history.

Steiner: Well, you and I are teachers and we are living in a period in which education is planned amnesia. No date, no background, no name, no text. I still grew up – being a good deal older than you – in a *lycée* or gymnasium system, where learning by heart was a perpetual discipline. I owe the world to that and I continue to learn by heart right to this day. I think if you love a poem, you want to know it by heart. But you are entirely right. What lies behind that is an anguish about the second death, which is that of forgetting. In my essays and in the first novel, *The Portage*, I speak of that moment when you stand in front of a list of names: it could be a war memorial in any English village, or the ninety-six thousand names on one wall in Prague, or the overwhelmingly moving Vietnam Memorial, which lists all the names of the fallen. And when I go to those I practise a very tiny device. I learn ten names by heart, arbitrarily. I take one block in front of my eyes and I say to myself that perhaps by doing this I am not only honouring them but trying to say to them, 'Look, there is not going to be the second death, the total ash: somewhere you are present in other human beings.' And I think that is worth doing. In Hebrew we call it the *kaddish*, the prayers of the dead. It seems to point to the history of a people always in motion, always in danger, and trying to have a passport made up of the past.

Bigsby: There is another aspect of those times which seems to concern you. It is a subject you come back to repeatedly, namely an anxiety about the function and value of art itself. There is a temptation to ascribe human values to art. We assume that it is a humanizing experience. Yet you have reminded us that it is quite possible to listen to Beethoven or to read Goethe and then go outside and smash the skulls of children. Are you any closer to resolving that conundrum in your own mind?

Steiner: I wish I could answer you very clearly. One would have to have genius to get out of this trap. I have painted myself into a corner. I am utterly convinced that it is a central question. Why did the great culture of Europe not resist more effectively when the inhuman came? Why did the nation of Beethoven and Bach, of Kant and of Goethe, become the nation of Auschwitz?

In the early books, in fact in perhaps the first thirty years of work in writing, I kept asking the question and was forced to the conclusion that people trained to love art supremely, people like you and I for whom a great play, novel or poem was of true significance, must acknowledge that the cry in fiction blots out the cry in the street. I came to the guess – it is not a conclusion, that would be arrogant, but to the intuition – that when you have been pouring over Cordelia, you actually do not hear the whimper, the pain, the messy humiliations, the ugliness in the street or across the wall of your courtyard; that imagination trained to imagine, to fictionalize, is somehow lamed in the face of actual, concrete inhumanity. I have painted myself into a total corner because, no less than you, I cannot imagine a world without the texts we love, without the music, without the art. Hence, my awkward, hesitant, stumbling move which starts in *The Portage* and then in the book on the Antigone myth, *Antigones*, towards something one can call – or not call, as one wishes – the religious, or the hunch that unless we can bring back certain relationships between secular art, literature and thought and the possibility of a metaphysical-theological dimension, we cannot get out of this, to me, otherwise unanswerable conundrum. It is no more than a wager on the possibility of another dimension.

On a much more modest and pragmatic level, I think we should be able to teach *Lear* or *The Brothers Karamazov* in a way that makes us and our students more alert to the crime in the street. But those who are able to do that seem to be very few. And there clearly isn't a technique for it. At best they should make us realize that fiction is a prelude to certain obligations of what I call concrete imagining, what actually happens to this human being I am reading about if it is translated into fact. We are both teachers. We live in this uniquely tense relationship to our students and to their challenge to us, but I just do not know a good answer. At best I hope I can keep asking some good questions.

Bigsby: One way of finding out the answer is to go through to the other side of the mirror and write fiction, which is what you have done.

Steiner: Many, many years ago I began publishing stories. And, God help me, in libraries, which are the graveyards of our false hopes, if anyone ever wanted to look there is early poetry. One morning I woke up and realized that the crucial difference for me was not between poetry and prose but, much worse, between poetry and verse. What I was turning out was verse. Like any well-trained English public-school boy, *lycée* student or gymnasium student, I had been taught to write verse. And a kind of horror shook me when I realized the light years between what I was producing and the real thing. I know that there is also light years of difference between my fiction and, if you want, the real thing. Now what is it? I think I can put my finger on it. In the real thing there is an absolute creative innocence; there is a mysterious immediacy of shaping. What I write are, in almost every case, allegories of argument or ways of translating the life of thought, of ideas, of passion, of debate, into a fictional form. There is no need to be ashamed of that. At the supreme level I would respectfully pitch certain dialogues in Plato as high as the highest of all drama, as dramatic and as moving. But that is the Everest, of course. There is room in the foothills for those who want to give their questions a lyric human voice – a setting. It is fun to do, it is exciting, it is very demanding. Once or twice I think I have at least had a whiff, a smell of the real thing.

In the new volume, *Proofs and Three Parables*, the last parable is called 'Conversation Piece'. It tries for a moment to imagine the unspeakable, the last dance of those who were dying as the spigots opened in the ovens, and the moments before that. That was written in one single night and the only way I can put it is that – and forgive this bad grammar, bad English, bad everything – it wrote me. One of the wonderful things about German is that you can get away with that kind of sentence. In German you can actually say a thing writes you and you do not write it. At which point, of course, English common sense rears on its magnificent hind legs and says, 'Come off it.' But the speech of the imaginary Hitler in *The Portage*, possibly, wrote me, as did the long preceding speech, the long litany for the dead.

A couple of times I have been just within smelling distance of the real thing. And if you have, then you do not fool yourself. You know what the real thing is: it is something very different. A few times I had the privilege of watching Henry Moore, who had accepted an honorary fellowship of my Cambridge college. When you asked Henry Moore about a political issue, or some nonsense from the day's news, what emerged was really not very exciting. You then shut your ears and watched his hands. When you saw the transcendant intelligence of those hands moving, you then knew what the real thing was. It can neither be faked nor imitated. You know that in a supreme artist of his kind, the – intelligence is the wrong word – the knowing, the total intuition, the economy of motion, which only very great minds have, was in those ten fingers, in those fantastic wrists. And that I do not have, of course. That is quite clear. I do not think one should ever fool oneself about the difference.

Bigsby: But if you have come close to the real thing, you have also come close to a kind of danger. Maybe they are aspects of the same thing. The story about Hitler, which plays with the conceit that Hitler lives on to be able to offer a justification for the Holocaust, brought you considerable trouble.

Steiner: It was an attempt to understand a very simple thing of the kind you and I read in newspapers or in *The Scientific American*. As it happens, part of my first university degree at the University of Chicago had some mathematics and physics in it. I was then under Dr Oppenheimer at the Institute in Princeton, and I am a founding fellow of what is essentially a science college – Churchill College, Cambridge. My lifelong fascination with science has never ceased, my delight in being among scientists. And I heard a very fine, simple lecture some years ago, when it was a new concept, about anti-matter. I noted down this extraordinary statement: for every particle we know about in our universe there is an opposite particle called anti-matter and when they clash there is a terrible destructive effect. I thought I would love to be able to express that in a fiction, and the thought arose in me that in the *kabbalah*, in Jewish mysticism, there is a very tenacious belief that it is not the unpronounceable name of God in Hebrew that is at all dangerous, but a secret name of God which would release the utmost horror and destruction in the world if anybody knew it and cared to use it. It is an idea that other mystical traditions also know, black magic and so on. It does seem that Hitler came very near to knowing that name, to being the anti-matter of language, that which can destroy the hopes, the face in human speech. And he was – of this I am convinced, or practically – a transcendant master of the word, or the anti-word. I wanted to try and show that in a fantasy. Now, unquestionably – and that is what happens to real artists, and that is why I say that was one of the moments I was in reach of the real thing – real artists not only paint themselves into logical corners but into deep emotional ones. It was pointed out to me by the many, many ferocious critics of this work, and by the crowds that tried to stop the theatre performances, both here and in the United States, that some of the arguments of my imaginary age had already appeared in my own voice in *In Bluebeard's Castle* and earlier works. And that to me – that unplanned element – is the evidence that for once I was writing, as one should write, not as a master planner or arguer, but in the grip of something larger than oneself. This is, as you say, also a very terrifying experience. And I at least hope I have some tiny inkling of what great artists have told us of the way they then look at their own creations in disbelief, in terror.

Bigsby: One thing that you allow Hitler to say is that his own desire for racial purity is an echo of a similar desire for racial purity on the part of the Jews, as the chosen people. He claims that his was a pursuit of a particular kind of ideal, and that that is what the Jewish people have also presented to the world.

Steiner: In *Mein Kampf*, and in other texts there is a conscious counterpoint to – an other side of, a mirror of – certain elements in primitive monotheism: the claim of an eternally elected ethnic group, the claim that this group has a unique territorial claim, aspiration, possession. He knew his enemies very, very well. One is haunted by the fact that in those two towering Jew-haters – and creators, in their own different ways – Wagner and Hitler, there seems to have been at some level some peculiar, sick, sick fear lest there be something Jewish in themselves. Now Dostoevsky would handle that much better than I did. It is a Dostoevskian challenge that Kafka would know what to do with and I certainly was not able to press home as a great artist could. But I do not think there should be any taboos to the danger of our thinking. We are an animal that should keep opening the doors in Bluebeard's castle, right to the last one.

Bigsby: The principal character in *Proofs* is a proofreader; he is very efficient, very precise, but his eyesight is fading. He is also a Communist, who sees the Communist empire beginning to fall apart. In other words, it is a world which is beginning to lose its definition in one way or another. It has an end-of-millennium feel about it, that story.

Steiner: That is entirely right. This is a novella which arises, again, perhaps from one tiny seed. Proofreading is a peculiarly difficult art; it is beginning to fade because of new technological means, disks and so on. But until very recently, and for some time longer, the Gutenberg revolution has depended on proofreaders. Great proofreaders are very, very rare. And we are talking together in a town which has the most famous of all proofreader stories. It relates to Whitehead and Bertrand Russell's three-volume work in mathematical logic, which consists only of formulas, with very few connecting words. Questions about theorems and certain developments of argument were put to them by proofreaders simply because the proofreaders were so exquisitely alert and accurate that they spotted anomalies or irregularities and said there must be something wrong in the argument. Russell writes about this. Skill of concentration led to the heart of the argument.

Marxism can be read, and I am using 'read' quite consciously, of course, in talking about a novel which features books and proofreaders, as an attempt to correct the text of human history, human greed, human enslavement, human exploitation. Marxism was, after the Mosaic Decalogue and Christ's Sermon on the Mount, the third great Jewish attempt to blackmail humanity into perfection, to tell human beings that if you have two rooms you will share one with somebody else, if you have a coat in winter which is thick enough for two people you will cut it in two, and so on and so forth. Marxism said, we will have the kingdom of justice not up there in heaven but next Monday morning, down here on earth. It is the great millennial claim to locate in this world the utopia of justice. Marxism set out to get it right. The genius of Lenin was so much that of a man trying to get it right, to blot out the errors, the stupidities, the misreadings, the wrong footnotes and so on. It ended, as we know, as a nightmare in many ways, though whether it has really ended is a large and complicated question. We have the whole of the Third World ahead of us, Latin America and so on.

Then again, proofreaders are owlish creatures who tend to work at night, so they can be identified with the other side of our lives, the clandestine side, the suppressed side. They also want to get it right. Quite desperately. That is their faith; that is their credo. And I try to show, in this little text, that it does not matter so terribly what you get right. It can be a bill of sale, it can be a telephone directory. We do know of people who were correcting proofs in books they had smuggled along right to the edge of the gas chambers, or who had seminars on Talmudic texts where the question of the right reading was as passionately debated, as angrily debated, as it would have been in any other circumstance. There is a kind of crazy, autistic dreaming of perfection in Messianic Marxism and what I ask myself is, 'What is it like to live the collapse of your god, the collapse of your temple, the collapse of your world, of its references, during the months around the collapse of the Berlin Wall, and everything that has happened since?' And proofreading, because of the play on words in 'proofs' – we read proofs, we need proofs, proofs prove things – gave me the image for this story.

Bigsby: So there is an ambiguity about the ideal. It may actually contain evil at its heart?

Steiner: The ideal seems to lead very often to disaster. Poe called it the imp of the perverse. What is it in the texture of our best efforts which turns them to sadism, to waste and to failure? I fully articulate that question in this little text. But careful! If man is here in order to invest in, produce and visit more Disney Worlds, more Disney Lands, if the end and object of our vast suffering and efforts is some kind of 'valium California', not so much the actual place as the dream of every T-shirt, of every Walkman, of every video cassette store from here to Vladivostok, if what human hope is about is to have more McDonald's – and I have seen them being opened at the foot of the marble steps of the Great Wall of China – and have a Kentucky Fried Chicken concession in every town of Africa and Asia, if this is what it has all been about, then I would feel a sense of utter despair and bewilderment. Nobody, I hope, needs to tell me about the Gulag. Nobody, I hope, needs to tell me about what is even worse, the lies to which human beings were compelled in order to survive Stalinist and post-Stalinist despotism. I want us to think a little more about the possibility that what we are stepping into may be a dark vacuum, a kind of zero of genuine human hopes and dignity, that the Western message and contribution is not that which really honours man. It flatters him endlessly, it seduces him, but I keep thinking that we were meant for something else.

Bigsby: That raises the question of this element that has become central to your work: namely, faith or mystery. But the more I think about it, the more I realize that that has always been there, behind the debate about language, tragedy and literature.

Steiner: Bless you! One of the lovely things about getting old is that you suddenly realize how little you have understood about what you have been doing. The first sentence of the first book I published, now over thirty years ago, is: 'Great criticism is a debt of love.' It is the first sentence of the first book on Tolstoy and Dostoevsky. And the first three pages say you are not going to get novels of that kind if the question of the existence or non-existence of God is not a legitimate object of enquiry, of worry and of imagining. The difference between a *Moby Dick* or *Brothers Karamazov* or *Anna Karenina* and most of what passes for fiction lies somewhere in that dimension of question. And now I realize, *Real Presences* being my fifteenth book to be published, that maybe they are one book and that, if I am very, very lucky, they are really hooked into one essential question or one obsessive searching and enquiry. Yes, it was there from the start. It may have taken me quite a long time to come back to the beginning, but to come back to the beginning is also, for artists, just about the most difficult thing of all.

Bigsby: *Real Presences* argues that at least the idea of God lies behind the notion of art and music, or that without the idea of God they would lose some of their power and their force. But with the idea of God, art can also produce kitsch.

Steiner: It can produce kitsch with any idea. We only need look at Stalinist socialist-realism to know what kitsch is. I meant something, I suppose, rather specific. First of all, as you know, and you are being very generous by not pushing it harder, what marginalizes me so deeply in the world of the academic, which I love in many ways, is my absolute conviction that the people you want to listen to are not critics, not professors, not pundits, but the artists themselves. As I try to show in *Real Presences*, maybe 95 per cent of all those who have left us testimony say, with D.H. Lawrence, that to create is to have a great and terrifying flame of some relationship to God pass through them. I try to show that it can often be that of a rival. Picasso, most wonderfully and angrily, keeps saying, 'He is next door, the other maker.' Matisse at one point says, 'Now we don't need him any more. I have just done it. I can create like him.' There are Michelangelo sonnets which explore this, saying, 'Dammit, he is trying to get my hammer.' And, after all, the David which Michelangelo sculpts is probably more beautiful than anybody ever created by nature. And so the rivalry is very, very real. For others, it is a celebration and an act of faith.

Blake is one of the writers I feel closest to in the English tradition. The sense of almost crazed intimacy between Blake and the process of creation in nature, or in theology and music, has moved more and more to the centre for me. I know people can say to me, 'Oh, come off it again, this is rhetoric, this is just a way of making words seem to say more than they do.' They can also say of great painting, 'It does not work for me at all.' But I can see them fall silent before music. Roughly since Plato there have been six or seven people who have had anything to say about music worth hearing. What in the world is music like? I just keep asking that question and get no answer. After all, if we had Aristotle come into this room and showed him a total modern abstract of black on black, Aristotle would smile and say, 'That is a picture of midnight.' And he could cope with it very well. If we showed him a white on white he would say, 'A snow storm, a blind owl in a storm – no problem.' Music – nothing. No one has come close to saying what happens to us when music possesses us.

The great French anthropologist Lévi-Strauss says, 'The supreme mystery of all sciences of man is the invention of the melody.' And that utterly convinces me. No one has ever said a single word about what it is to invent a melody which transforms you, which you can never forget, which you walk to and love and perhaps die with. So my challenge is: in an age of theory – in an age of unbelievably arrogant and often pretentious and jargon-cursed literary theory, poetic theory, aesthetic theory, deconstruction, post-structuralism, and so on, need I take seriously any reflection on meaning, and on the human relationship to meaning in form, that has nothing to say about music? I find myself listening more and more to music and just knowing that there is in the human capacity to create and to respond to music something which, quite simply, at the humblest, daily level, so far wholly escapes us.

Bigsby: That is presumably because language has limits. Anyone who has ever tried to write to somebody who has just lost someone very close to them through death knows that there is no usable language. You fall back on clichés as a way of acknowledging the fact that language has run out. Is music something that starts at the point at which language ceases to be able to function?

Steiner: Again, we are speaking in Cambridge where Wittgenstein lived and taught, and generations have quoted or lived by his affirmation that the limits of our language are the limits of our world. But I say no, they have not even begun where music starts. That seems to me one of the really crucial divisions in sensibility, in philosophic understanding. It is not just that you cannot paraphrase or metaphrase music. It is that language, even at the remotest abstraction, finally and laboriously can be brought back to being something like the world. Music can't. Yes, there is birdsong, I know. And there are rudimentary imitative sounds. I.A. Richards in this very town once said, 'The most complex event in the universe is the balance of a quartet.' Fine. It is a lovely teaching overstatement but I do not think he is very far wrong. No mathematics, no philosophy, no logic, no acoustic analysis even begins to tell us what the balance of a great quartet is and why each performance is totally unique, can never happen again, has never happened before; nor can it tell us what it is that is being said about the meaning of meaning between four pieces of wood with catgut strung across them.

That is where my difficulties begin, and it is among musicians that I have of late found some of the most immediate understanding and response to my kind of worries. That a musician, through his music, can communicate immediately and overwhelmingly provokes profound envy, exasperation and anguish; but it also provokes enormous joy and celebration. You speak of trying to reach someone in their grief. In most so-called primitive societies, as you know, with very great grief language largely stops and it is indeed in music, or in a group song sounding in the house of the bereaved person, that something is trying to be not said but lived. Language says: music lives.

Bigsby: Why can we be moved by bad art?

Steiner: Isn't that a difficult and an exciting question? There lies behind your question, with your knowledge of modern drama, something you must often have puzzled over: Noel Coward's famous line about bad music being so unbearably moving. I don't know what it is about bad art that moves us so. I don't know that we can apply aesthetic criteria to that which comes wholly to possess us. It may be that, for most of us, great art has a forbidding, didactic presence and authority. It may be that we feel more comfortable, more relaxed, more part of the family with what is called bad art. But the moments which change human perception are so close to a child's game. I will just give two examples. Millions and millions of people have walked down London streets, Paris streets, Moscow streets, for generations, and children have come by on a tricyle. Picasso walked down a street, flipped the saddle and the bull charged. All tricycles since that day have had the saddle as the bull's head and the two great arms as its horns charging at you. Those things can either give you journalism, a Campbell's soup can or something absolutely new in the range of our perceptions. I hope there will never be a critical system that will foolproofedly distinguish between the two.

Bigsby: Can you explain to me, or to yourself, why you haven't followed the logic of your own work, that is, why you haven't moved from a belief in mystery and the idea of God to a belief in God?

Steiner: Here I will avail myself of the privilege of English decorum. This is an area in which I do not yet feel able publicly to articulate. Besides, your assumption may not be wholly justified. I think the question that can be debated publicly is: do you feel that the wager on the possibility of God should entail, for example, religious practice? There is a rabbi who has made almost a reflex sport of attacking me, in all possible connections, precisely because he believes that the only kind of acceptable Judaism, at this time in history, is the one that practises and is seen to practise. I think this is probably nonsense, utter nonsense, because the domain of one's inner imaginings and structures may be serious and intense and dangerous in inverse proportion to the facilities and public comforts and homecomings of practice. I would go that far. But on a much gentler and more speculative note, I suppose, if you have me absolutely against the wall, somewhere I am a Manichaean, that is to say, the principle of evil seems to me a very real possibility. I have the coolest, calmest, greatest philosophic mind of our history on my side: Immanuel Kant, a man who breathed reason, lived reason, ate reason and who very calmly states that there is an incarnate principle of evil because nothing else makes sense of the mess we are in.

The example that I now ponder, and ponder because it comes, alas, from personal acquaintance, comes from America. When you had a wisdom tooth out, even if it went very well, they gave you a little blood transfusion, just against shock or loss of blood. It was routine. There was a lovely young woman. Twenty years later, the foetus, conceived in a happy marriage, has Aids. Once you are confronted with that, a number of reactions are possible. The first is, 'Oh, come off it, Steiner, it is a statistical accident. Across the random totality of men and women on this planet it is of very limited significance. Life is a biogenetic lottery. You get a good number or a bad number.' Those who can live by that, I shut up in front of. My colleagues can live by that; a great scientist can perhaps live like that. I say 'hats off' and I shut up. I wonder to myself whether they live by it on the day their child is in a traffic accident, but that may not be a fair challenge because they would then say, 'We are going hysterical with grief and agony. That does not prove our rational insight was not the right one.' That is one possibility.

Another one is a kind of Calvinist fundamentalism: we are being punished for some inherited original sin. This is not as silly as it sounds. The notion that history is a form of punishment for fallen man has as much logical persuasion to it as many a scientific theory which cannot be demonstrated, cannot be proved. Certainly, Freud and Marx held that theory in one form or another: the primal fall, primal crime, primal error of man. Or you can say to yourself there is active evil in the affairs of men. The men who dreamed of Zionism and wrote its great documents were socialists, dreamers, humanists of the deepest passionate idealism. Their dream is fulfilled and today Jewish police and occupation authorities torture and kill, out of that dream, in direct consequence.

What is the twist that turns good into the inhuman? Why are we so helpless in front of the inertial power of suffering? Why is it that when Trinculo and Stephano in *The Tempest* need Caliban and all is going well, Shakespeare has that kind of total millennial insight.

Suddenly, without a quarrel, Stephano says, 'I could find it in my heart to beat him.' It is a line that leaves me helpless with terror, with wonder, with a sense of an imaginative intelligence so much greater than anything I can conceive of. The whole of our history is in that line. No revolt yet by Caliban, no quarrel between them. They are all embracing each other and then: 'I could find it in my heart to beat him.' The beginning is there of all that will happen to the Third World, to our present situation and so on. Shakespeare needs no further explanation. There it is. How is it that we find it in our heart to beat, to torture, to destroy? And these are speculations which a positivist, scientific logic and the presently fashionable secularism will not tackle.

Bigsby: Does that mean that because you have been forced to accept the existence of something called evil, perversely you have been forced to accept the existence of something called good?

Steiner: I hope not 'forced'. How could you or I be teachers if we were not people who dream forward every day. That is what teaching is all about. We could not bear it otherwise. We are also betting on moments of good. But it has become a little difficult. Heidegger, the great German philosopher and man of considerable personal evil, said, 'tell a good story or anecdote and you kill thinking', which is a savage thing to say. I know exactly what he means, so I have to conclude in a very personal way. When the killing fields episode came in Cambodia we took one quick step back. It is absolutely certain that during the time of the gas ovens and Auschwitz, very, very few knew. That is absolutely certain, a handful. And only few even of those few believed it. So, even within the handful, it was a handful. This time, television, press, CNN informed us fully.

It emerged that about one hundred thousand people were buried alive by the Khmer Rouge, and I can only say to you, upon an oath and trust of friendship, that I was idiotic enough to believe that the great powers, but also Israel and England, would issue a statement saying: 'Look, we don't know who is right in this cockpit of local political imbroglios. Nobody can figure this one out. So we are coming in, we are stopping this because, forty years after Auschwitz, when we shave in the morning or put on our make-up, we are not going to look in the mirror when a hundred thousand people are being buried alive, because man cannot go on this way. We're going to stop this.' At the time, Russia was fully stable and had its own vast political power.

America was fully stable. As you know, nothing happened. Absolutely nothing was done to stop this and, as we speak in Cambridge this afternoon, in this home, the fact happens to be that governments you and I elect by our votes and pay taxes to are rearming Pol Pot's Khmer Rouge. And it is in the dark light of that kind of deepening astonishment that I sometimes feel that a Manichaean vision of reality may be the most modestly accurate.

Bigsby: You have said that our lives depend upon our capacity to speak hope, that we are leaning into the future in some way. But you have also commented on the ironic hope that the concentration camp victims clung to, to the very doors of the crematoria. Hope is obviously a human characteristic, but is it redemptive or is it the heart of a terrible kind of absurdity?

Steiner: One would have to be one of the world's greatest visionaries to come anywhere near answering such a question. But, contrary to official linguistics, I am overwhelmed every day by the scandalous wonder of the future tense. That you and I, in every known human language, can speak of the Monday morning after our own burial, can speak of the billion or billion and a half years when certain galaxies will be in certain positions: that crazy, incredible gift we have, and probably animals do not, of using future tenses can be one of fear and dread; it can be one of total fantasy. 'If' – that insanely powerful word 'if' – if it were so, if it became so. Every time we use this feature of grammar we should, in my opinion, pause with a sense of enigmatic miracle. But it can, indeed, also go both ways. You are quite right. A nightmare is also a projection. Nevertheless, I come back to teaching. Teaching is the wonderful tomfoolery of unbroken hope. You know, as well as I do, that there are days when one can go up the wall with despair. And then comes something – a moment with a student, a moment in class, a rediscovery of a line one thought one knew totally, a quiet sunburst of hope. Isn't it interesting that those who designed what was meant to be a world language chose a name for what was to be the new international tongue to resolve conflicts and bring mutual understanding, which was an anagrammatic construction of the word for hope in all Romance languages. They called it esperanto.

IN CONVERSATION WITH PAUL THEROUX

Journeys, of one kind or another, have been a stock-in-trade for a writer born in one country, America, but who lived for many years in another, Britain. Professionally, Paul Theroux has divided his time between travel writing and the novel. *The Great Railway Bazaar* (1975) is about a trip which took him halfway round the world: through Europe, across India, Burma and Vietnam to Japan. *The Old Patagonian Express* (1978), another railway saga, took him to the tip of South America, while *Riding the Iron Rooster* (1998) is an account of a journey through China in the late 1980s. Even Theroux's novels often have an international setting. *The Family Arsenal* (1976) may be set in London but *The Mosquito Coast* (1981), later made into a film with Harrison Ford, takes place in the Central American jungle, while *My Secret History* (1989) transports its hero from America to Africa to England and then back again to America. In *Chicago Loop* (1990) he takes a double journey, into a bleak social world and into the mind of a psychopath. Later books include *Millroy and the Magician* (1983), *The Pillars of Hercules* (1995) *My Other Life* (1996) and *Kowloon Tong* (1997). Paul Theroux is a winner of the Whitbread Prize for Fiction. This interview was conducted in April 1990.

Bigsby: In *My Secret History*, the character says that he was born poor in rich America. Did that apply to you?

Theroux: No, it didn't. Like many other things in *My Secret History*, it didn't apply at all. I was born, I would say, middle class in rich America, in a very large family of seven children and a very talkative family at that. So it didn't apply to me at all, but it was something that I could relate to because the subject of money was always on my mind. In the States you have no status if you have no money, and if you don't have very much money you don't have very much status, so even middle-class and lower-middle-class people worry about money. I must say that one of the things that really delighted me when I first came to England, when I first got to know English people, was that money didn't matter very much to them.

Bigsby: Yet when you went up to university, you were taking pre-med courses. Why today are you not sitting in a Boston surgery counting your money or having your hands in somebody's chest doing triple bypass operations? What went wrong?

Theroux: Something did go seriously wrong. I wouldn't be in Boston doing bypass operations or counting money. If I had a fantasy it was to be in Central Africa operating on someone with a strangulated hernia and not making any money at all, or pulling someone's teeth or working among lepers or Aids patients in Uganda. I always thought that I was interested in tropical medicine, and I saw myself going abroad and working in a sort of jungle hospital. That was my fantasy; it was never suburban surgery or triple bypasses. They never interested me.

Bigsby: So it was Albert Schweitzer?

Theroux: It was. I'll tell you who it was; when I was growing up, it was Dr Tom Dooley. I grew up Catholic and Dr Tom Dooley was a very, very important symbolic figure. He was so important that a few years ago when I was asked to write about his life, I willingly agreed although it wasn't a great sort of commercial deal and I discovered that Tom Dooley was an enormous fake. He had flunked out of medical school and been kicked out of the Navy. He was a doctor in Laos and in Vietnam in the 1950s, and he ran a sort of jungle hospital, but he was a totally hollow man.

Bigsby: How did those medical ambitions founder?

Theroux: I think that the urge to write, the desire to write, and the pleasure of writing overwhelmed those ambitions, as they overwhelm a lot of things. They overwhelm friendships, they overwhelm normal life, they overwhelm so many things, and I think it was just that. I realized that I couldn't be like Chekhov and combine both. Chekhov had genius both as a doctor and as a writer and I maybe had talent as both, but I couldn't obviously do both. It was with great regret that I gave it up. But I will tell you something, I think about it a lot. I won't say I think about it every day but I think about not being a doctor a lot. Every few days I think maybe I should have done it, maybe I could still do it but, like a woman who realizes that she can't have a child any more, that her childbearing days are over, I think I have now realized that I will never go to medical school.

Bigsby: Does that mean you think that in some way being a doctor is more worthwhile than being a writer?

Theroux: I think that in many ways being a doctor, in certain places, is more worthwhile, yes. When you hear writers talking about themselves or their books or going to conferences or worrying about literary freedom and persecuted writers, I think, in the real world – in the world that I enjoy being in: in Africa, South America and Asia – writing doesn't matter very much. One of the pleasures of illiteracy, I should say, is that people seem much happier; they seem to depend on an oral tradition. Maybe this opens a whole other subject, but I do think that medicine, and I am talking about medicine where it is crucial, where it is a matter of life or death, not where it's cosmetic surgery or heart transplants, necessarily, but where a person dies because he steps on a stone fish or gets an infection or dies because of a simple reason, I think that was the sort of thing I regret: not being in a place to save such lives. I don't know whether writing saves anyone's life. I don't even know whether it makes people freer or happier. I think it does liberate people. Writing is liberation, but I tend to think that it liberates the writer more than it does other people.

Bigsby: You did, however, go to Africa. Was this a writer looking for experience or was it a member of the Kennedy generation going out to do good in the Third World?

Theroux: I had always had a fantasy of going away, partly because of this big family. I had a fantasy of having my own room, of being in my own house, of having my own space, to use the current jargon, and I felt a tremendous lack of privacy in a large family. I also had the fantasy of going to an exotic place, an exotic country, and living in a solitary way. It is the fantasy of being Robinson Crusoe or Columbus, of being Adam or Noah or Henderson the Rain King or maybe Allie Fox. It's a fantasy of going to a place and doing something, creating something. But I knew I could only do it alone. I wanted to be isolated, and I think I had a very strong urge to prove myself, to prove that I could do something. I felt that I didn't want my family or people that I knew witnessing this. I wanted them to see the results, not the work.

Bigsby: What was it that you wanted to prove? Where did these feelings come from?

Theroux: When you deal with writers you are dealing with a very eccentric, very odd group of people. Generally speaking, when you talk to a writer you very seldom talk about books; you are much more likely to talk about eccentricity or loneliness or lack of love or, in some cases, lack of money or whatever, lack of status. It is very seldom, I think, that a writer becomes a writer because he has read a lot of books or because he has had a good education. I felt deprived of other things. I felt very lonely. I also felt that in a large family I was a bit lost, I suppose, but, along with that, politically, I felt that it was a good thing to write. I felt as rebellious as many other people did in my generation; I felt that we were being lied to. For example, in the 1960s we all knew that the Vietnam War was a sham, that it was stupid, that it was a waste of human life, of effort. When you refer to the Kennedy generation the fact is that I rather disliked Kennedy as a president. I thought he was a bit of a crook and a bit of a hypocrite. I also thought that he had everything going his way and that he led us into Vietnam. So, when he died a lot of people were very ashamed. I think that people remember his death because they disliked him so much. But I left. I didn't want to go to Vietnam. I wanted to prove myself. I had political reasons, but I also had reasons to do with fantasy, emotional reasons, whatever, lots of reasons for going away and staying away.

Bigsby: My impression is that you really enjoyed those African years.

Theroux: Yes, I enjoyed being in Africa very much because I felt that I had discovered something on my own. I had discovered how to speak a language that very few other people knew. I was in the bush. I was alone and I think, for the first time in my life, I was succeeding at something independently and actually making my own decisions. I was running a school, more or less, and I was being useful. It mattered to people's lives. The curious thing was that every night I used to go home and write, and I wrote like mad. I used to stay up late pumping a tilly lamp, one of these pressure lamps hissing away while flies buzzed around, and I used to write. I wrote and wrote and wrote and no one there read anything; no one knew that I was writing. Most of the people I talked to were totally illiterate, and I felt a kind of secret joy that I was doing this, that what I was doing for them didn't have anything to do with my writing life. My writing life was totally separate. And if I failed in it I failed and no one would ever know. I could just maybe show up a little weary the next morning having failed at that, but I was succeeding at being a teacher and I was writing a textbook. I actually published two volumes of a textbook with Longmans under a different name, and that book has never emerged.

Bigsby: You managed to get thrown out of Malawi.

Theroux: That's a very long story which I told in an essay called 'The Killing of Hastings Banda'. Briefly, it was an assassination attempt that I was involved in unwittingly. Then I became a sort of patsy and was ejected from the country. Oddly enough, twenty-five years later I went back. I still spoke the language. People remembered me. I met the students and, although I had been ejected from the country which was my first love – your first country is a very important thing, the first country you go to as a young person – the people were still alive. They were fairly happy and they had children. They were old. Indeed, they had aged a lot, much more, I felt, than I had, but that's the way it is in a poor country.

Bigsby: From Malawi you went to Uganda, from there to Singapore and then England. Are you by nature a traveller or wanderer?

Theroux: That's a very difficult question. I think that by nature I am very restless. I feel that we have a very short time on earth and that there's a lot to see. I actually have a sense – probably more lately, say since I turned forty – that I have begun counting, keeping track, asking myself, have I seen this? I want to do this while I am still healthy. I want to try this while I can still do it. When you get older you start buying clocks and speedometers. I put a speedometer on my bike. It clocks the miles. You start thinking about mileage, you start thinking about counting. There is a line in Samuel Beckett where someone, I can't remember who, says, 'Counting is the only pleasure on earth.' It is the sort of thing you expect of an elderly person and there's this Irish fellow counting. If there's a difference between travelling and wandering, I don't know. I think that wandering is something that someone does who doesn't have a home, who doesn't have a place to go back to, and I have always felt that I am a traveller who leaves home and then goes back home, and that is a very, very important distinction.

Bigsby: You began your writing career as a novelist and were beginning to get established. Then, in the early 1970s, you launched what was in effect another career, that of a travel writer. What led you that day to take a train at Victoria Station and go on a journey that eventually became *The Great Railway Bazaar*?

Theroux: I think it was calculation. I had been travelling a lot before that. I had been travelling, say, since university, since I was nineteen. But in 1973, when I set off on that trip, it was a calculated attempt to travel with the intention of writing a book about it. From the day I left to the day I came back I kept notes and I had very, very copious notes. I even bought a camera and I took a lot of pictures, because I thought travel books should have pictures, and I've looked at these recently. They are sort of funny because they are just snapshots, but I thought that's what a travel book was. It was a series of your adventures and then you had pictures, a bit like a geography book. This is a man in native dress. This is the time I was on a train. I took pictures of trains and landscapes. But it was deliberate, and I don't think of a novel as such a deliberate thing.

Bigsby: I learned from *The Great Railway Bazaar* that the Russians have something called 'hard class' on their trains.

Theroux: And soft class.

Bigsby: Reading your travel books you don't seem to go on soft class. I get the feeling that there is no other class than hard class. Travelling and suffering do seem to go hand in hand. Why pay the price that you have to pay in writing travel books?

Theroux: I think the price is worth it. First, I have paid in real money. I think I am one of the few travellers who doesn't take free rides. When I am offered a trip I generally don't take it. I discovered there was a travel industry, long after I began writing travel books, and that there are people who never pay for hotels, who never pay air fares, train fares or whatever, so I always paid in money. And I discovered that is a unique thing, almost, and that most people write books full of acknowledgements thanking people for tickets. The price in physical and mental distress, I suppose, is something else. I think that I would do it anyway. The difficult thing about writing is not the physical discomfort, because all travel is uncomfortable, all travel involves delay, irritation and nuisance, all travel is less than it appears, much more trouble than you would ever imagine. People go on one-week skiing holidays and spend two of those seven days travelling and five days renting equipment and getting ski passes and waiting in line and being pushed around by French people and stepped on by bratty children. What they call a one-week skiing holiday is a couple of days on the slopes. It is terrible most of the time, I think. The difficult part of travel is writing about it. It is waking in the morning and realizing that you have a long day ahead of you and that you have to get something out of it. You have to bring something back.

Bigsby: Can that get between you and the experience? We are used to people who travel and see the world through a viewfinder but, in a way, don't you do that?

Theroux: That is partly true, but my travel books have all been different and I have always had a serious intention. In China, for example, although I had read a lot of books, I had no idea about the Chinese landscape. I was very keen on showing what China looked like, describing what it smelled like, what it sounded like, and the jabber and chatter of people, by actually talking to people. I often feel that the writing I do or the life I lead is much closer to that of a painter than a writer. The other day someone asked me on the radio: 'You've written thirty books in twenty years, isn't that too many?' My reaction to that was, I suppose, a kind of exasperation and disbelief. But no one would say Picasso did too many pictures. You do as many pictures or sketches as you feel that you have to. And I see myself in that role: as sometimes sketching, sometimes painting. Sometimes it is a large canvas, sometimes it is a small one. In China I used to look out the window and feel that I was sketching a landscape with figures in the foreground. Sometimes I would meet those figures. And I do a portrait of a person. Is it a deliberate intention? Yes, it has to be deliberate, you have to screw your courage and your will up so that that day will matter, so that you find something. But the same is true with writing a novel. With writing a novel you wake in the morning and you have to get something done. You have to get yourself in the mood. I always find it terribly difficult to do, to get into the mood, but all writing in that sense is deliberate.

Bigsby: Doesn't it make a difference whether you do or don't speak the language of the country through which you are passing? You do speak Spanish; you don't speak Chinese or Russian, do you?

Theroux: No, I studied Chinese for three years in Singapore. I studied Mandarin. My wife and I both did, in fact, because the place was really so dull. Before I went to China I mugged it up again so I could have a rudimentary conversation in Mandarin, an ice-breaking conversation. I know when people are lying. I used to know when two Chinese people were speaking to each other about me and I could usually tell what they were saying. Or if a man was translating something and there was a word or phrase that wasn't being translated I usually knew that because of this rudimentary knowledge. The longer I was there, the better I got at it. Mandarin is no more difficult than any other language. But I wasn't fluent.

Bigsby: But what of Russia? Do you see a different world when you have access to the language?

Theroux: Yes. There's no question about that, and I felt that when I was writing *The Great Railway Bazaar*. I don't speak Hindi, obviously, and I don't speak Urdu or Farsi, and I feel that that book is a funny book because I didn't speak the language and wasn't getting to the heart of things. When you do speak the language, for example, when travelling around England, a country can seem very, very sad. That is when you learn about the ordinariness of people's lives. I had an experience once in France. My French isn't very good but my wife speaks it very well. We were on a train just riding along when I saw two ancient, black-shawled women talking. It was the sort of conversation in which you assume they are talking about the harvest or the cows, and I said, 'That's picturesque.' And my wife said, 'Do you know what they're talking about?' I said, 'No' and she said, '*Dallas.*' They were going home to watch *Dallas*. There are two kinds of travel books, one in which you refer to 'these two charming women' talking about the harvest, and the other one in which you confess they were talking about *Dallas*. It is like D.H. Lawrence seeing those Mexicans standing by the road and thinking they were melancholy, thinking metaphysical thoughts, when in fact they were waiting for a bus. I have written both kinds of book but I'm happier writing a book where I speak the language. First, because I think it is more truthful; second, because I think when you do not speak the language you inevitably end up writing only about yourself. Here I am boarding a bus, here I am getting on a train, here I am having a terrible meal, here I am trying to be understood by this native who is jabbering away: that sort of book. It is the kind of travel book that I really do not like. I think I have written things like that but I am somewhat ashamed of myself.

When I am flummoxed in a foreign country, when I do not speak the language and end up writing a piece, a book, or whatever, about that experience, it is not a happy experience. But when you speak the language you do get at some truth in the country and are removed from yourself. I think I managed it in China. I think I managed it in South America, and I think I managed it travelling around Britain. A lot of people objected to my book, *The Kingdom by the Sea*, but to me it is one of my funniest and most successful books, and I think it is a period in Britain – a couple of months in 1982 – which are frozen in my mind. If anyone wants to know what the country was like then, they only have to read my book. It wasn't a put-up job. I did not look for horrible and ridiculous people. These were people I met and they were speaking to me in their own language. I understood exactly what they were saying.

Bigsby: You are a central figure in the travel books. Is the Paul Theroux in those books quite continuous with the Paul Theroux I am talking to now across the table, or do you become a kind of picaresque figure?

Theroux: When setting out with an intention to write a travel book you may be a different character, but I don't think so. It is hard to sustain a different tone. The best thing to do in writing a travel book is to be yourself, to tell the truth and to report on your experience. I tend to report on everything because I started out doing that and I realized people wonder about the ordinary details of travel life: they do not want to read simply about arriving in a place, the high spots. They want to know about the low spots and what you were reading and what you were eating. I missed that quality in Bruce Chatwin. In fact, we were having a truthful between-writers conversation once and he said, 'What do you really dislike about my books?' And I said, 'What do you dislike about mine? What did you really feel was missing?' I can't really remember what he said. I think it was that I hadn't gone deep enough into Argentina, and he said, 'What is your objection to my work?' I said, 'All right, do you want to know my serious objection to your work? It is that you don't come clean. I always want to know how you got to this place, what you were wearing, what you ate, where you slept. It took you two days. Were you sleeping in a sleeping bag under a tree, in someone's house with your posh friends? You never come clean.' He said, 'I don't believe in coming clean, do you?' I said, 'Yes, I do.'

Bigsby: But if a travel book is about places, it is also about the person writing it. Have you in the course of those journeys learned something about yourself?

Theroux: Yes, I have learned a lot of things and I have tried to put them in the books. I think what I have discovered is that it is impossible to attach yourself to another country; that where you come from is what you are and that you have only one home. I found I have only one home. I don't know what other people find. I meet people, English people, in California or Boston or Chicago, and they say, 'Well, I am an American now,' but you don't find Americans saying that. I would find that impossible to say. People say to me, 'You live in England, did you vote for Mrs Thatcher?' I do not vote at all, I haven't got a vote here. I am not a citizen. I am not affected by things that go on. I don't even get angry. I look. If I come up Regent Street and see broken windows or bits of wood in the windows where there has been a riot, to me that is like a riot in Costa Rica, Uganda or Singapore. And I think I live successfully in England because of that. That is one of the things, I suppose, I learned by going away from home: that I have a home and that I have to go back. Although at times I feel at home in Britain, and people have been very kind to me here, in a sense I have no business here and I don't belong.

Bigsby: You seem, both in your travel books and in your novels, to have a fascination with the seedy and the extreme. Anthony Burgess, in reviewing *The Consul's File*, talked about the Malaysia that you were addressing as being 'glamorous with impurity'. You do have a fascination with the impure, the marginal, the extreme, don't you?

Theroux: Well, so does he. I think a lot of writers do. You tend to distrust people who put their best foot forward. I suppose that when people talk about London and only talk about the West End, or talk about England and only talk about London, when people glamourise things, you know that it is a lie. My concern is to get behind things: the complexity of people, the seediness, the disturbance, the upset. That is what life is. Life is not the smiling face that we greet the world with. It is the disturbance behind it. That is probably a cliché but if that is not your subject then there is nothing to write about. Everything else is a waste of time. The fact that Burgess says that suggests that it is true of his own experience, too. If there is a broad statement you can make about his work, you could say that it is about messy people leading messy lives. That is what most of humankind does.

Bigsby: You say at the end of *The Great Railway Bazaar* that you had always believed that the difference between travel writing and fiction is the difference between recording what the eye sees and discovering what the imagination knows, and you lament that you could not actually reinvent the trip as fiction. But isn't that what you do? Isn't that what travel books partly are: reinvention as fiction?

Theroux: It is reinvention and it may even be fiction, but it is not a deliberate fiction. I think it is an accidental fiction. The travel book ought to be as accurate and truthful as possible, and it should have as little invention as possible. The conversations should be as they have transpired; descriptions should not be prettier or better or worse than they are.

Bigsby: This is another distinction between you and the character in *My Secret History*, in that there the character who appears to be writing a book very much like *The Great Railway Bazaar* describes writing that book as inventing and enlarging – fabulating is the word he uses.

Theroux: Yes, and I feel that I don't do that. I have a great objection to invention in travel writing. In fact, Jonathan Raban and I occasionally cross swords on this very issue because he feels that the travel book is a kind of novel and I know it is not. I think people who say that wish they were novelists. I don't know about Jonathan but there is a kind of novelist manqué who doesn't have a subject, who goes off with a publisher's advance and writes a travel book. That is a very worthy thing to do, but it is not what I do and I don't think it is the same thing as writing a novel. Writing a novel is such a distressing, difficult, interior examination, such a groping in the dark, that it is not to be compared with, let's say, going to Istanbul and writing about funny people.

A travel book may be revealing. I think that I am the character that I say I am in my travel books, but anyone who really wanted to know me would have to read a novel that I had written to discover me. People say to me all the time, 'Where did you get this character in *The Mosquito Coast*?' Someone asked me the other day, 'Where did you get him, this Allie Fox. He is quite a guy. Where did he come from, then?' as though I had once met someone called Allie Fox who had gone to South America or Central America and done all these things. He is within me. These characters are within me. I wanted to shock this person by saying, 'I'm Allie Fox, don't you see? Don't you see, that is me?'

Bigsby: There is a dedication at the front of *Mosquito Coast* apparently to Allie Fox's son.

Theroux: Yes, because I met a man who had a horrible father and he inspired me to write this book. He hated his father and I have only ever heard of two people who did. One was a man whose father was in the SS and the other was this man, whose father used to do horrible things. But I had also been reading *The Narrative of Arthur Gordon Pym*. *Pym* is a wonderful and truthful novel. It seems to be a story about Arthur Gordon Pym, someone Edgar Allan Poe met. Poe is supposedly writing this book for Pym, editing it and writing about this nightmarish journey. And I liked that. I wanted people to accept *The Mosquito Coast* as a truth, or like *Robinson Crusoe*. But that book was inside me; the man was inside me.

Bigsby: One link between your travel books and your novels seems to be your concern for dialogue, which matters in both forms.

Theroux: I find patterns of speech and individual words extremely interesting and if I make regular notes, it is about the way people talk. Often I talk to myself. They say that is a sign of madness. If it is I have been mad for thirty years or perhaps forty-nine, because I have talked to myself almost my whole life. I think that one of my ways of being a writer is by chattering to myself. I suppose it is impossible to write dialogue unless you have some kind of gift for mimicry.

Bigsby: Do you feel the lure of the theatre, then?

Theroux: I don't feel the lure of the theatre, or only in the sense of thinking how wonderful it would be to write a play. A play seems a simple thing to do. You just sit there watching people do the real work, being the characters. Writing a novel is such hard work because you have to do everything. But the lure of the theatre, in the sense of being an actor or being involved with the play, no – although I have written a play.

Bigsby: One other reason the theatre might prove attractive is that you also seem very interested in people who play roles. Your characters are often actors who manage to keep different lives going at the same time. It is true of *Doctor Slaughter*, *My Secret History*, *Chicago Loop*.

Theroux: I suppose the sense of multiple lives or role-playing is fairly important in the work, but only because I think that true of most people. When I was travelling around Britain I used to meet people occasionally and I would say, 'What do you do?' and they would say, and this is a very English thing, 'I have a farm' or 'I mend shoes', 'but what I've always wanted to do was go to the Highlands and herd sheep'. People would talk about what they wanted to do rather than what they were doing. It is a lovable characteristic of people in Britain, and not only in Britain. I think that in each person there are two wheels turning. One wheel is what you do, but a much larger wheel is the wheel of fantasy, of dream, of desire, and that is the wheel of life. It is like my being a doctor, so I read about doctors. People often say, 'I bet you have a lot of books in your library.' I have very few books. The books I do have in my library are about the North and South Pole, places I never imagine that I will ever go. Otherwise it is books about medicine and science, things that I don't do but wish I could do. I have an abundance of books of that kind.

Bigsby: It is very tempting to trace this sense of doubleness, which is certainly there in your fiction, to your sensibility. You are an American who lives in Britain. You are a novelist who is also a travel writer. For years your publicity photographs used to show you in dark glasses, almost as though you deployed those roles as a way of evading definition, of avoiding being tied down.

Theroux: But couldn't that be simple loneliness and insecurity, and the fact that I realize that people want more out of life than just a nine-to-five job? I began to see myself as this solitary adventurer so that this sense of a multiple life became very interesting. Maybe that is the stuff of fiction, the person who is within you and whose heart is ticking away inside you. Perhaps this is a theme of mine. But I recognized that sense of multiple selves from a very early age, from a very early stage of my writing. It is not a double life. It is that people lead successive lives, triple lives or quadruple ones. It is not a simple sort of schizophrenia.

Bigsby: Would that interest in different lives account in part for your fascination with genre fiction? You have written a thriller, *Family Arsenal*; a ghost story or a gothic story, *The Black House*; science fiction; *O-Zone*, crime fiction. Why the attraction of these genres? Do you want to climb into the ring and have a championship fight with a series of different champions?

Theroux: No, that would make me sound competitive. Even when you describe these as genre books, I don't actually know that they are.

Bigsby: I don't mean that they are only genre books. I mean that you've taken the structure of a genre, then inhabited and used it.

Theroux: Perhaps I have done that, but not consciously. I think perhaps I have skipped around, tried things to see whether I could do them, to say what I had to say in that form. The ghost story has always been attractive to me. I love reading them. I find very few that really scare me, but when I do find one – like an M.R. James, or several Elizabeth Bowen ones or L.P. Hartley – I think that is something I would like to try. I used to tell ghost stories to my students and, as I say, I like reading them, but I never thought of it as my trying a ghost story.

I was thinking the other day that I haven't written the same book over and over and perhaps that is because I have a fear of being a bore. I have a fear of people saying, 'Oh, here comes another one and it's just the same.' I suspect that what looks like variety in my work is simply a change of setting. I have set books in England, in the States, Africa, South East Asia, and it looks like a different book because the setting is different, but it is only the setting. If you look at an Edward Lear landscape – he did landscapes in Corsica, India, France and England – the pictures look different but it is definitely Edward Lear doing it. It is the landscape, the tone, the smell, the taste, the sound of places that make the book look different. There is a sort of frame, of course, but that is something else. The word genre wasn't even in my vocabulary until recently.

Bigsby: For you, what is the difference between writing a novel and writing for the cinema?

Theroux: I think writing for the cinema is as near to a waste of time as any human effort, any literary effort could possibly be. The only thing that is slightly worse is probably writing for television. Writing a script is a horrible thing and I am not saying that because I do it badly. I have written scripts and they have been made into films and I have made a lot of money doing it, but it strikes me as a low, unworthy thing to do. You could only do it for money or for approbation. That is what Laurence Olivier said about actors. When asked, 'Why do actors act, what's the metaphysics of it?' he said, 'There is only one: look at me, look at me, look at me, look at me, look at me.' And then there is the money. There is no literary dimension. When you write a script it is like writing a recipe. Add two eggs, add a cup of flour. Man enters room, looks around. Everything you try to do in writing – be subtle, describe something, make an image, a metaphor, have a reader see and smell what is going on – is done in the crudest possible way in a script.

If you look at most films they don't have much dialogue in them. Most films are scenes – car going down a street, man entering a room, opening a door, frowning, dead body on the floor, whatever, marriage, divorce. If there is a phone call, it is two words. I was in a script conference once and a man was talking and he said, 'OK, so the man comes in a room, sees so-and-so, the woman, er, all right, let's skip over that.' I said, 'What about the dialogue?' He said, 'Well, let's just say the man said, "bullshit, bullshit, bullshit." And then cut down to the street where something's happening.' And I said, 'Do they talk?' He said, 'No, they don't talk. Further down we'll have them talk – "bullshit, bullshit" – and then, let's see, then they get on the train.' I thought, 'That is the truth of it.' Their idea is that a script is written, it is rewritten, discussed, then there is a script conference. It does violence to the creative mind. It is a terrible thing, a waste, and the people who do it have, I guess, made a Faustian bargain or something. Maybe it is to do with flattery or is a result of loneliness, because I have succumbed to it at times. But I think it is horrible, really horrible.

Bigsby: You have said that it is ego that might lead you to do it, but isn't it ego that leads you to distrust it in that you are afraid of losing control of your work and the language that you generate?

Theroux: Yes, but that is not ego, that is the artist's vision. The only thing you have is your work. You have a character, you have a scene, you have an idea. Forget the money. You are a writer and you want this idea you have to be your idea, not to be messed around by other people. It is a simple enough thing. One of the honest things about writing a book is that you write it, it appears, and it either stands up or it falls, but it is yours. But a film is not yours. A film belongs to everyone who ever had their sticky little fingers on it. And most of them are made for eight year olds, ten year olds, twelve year olds. A film made for adults will fail because they want it to have a broad appeal. The sort of people who make movies, Mickey Mouse movies, violence movies and car-chase movies, simply want to get lots of folks there in the cinema. I am not speaking of Satyajit Ray or Ivory and Merchant. That is a slightly different thing. That is way out on the fringe.

Bigsby: Can film do things that the novel can't?

Theroux: Yes, it can play music and it can shock you, it can frighten the hell out of you just with a squeaky door or a bang. But that is a cheap trick, that is like a ghost train rattling through: bang, bang, you see a skeleton. I like the music in films, and it is the sort of thing that is lacking in a novel – no soundtrack. But what do you think a film can do apart from that?

Bigsby: It can communicate without language. The slightest gesture, a single image, can communicate.

Theroux: Yes, it can. I don't want to downgrade that, but what is a writer's role in that? That is done by the photographer, the editor. After they have made the film someone says 'there's a good piece over here' and they take fifteen yards of film and splice it. That is nothing to do with the writer, absolutely nothing.

Bigsby: So, you have not been happy with adaptations of your own work?

Theroux: I'll tell you something. I go to films all the time: partly to kill time, partly for the brainless amusement of it and, I suppose, to be stimulated. Sometimes I am; usually I am not. I thought that *The Mosquito Coast* was a decent film, but as for that film being anywhere near the book, forget it. I mean, pick up the book at any page and you will see that there is more to think about on one page of that book than in that whole film, and I actually liked the film. Think of the density of prose or the humour, or the smell and look of things. I think the experience of reading a book is one that never leaves you, but after you have seen a film you go out and it is a bit like a Chinese meal, really. In fact, my whole experience of film is like a Chinese meal: you eat it, *mmm that was very good*, and then about an hour later you are hungry again.

Bigsby: Your books all have a very strong narrative drive. They are apparently written with great fluency and facility. Is that so, or do you have to work hard to give that impression?

Theroux: I have to work very hard to give that impression because I write books steadily but over a long period of time. *O-Zone* took me years, *The Mosquito Coast* took me years, *My Secret History* took me years. I tried to make it look as though it didn't. Even a travel book, where I seem to be just scribbling things down, I find very painful and slow. But I hate hearing people say that. I hate hearing myself say that. If I was listening to the radio and someone was talking about the torment of being a writer, I would switch off. I don't like hearing it, because everyone's life is difficult, everyone's work is difficult. The thing is: don't make it look difficult. Writing has to be lucid. It has to sound fluent and it should give some joy, some pleasure, and it should be effortless. You should not be constantly drawing attention to your style. I hate it when I have to notice a person's style. I think that writing should look easy.

Bigsby: I wonder if it wasn't particularly hard with *Chicago Loop*, not merely because you are trying to get inside the mind of a psychopath, but because you are also developing a kind of attenuated, flattened prose style, an alienated prose style.

Theroux: Yes, with *Chicago Loop* the point of view is that of the main character, who is a psychopath. I wanted to see things and to write the book entirely from his point of view, and not in a more olympian sort of way. That made it difficult because I wanted it believable and I didn't want his world to be one of total distortion. The mind of a criminal does not necessarily have to be different from the mind of a person commuting from Tunbridge Wells, but I found that the book was very single-minded and had to be single-minded. It made it difficult, but the difficulty of that book arose more from the subject matter. When you are writing about a murder, and taking it seriously, and writing about a man who then becomes a transvestite, those are disturbing things. For me to wake up in the morning, have breakfast and then face him was not an easy thing to do. But that was my subject. When I went to the Robert Mapplethorpe exhibition in New York with my wife, I had more or less the same reaction that Parker had, and I thought it was something I wanted to write about. I knew it was going to be part of that book and part of that world because so many of Robert Mapplethorpe's pictures look like crimes or victimization to me.

Bigsby: You have been described as Graham Greene without the sin. You do seem to have a tendency to withhold judgement, certainly in *Chicago Loop*, because of the methodology, because you are inside the mind of the character. Is there a moral danger about that suspension of judgement?

Theroux: As far as the Graham Greene reference is concerned, I don't know whether there is a sense of sin, but I do have a sense of right and wrong, let's say. I don't have religion and I do think that mine are books without God, but they do have spirit. My whole life, I've also wanted to write books that are funny, books that have real serious humour in them. Albert Camus once said that he wished his books had been funny – and they are pretty unfunny – but he was a great hero of mine and when I read that comment I thought, well, I may not be Albert Camus, but at least a lot that I have written has been humorous, so I have done something that he wished he had done.

As far as your question about suspending judgement is concerned, no, I don't think that it is a cop-out. If you ask the question seriously and present a situation truthfully, that is all you need to do. In fact, the only thing that you should do is to present someone. I think the thing to do is to be as truthful and as lifelike as possible. That is the most anyone can do; and when you are drawing conclusions, when you are picking characters and condemning them to hell, as Greene and lots of other writers often do, then I think you are doing a grave disservice.

Bigsby: I don't know if you ever envisage a reader for your books, but how do you imagine a woman reader might respond to *Chicago Loop*?

Theroux: A woman reader would see that men are pathetic, weak and frightened, that they fear their masculinity, and that what drives men to violence is this sense of inadequacy. Very few men hate women; what they do is hate themselves. It is very hard to be a man. It probably isn't roses to be a woman, but it is very difficult to be a man. If women only realized how insecure and deprived most men feel, then they would probably be happier being women, and probably wouldn't hate or fear men so much. I think in *Chicago Loop* the man really is pathetic. He does not know who he is, where he is going or what he has done, and in a sense when he becomes a woman he sees that it is just as hard for a woman, perhaps. He is a bit more vulnerable as a woman, but a woman who stands up to a man often finds that the man caves in. It is very seldom that a woman stands up to a man and the man beats her up. That is not the message of the book, but at least the book might reassure some women on that point.

Bigsby: In *Chicago Loop* it strikes me that Chicago itself is perhaps one of the most important characters.

Theroux: It is certainly a feature of the book. Chicago is a rough, tough city, with extremes of temperature, very hot and very cold. It was very hot when I was there and it is very hot when this book takes place. Yes, it is a factor. The other significant aspect of Chicago is that it has such extremes of suburbia and downtown. It has the most beautiful buildings in America, without question. It also has some of the grubbiest, most terrible slums. It is one of the most dangerous cities as well as a city where very, very wealthy people live. So the city has as many aspects, as many characteristics and moods as its people.

Bigsby: What is it that determines the rhythm of your books? This time a novel, that time a travel book?

Theroux: It used to be the children's school year and the school day. I used to take the children to school, or to the bus-stop, then come home and write all day until the children came home from school, say at three-thirty. Then I would stop working. My younger son always used to say, 'What page are you on?' and I'd say 492 or whatever, and he'd say, 'How many pages have you written?' The school year was important because I would try to work from September roughly till June and then take the summer off. When my children grew up and went to university my life was shattered and the rhythm of my books was different. You asked about this time a novel, this time a travel book; the fact is they were the same to me. After I had spent a period working in a room, writing a novel, I felt the need to get away. After a couple of novels I would feel such an intense sense of confinement that I would try to invent a trip, go to Patagonia by an interesting route, walk around Britain or go to China. The travel was a sort of antidote to writing fiction. But as far as the rhythm of my life is concerned that was all to do with being married and having children.

Bigsby: Do you live in Britain because of your family or for other reasons?

Theroux: Mainly because of my family, though not only that. I find Britain congenial in many ways. People have been good to me here. But I also feel that I don't belong. I feel very much an alien and I need the smells and sights of home, so I often find, much more now than before, that I spend a lot of time in the States.

Bigsby: So you're not going to do a Henry James and become a British citizen?

Theroux: Not in the least. In fact, I read James a lot. I am reading *The Aspern Papers*. That is my bedtime book at the moment, and I have just read 'The Beast in the Jungle', so I have been reading and thinking about James a lot, and thinking how much of England James had taken on board and how he needed really to be an OM, an Order of Merit. He wasn't anti-American, it was just that he really was English. He liked this little life, this bachelor life, shuttling back and forth and going to dinner parties. My life is not like that at all. I don't ever go out to dinner. And I don't go to parties, so I have no social life here at all. It is very odd. His life was totally different. He had a real life here. I have a house, a family, a home here, but the rest of England is alien territory to me.

Bigsby: Has England become more like America than it was when you first came here?

Theroux: That is definitely true. One of the interesting things that has happened to me in the past eighteen years is that I have been able to witness England passing from a period of pounds, shillings and pence, and frugality, and people being polite, with a lot of old-fashioned courtesies, mending and making do, to a kind of trashy, throwaway, rude and fairly unproductively slick society. They have become Americanized without realizing it, which is the worst thing. It is like being very unhappy and not knowing that you are unhappy. People who know they are unhappy have got something, but to be in despair and not know that you are in despair, to be Americanized and not know you are Americanized, telling yourself you are really Europeans or really British is a terrible thing. I have also noticed the destruction of the countryside, how the countryside has been plundered and changed, with people turned out of their houses, farm labourers turfed out of their cottages and so forth. That has been an interesting thing. The passage of time, what time does to people, both here and elsewhere, is probably the most valuable thing for a novelist.

Bigsby: You are beginning to sound both like Allie Fox and, to some extent, like the protagonist of *Chicago Loop*, who also has this sensitivity about trash food and a trash culture.

Theroux: But I am the character in *Chicago Loop* and I am Allie Fox, so that is not so disturbing. Whether I am also the woman who narrates *Picture Palace* I don't know, but I sometimes think that even that is an autobiographical book.

Bigsby: Have you begun to scan the railway timetables again recently?

Theroux: No. I have begun to think that perhaps if I take another trip, if I am spared to take another long trip, it will be a different sort of trip. Lately, not too long ago, I was in Australia and New Guinea, and I have a portable German kayak, a canoe. I finished my business in Australia and I paddled up the coast, camping on an Aboriginal reserve in North Queensland. Then I packed up the boat and went to New Guinea and I paddled around the Trobriand Islands, lovely places. And I was paddling, camping, meeting local people and just making notes in the sort of sketching way that I normally do and I was thinking, this is paradise. I could take this boat and go to Fiji or New Caledonia, Vanuatu, Samoa, Tahiti. What a life. I might not even write about it but it would be a wonderful way of travelling and living. I think that is probably the best reason for travel, not to take a trip and say 'this is a trip, this is a deliberate trip and I'm writing about it', but to say, 'This trip is my life. This journey is my life. Something may come of it, something may not come of it, but it doesn't matter. I am alive, I am healthy and happy. I am living.' And that is probably what I should be doing. The Pacific is a very large place, and I have a slight inclination to do that: to set off and live, not necessarily to write.

Bigsby: You seem to have laid your dark glasses aside. Do I read any significance into this?

Theroux: No. It was just a habit. I was in Africa for five years and then Singapore for three, and for those eight years, in that equatorial light, I always wore shades. I just got into the habit of it. And once you have worn them, it is very hard to break the habit, for two reasons. First, the light does bother you if you have worn them for a long period. Second, people look more intently at you. It is wonderful, wearing dark glasses. You give nothing away. They weren't opaque Jim Jones glasses, but they were like a little mask, I suppose. Have I lain them aside? Yes, because I haven't been in the tropics since, at least not to live steadily; but, no, you shouldn't read anything into that.

Bigsby: Not that you have come out from behind the mask?

Theroux: No. Writers don't have masks. If you read even the worst writing, even the most inaccurate, inept, incoherent writing, it has truth in it and it reveals, reveals. I mean, this is why you read a book by any popular novelist that you can name: something is revealed there. I feel as if I, as a writer, have lain my life, my heart, my mind, my fantasies open to the gaze of the public. But that is one of the problems about writing: you give everything away.

IN CONVERSATION
WITH
ALICE WALKER

Alice Walker was born in 1944 in Eatonton, Georgia, and educated at Spellman College and Sarah Lawrence College. She subsequently taught at both Wellesley and Yale. Her first publication was a volume of poetry: *Once: Poems* (1968). This was followed by *Revolutionary Petunias* (1973), *Good Night, Willie Lee, I'll See You in the Morning* (1979) and *Horses Make a Landscape Look More Beautiful* (1984). Her first novel, *The Third Life of Grange Copeland*, appeared in 1970. It was followed by *Meridian* (1976) and, in 1982, *The Color Purple*, which won a Pulitzer Prize and was made into a film. Later work includes *The Temple of My Familiar* (1989), *Possessing the Secret of Joy* (1992) and *The Way Forward Is with a Broken Heart* (2001). Alice Walker is also the author of an influential book of essays, *In Search of Our Mothers' Gardens* (1984). This interview was conducted in London, in 1989.

Bigsby: You have travelled a long way from Eatonton, Georgia. But in your work you return there again and again, as you do to your early experiences and relationships, particularly that with your father.

Walker: My father was a victim of sexism but he had no way of understanding that. When he was a boy his mother was murdered by a man who wanted her to be his lover. She refused, and he killed her. And it was one of the great puzzles of my father's life. He had never understood – he was eleven – why she, then, in memory, was always blamed for having been killed when she was only saying no. So this coloured a lot of my life with my father, because he never quite understood that there is sexism in the same way that there is racism, and that this was operating in that case. Instead, he thought that the answer to this was to make the girls stay in the house, not to go out with boys and to be unnecessarily circumspect. I don't think any of this was really quite conscious. In so much of my writing I have been trying to get at that particular secret, misunderstood murder and its impact on the whole family.

Bigsby: When children are growing up they tend to accept everything as simply the way things are. Can you remember the moment at which you became aware of the fact of racism and discrimination?

Walker: I think there must have been a moment, but the only thing I can come up with is an early memory of noticing that my parents changed whenever white people appeared; they just lost their vivacity. I have seen this all over the world where there is a master–servant relationship. The servant just does not exist as a real person; the servant, in an attempt to conserve his or her humanity, just shuts down. Seeing my mother working for white people in their house was a very traumatizing experience because she was just a different person from the mother I knew in my house.

Bigsby: Your own route out of those experiences was largely through education. Where was that enthusiasm for education born?

Walker: First of all, I come from what I like to call a kind of tribal or oral tradition community. There were stories everywhere. My parents could tell stories to make you weep or laugh or whatever: they were wonderful, and they loved books. So we always had books, people gave us books, my father found books. I was really amazingly well read considering where I was. I was in the middle of nowhere; I was in the middle of a cotton field.

Bigsby: When you were eight, you had an accident. One of your eyes was damaged, and, indeed, looking across the table, I can see that one is a different colour from the other.

Walker: Oh, yes, isn't that wonderful? I finally realized that all witches have different coloured eyes, you know. One is blue and one is brown.

Bigsby: I don't mean this question literally, but did that accident change the way you looked at the world?

Walker: Yes it did. And I share this, I think, with every writer I have ever read. I think almost every writer has some kind of trauma around the age of eight, nine or ten that puts them outside the usual round of activities and, during that period, they change. It is like a time-out. Before that period you are really right in the web of life; you don't even see the design. But this kind of trauma, illness, or whatever you have had makes it possible for you to be outside for a bit: then you see everybody else and you see a design. And I think that is what happened to me. It was a trauma and very hard to bear, but it certainly made me look at the structure of my family life, look at the structure of the society. So in a curious way it was very helpful.

Bigsby: You say it made you look at the structure of your family life. Is that because it was your brother who damaged your eye and that it became necessary to help him conceal the accident?

Walker: Yes. For one thing it helped me to understand at that early age, although there was no name for it at the time, another aspect of sexism. My brothers were all given guns because they were boys; me, a girl, didn't get a gun, not that I wanted one. So, in a sense, my parents then sent me out into the world with these two brothers, who were my playmates, undefended. And another thing was that we had always had bows and arrows and I was the Indian. That was another illumination: I could understand then how it was that the killers, the invaders, the Europeans who colonized the United States, did it. They had the guns and the Indians had the bows and arrows. So, early on, I could identify with native Americans.

Bigsby: You then went to Spellman College in Atlanta, which is a black college, and then to Sarah Lawrence, in the north, where you began writing poetry.

Walker: I had written at Spellman but I didn't feel that it was really appreciated, and so when I got to Sarah Lawrence I began writing stories and poetry.

Bigsby: Some of those early poems focus on suicide, which seems an unlikely subject for a young woman.

Walker: I think almost all young poets go through it really. There is every reason in the world to sometimes feel that there is no point; but luckily it didn't last.

Bigsby: How far was poetry a way of handling experience?

Walker: It is like a ladder that you can climb on, climb out of various kinds of depression and stress.

Bigsby: How does that mechanism work? Is it the formality of it, having to compress language?

Walker: No, I don't think so. What I like about poetry is that it is the raw welling up of the emotion of the experience. If you can bear not to repress it, it is such a liberating force; it just feels wonderful. I think it must feel like when you are just getting over an illness, that first day when you know that the tide has turned. I think poetry is probably given to us, like most art is, as a healing thing rather than anything else; not ornamental, not necessarily political but definitely something that we have to help us feel ourselves.

Bigsby: Do your poetry and prose come out of different moods?

Walker: Oh, yes. I feel I don't have as much control of the poetry. It just springs into action when it is needed. As someone else said, poetry gives you a place to put things for which there is no place. But with prose, writing novels, what I like is just to be able to create a whole world and then live in it with people that I am interested in.

Bigsby: And yet surely your poetry and prose are closely related? The prose of *The Color Purple* and the prose of *The Temple of My Familiar* seem in many ways to share the qualities of poetry.

Walker: One of the things I love about *The Color Purple* is that no matter what happens I can go to that book and, if I read the language to myself, I can hear my grandmother speak. That is the gift of the book to me.

Bigsby: It is an act of preservation.

Walker: Absolutely. And I wanted to show to people like my daughter, who has never heard this, its vitality and its beauty.

Bigsby: To be brought up in the 1950s, to be aware of the literature of the 1950s and early 1960s, was, as far as black writing was concerned, to be exposed to people such as James Baldwin, Ralph Ellison and Richard Wright – men, in other words. In reading their work, did you feel that they spoke to you or for you?

Walker: I felt they spoke very much to me and for me, and I loved reading Richard Wright. I loved Baldwin. Even to this day, I think of Baldwin as a kind of spiritual uncle. It is like reading Somerset Maugham, whom I also love, or other English writers, the Brontës, or Thomas Hardy, whom I just always adored, and gradually understanding that, though they could do perfectly well writing about what they knew, about their society and everything, they were not quite equipped to render my world. And then I realized that that was fine because I could render my world. We all have limitations, places that we don't quite see into. But I think good writers always touch us, even if we seem to be really different.

Bigsby: In the late 1960s, as black consciousness became more powerful, writers such as Ellison and Baldwin found themselves attacked for not creating exemplary characters. Did you feel that pressure being put on you as you began to write your novels?

Walker: People tried to put that pressure on me, but I really just closed my door to it because I am committed to expressing a way of life that I think is important and that I know. I think I know it better than the people who want me to change. I feel that I have come from a culture in the South in which truth really did matter, and this was really very clear in the civil rights movement and in the songs which stress that you must be truthful, forthright and upright. It was not ever about expediency; it was always about trying to be clear about who you were, and being just. I think that is because people really understood that if you are as true as you can be to whatever your vision is there is some chance of actually getting somewhere. The truth acts like a compass, you know. It really helps you get from one place to another. Whereas if you start fiddling around with it too much you never really get anywhere.

Bigsby: You have attracted some criticism from black critics. Your first novel, *The Third Life of Grange Copeland*, includes some fairly horrifying violence, enacted by black men on women. That is true again in *The Color Purple*. You have been accused of creating a kind of pathology of the black world. How did you respond to those criticisms?

Walker: I like to remind my critics that unfortunately the incident that so upset them in *The Third Life of Grange Copeland* was based on an actual case. There was so much violence in my home town. I don't think it is unique, either. I was thirteen years old when I actually saw this woman who had been murdered; I went to school with her daughter and I really tried very hard in the novel to understand the forces that caused this murder. A lot of it had to do with the oppression of share-croppers, like my family, by the landowners; but a lot of it also had to do with the failure of this man in being violent. He did have a choice. He need not have shot her. So, you see, I don't think that I am capable of seeing very bad, unjust situations and not doing something in my work about them.

Bigsby: And not only in your work. You were involved in the civil rights movement, a campaign to change America. But it was a movement that also inevitably changed the people who were involved in it. In what ways do you think it changed you?

Walker: I think it has given me absolute faith in people's ability to change. I am in no sense a pessimist, and that is because I have seen our people in the South change an entire system, and I have also seen them change it in a very beautiful way. I think I have never seen such beautiful people as the people involved in the civil rights movement, because they were ordinary people. Men and women and children.

And they had just had enough. They were sick of segregation and the economic oppression. They just said, No! They stood there and banded together. They stood against it. It was like a sunrise.

Bigsby: In 1982 you published your most successful novel to date, *The Color Purple*. How far is that a book which sets out to preserve a history? How far did you see your function as being a record-keeper, reaching back and giving names to the anonymous?

Walker: Oh, very much so. I am very, very clear about my function as someone who records and tries to pass along history in my work, because we don't get it otherwise. The schools are falling apart, the history books exclude us, and so I make it a part of my work to record things.

Bigsby: *The Color Purple* is told through letters. Was that a device, a mechanism, that took you a long while to discover, or was that the beginning of the novel?

Walker: It just seemed so right. I never write anything until it is ready, you know; I am not one of those writers who are always scribbling then crossing out. I will go for a whole year without writing anything, but it is all written in my head; then I will just sit down and write it morning after morning after morning until it is done. So I had all of those letters going and the letters were moving the story along. It was the perfect way to deal with two people who were on different continents.

Bigsby: That is Miss Celie and her sister, Nettie.

Walker: Yes, and they didn't have a telephone. There was no fax. So their letters had to do it.

Bigsby: Miss Celie's letters come out of an experience that you know very well, that was very close to home. Indeed, the characters in this novel carry the names of members of your own family.

Walker: Right, deliberately, but they are all scrambled around so that no name actually fits anybody. But I wanted to memorialize these names.

Bigsby: Did you have more problems with her sister, Nettie, who is writing out of an Africa which is more remote from your own experience?

Walker: I don't know. I know that there are people who don't like her letters as well, but that, too, in a way is part of the plan. I was trying to show the reader that standard English, missionary English, does not hold a candle to the southern, country vernacular which Celie speaks, and her letters, which you would think people would puzzle over, are always the letters that are the vibrant ones. They stick in people's minds, much more so than Nettie's. But, then, Nettie's letters are like Nettie. Nettie is a kind of proper, prissy, good person, but without the kind of grittiness that Celie attains.

Bigsby: A lot of people will have come to *The Color Purple* not through the novel, initially, but through Steven Spielberg's film. What did you most regret losing in that translation from novel to film?

Walker: I regretted very much that there was not more of an exploration of the relationship between Celie and Shug in Memphis. I would have wanted to have wonderful scenes which showed a lot more of the women's culture. If you had had scenes of Shug's house in Memphis, with all of her very woman-centred statuary, the way she lived as a freewoman, it would have been wonderful. The other thing I regret is that they didn't quite understand that if you say 'Daddy' it has a very different meaning from 'Pa', which I had called the stepfather. I think that when people saw the film a lot of them believed that Celie had been raped by her daddy when in fact it was the stepfather, who she always called Pa, which is slightly different. But it really made a difference to me.

Bigsby: So attached were you to Miss Celie and her friend, Shug, that they pop up again in your next novel. Why did you transpose them out of one fictional world into another?

Walker: I wanted to see what would happen to them, and I also wanted to give Fanny, the woman in *The Temple of My Familiar*, really wonderful grandmothers; it seemed important to me that she should have these wonderful women. And I wanted to see if Shug would continue to develop spiritually, since Shug is in some ways a modern representation of African goddesses and, true to form, she continues in this mode. She is very spiritual and, in fact, writes her own 'Beatitudes'. She decides that the Bible is not really her book, that she needs a somewhat different one. And so she sets out to write it.

Bigsby: *The Temple of My Familiar* is no longer rooted in the black experience quite in the same way as the earlier books, is it?

Walker: It goes back much, much further in time, and so it is different in that way. But, also, I am always concerned with religious questions and questions of spirituality, and I am showing how a black woman gets rid of the notion of a white god. In this book I am showing that if our first ancestor was a black woman, then that, essentially, is our god. And I think that in this book I am showing that to be really different from the white god, the black woman has to affirm everyone. The black woman, god or goddess, has to have everyone close to her. She cannot tell Hal, her friend of many, many incarnations, the two aspects of herself which would most frighten him: that she was once, or several times, a white man and once a lion. He is afraid both of cats and white men. But these aspects are really necessary parts of her if she is to be a real goddess, because a real goddess, or a real god for that matter, would love all parts of the planet, all parts of human beings and all animals.

Bigsby: It strikes me that that is the only kind of god that you can believe in. I find in this book a belief in faith, a belief in spirituality, but not a belief in religion and probably not a belief in any conventional god, not any god that transcends the people.

Walker: No, this is a very ordinary woman.

Bigsby: *The Temple of My Familiar* is a novel but I notice the book jacket uses the word 'romance', presumably in Hawthorne's sense. And this book does not have its root in a solid world of fact in the way that perhaps *The Color Purple* did, or indeed your earlier novels.

Walker: When you are dealing with five hundred thousand years, you have to admit that you may not have all the facts. But I mean 'romance' in the archaic sense that it is a wisdom tale, and a wisdom tale is a tale in which everyone reaches a new level of understanding. It also has an aspect of the fantastic.

Bigsby: Are you a believer in the non-rational world, non-rational elements of the human sensibility?

Walker: Absolutely, yes. I am very much at one with the earth itself, which is not rational, you know. The earth is just itself. It has its waves and it is full of wonders and mysterious things that I think will never be explained, and I don't mind that they never will be.

Bigsby: You seem to have written a planet novel, haven't you?

Walker: Right, exactly!

Bigsby: There is a character in this novel who is a teacher and, in a way, I think you have never quite got the teacher out of your sensibility.

Walker: Oh, I know, I know.

Bigsby: She says that in her women's studies class she has to explain about blacks, while to men she has to explain about women. It is a role that she resists, but that she accepts. Is that true of you, too? Do you resist this role but feel that somehow you have to play it?

Walker: I don't know. I think if you feel that in my work it probably means that I am playing it; but in my life I have stopped trying to explain. I have gone to the level now of just pure being.

Bigsby: You are sounding very San Francisco.

Walker: I know. It's great, isn't it? I love San Francisco and I love California. I know that people have a problem with it but that is really too bad; I mean, I respect the culture, really.

Bigsby: It does come into the novel, doesn't it? We have sensual massage, futons . . .

Walker: And why not? I have lived there eleven years; that is my culture now.

Bigsby: We are all obviously composed of a multitude of different roles. You are – among many other things – black, a woman, an American. Is there a hierarchy to those particular roles in your mind?

Walker: I don't think so. I think I am pretty much all of them, plus my Cherokee great-grandmother. So I think of myself as African-Amerindian.

Bigsby: I see why they had you play the role of the Indian when you were eight years old.

Walker: Right. Little did we know.

Bigsby: You once said that music, black music specifically, was able to express things that you would like to be able to achieve in prose. What were those things, and do you feel that now you may have succeeded?

Walker: I think if you could turn *The Color Purple* into a jazz piece by, I don't know, Miles Davis, Thelonius Monk or one of those really great musicians, it would play quite well. But I still feel that music is the higher art.

Bigsby: If it doesn't sound too grand, both you and America have come an enormous distance in the last twenty years. Looking back over that period, the period in which you grew up, do you have a sense of amazement that America has changed as much as it has and that your own life has been transformed as it has over that period?

Walker: I think it is an amazing thing. I really do. In Georgia, where I was born, it was so small and the houses that we always lived in were so awful; I was just explaining to my daughter this morning. And now to have a house that doesn't leak and to have fresh flowers whenever I want them is such an amazing thing. I mean, it is amazing.

IN CONVERSATION
WITH
TIMBERLAKE WERTENBAKER

Timberlake Wertenbaker was educated in France and the
United States. She worked as a journalist in America and
England and taught French in Greece. She was Resident
Writer at Shared Experience in 1983 and at the Royal Court Theatre
in 1985. She has won many awards, including the *Evening Standard*
Award, the Olivier Award, the John Whiting Award and the London
Theatre Critics Circle Award.

Wertenbaker's plays include *This Is No Place for Tallulah Bankhead*
(1978), *New Anatomies* (1981), *The Grace of Mary Traverse* (1985), *Our
Country's Good* (1988), *Three Birds Alighting on a Field* (1991), *The Thebans*
(1992), and The Break of Day (1995). She is also the author of radio and
television plays.

This interview was recorded in Cambridge, July, 2000.

Bigsby: Can you explain the name Timberlake Wertenbaker?

Wertenbaker: I am afraid I have to attribute it to the eccentricity of my parents. It is nothing more than that. I had an ancestor who was a librarian in Virginia, who was married to somebody called Louisiana Timberlake Wertenbaker, and I was named after her; so that is the Virginian connection. She was the first librarian of a university in Virginia.

Bigsby: You have an American passport.

Wertenbaker: I have, intermittently. I also have a British passport. It is very difficult for me to answer that question. In fact, that is probably the most difficult question you are going to ask me because my parents were Anglo-Americans who lived in France. They were essentially expatriates by nature. My mother flew to America so that I would be born an American and have an American passport. Then we flew straight back to France. I also have a British passport because I am entitled to a British passport. So I have two passports and I suppose three nationalities – or four, because being raised in the Basque country is a tremendous identity. The Basque country has been fighting for its identity, particularly for its linguistic independence, for many years; the idea that language gives you your power and your independence is something that I was brought up with. When I was going to school on the French side of the Basque country we were not allowed to speak Basque. It was completely forbidden. It was forbidden on the Spanish side by Franco and forbidden on the French side by the educational authorities. That is my Basque side. My education was French and I have lived mostly in Great Britain, so I think I am typically British, because I think most British people are of mixed cultural background and mixed nationalities.

Bigsby: When I first heard you speak I thought, yes, very English, of a certain class, and yet there is something else in the accent, isn't there?

Wertenbaker: Don't be deceived by the class because as someone who has lived in many countries I use what I can.

Bigsby: What was the pathway that led you to theatre, as opposed to anything else?

Wertenbaker: It was chance, and I think theatre is very much an area of chance. I was in Greece at the time, on an island, and somebody there decided to do theatre for children and simply asked me if I was interested. It was a discovery. I suppose it was the discovery of the collective, how wonderful it is to work collectively with various people. It was also a discovery of the immediate in that it took us three weeks to put on the play. It was for children and it was absolutely charming. The community was very grateful. It was a small island. We did it in Greek. There were several of us, some Greeks, a couple of English people and an American dancer who all happened to be on this island at that time. It gave me a great taste for public performance. I discovered I loved the public hearing your words. I didn't write many of those words, but a few, and it made me feel that there was something very immediate, that you are immediately part of the community you are in. You affect it. None of us who came after the David Edgars or the David Hares, particularly because we were women, ever claimed to change society. I think that was a very male, leftwing thing. But we felt you can shift things, you can move people's minds in certain ways, you can ask them to refuse to accept certain givens. That is what brought me to theatre and then I thought, well, if I like theatre I had better come to England and settle there.

Bigsby: What was your sense of the British theatre when you came here? Did you find you had to elbow your way into it?

Wertenbaker: It wasn't welcoming, but I had very little confidence so it didn't really matter. I gave myself a year and I liked what I saw. It was quite rough and ready. It was companies like 7.84 and Joint Stock, and it had great verve and great roughness and it had its roots in early English literature. They were big companies doing big plays rather roughly, and I liked what I saw. I loved the plays. Then I became very keen to be part of the Royal Court for historical reasons. It wasn't doing very interesting plays at that point but Caryl Churchill was around and you began to feel that maybe you could write plays as a woman. I wouldn't say you were welcome but, on the other hand, the doors weren't closed either. In fact, they were much more open than they are now, I would say. There was, then, at the Royal Court, a dramaturg who was very political. He had studied Trevor Griffiths. He said, 'Where are the women playwrights?' And of course people said, 'Oh, there aren't any women playwrights. They don't write plays.' He looked for women and the minute you look you find. I happened to be one of the people. I was having a reading somewhere and he came, and that was the beginning of my association with the Royal Court, which was very fruitful at that time.

Bigsby: I want to ask you a little later about the development of that relationship at the Royal Court. But first I want to ask about an early play that drew attention to you, *New Anatomies*. This features a woman who dresses as a man. Wasn't there an early version of that play in which there were to be several women dressing as men?

Wertenbaker: Yes, that's right. Somebody asked me to do something and I thought I would write about three different women. At that point I was going to do it as one play but then I thought, no, each of these plays is full length, and so *New Anatomies* was the first one I did. I did write the other ones, though.

Bigsby: There is a feeling in that play that, for her, dressing as a man is a process of liberation. Can you explain how that works in that play?

Wertenbaker: It is a question of identity and how you are seen. In her case, and at that time – late nineteenth century, early twentieth century – you couldn't move in those tight dresses of the period. She couldn't move. Also, to be seen as a woman was immediately to risk being victimized, ridiculed, not taken seriously. She didn't just dress as a man, being a western Russian woman, she dressed as an Arab: she became an Arab man, which is an extraordinary gesture. I had a terrible time with the women's theatre group who were putting it on because they got very worried politically. They said, 'Oh, Arabs, they don't like women. We can't do a play about Arabs.' I said, 'This is ridiculous. This is Algeria. Study your history.' So they went along with it. Once you stop thinking of yourself as a woman you do stop limiting yourself and I think it is one of the great difficulties of being a woman writer. Can you just forget that you are a woman, can you just forget that and not keep seeing yourself as such, and can you simply write or can you simply act, can you simply take some kind of action? She wandered through the desert, and went to various monasteries. The play is completely historical. You only need to see girls now, if they are wearing very high heels or very tight skirts, to know that in the simplest physical way the limitation of the body will limit your mind.

Bigsby: Did you at that time feel pressure on you, as a woman writer, to write a particular kind of play?

Wertenbaker: No, I didn't feel that pressure, but I always wanted to write quite big plays. I think it surprised people, that's all. I think they didn't quite expect it, and they didn't quite expect the plays to be as crude with the use of language. I was slightly discouraged by some of the plays that I saw by women which were about relationships and about being in the kitchen. It didn't interest me, but I have to say I was not under pressure. If I was under pressure I was resisting the pressure because I couldn't write those plays.

Bigsby: The reason I asked is that in 1980s America three women won Pulitzer Prizes. Each of them was denounced by feminists because the model of women that was being presented was not the one being promoted at that time by the women's movement. You felt none of that?

Wertenbaker: Oh, I did feel some of that. There was pressure from the feminists, who themselves portrayed perfect women, to portray heroic women without flaws. The woman in *New Anatomies* is very flawed and actually rather despised. There was also pressure in *Three Birds are Alighting on the Field* because in the last scene the main character takes her clothes off. I was very much attacked for that. How could I exploit women? It is a gesture in which a woman discovers her sensuality, and it was meant as such. It was a kind of liberation. The woman simply discovers herself for the first time in her sensuality. I was particularly attacked on radio for that, rather nastily. And I was so surprised. It came out of the blue I hadn't realized there was this ground swell of disapproval. So, there was pressure. There will always be pressure from all sides, but it wasn't extreme. Maybe I just ignored it, but there were some rumblings.

Bigsby: The character you were describing in *New Anatomies* goes on a kind of a quest, a journey of self-discovery. That is not the only time in your work that that occurs, and you have said that the idea of quest is important to you. Why, and in what sense?

Wertenbaker: Because I think that is where women really are limited. If you look at all the literature, including *Harry Potter*, it is always the boys, the men, who go on the quest, whether it is *Peer Gynt* or the *Three Musketeers*. All of the literature I had read was about men having adventures, and I didn't understand that. So I thought, why can't a woman go on a quest? What keeps a woman from going on a quest and why hasn't it been written about before? I decided this was what I wanted to write about. Hence, *New Anatomies* and *The Grace of Mary Travers*, the latter about a Faustian pact in which a woman seeks knowledge by going on a quest. If you don't have the literature, if you don't have the model, then that perpetuates itself. Women are usually portrayed by men, and always portrayed as being very still, as rather symbolic of something. All our great male leftwing playwrights always had these women at the end of the plays: the perfect woman who goes to Greenham Common and is a saint. It is not the woman who changes, who makes mistakes, who offends people. That simply was not in anything I read or saw, and it made me very angry. It still does, actually, because it is still going on. Women are portrayed as still, and I think this is a problem not just for women but for men, because if you have this polarity you are defining humanity in a way which is arbitrary and probably wrong, erroneous.

Bigsby: In *The Grace of Mary Travers* there is a woman who seizes power, in various forms, and the result is not attractive. It is a kind of corruption. Does that mean that in some senses that play is not really about women, but about power?

Wertenbaker: It is about knowledge. It came from the feeling that, towards the end of the twentieth century, we have more knowledge but that it has brought us to some kind of intellectual despair. It is a point that can be argued but I just wanted to look at that. And, of course, we are facing that now again with the genome project. Knowing so much brings with it this very heavy price because you are in danger of losing hope and I think that we are always balanced between hope and the despair that knowledge brings. You see it again and again in history. Every time we gain knowledge – whether it is about the universe, whether it is about the theory of relativity – it puts us in a state of despair which we then seem to climb out of. But I felt that the knowledge we have of history, and of the depth of depravity to which humanity can descend, does pose the question of whether it is worth it. Is there anything in humanity that is worth saving and will we just destroy ourselves anyway? That is what I was getting at.

Bigsby: You mentioned the past and history. I know, of course, that you have set plays in contemporary periods, but you have also turned to the past. Why? Are you looking for a paradigm, a model, a parallel?

Wertenbaker: I think so. I think it is also something to do with the fragmentation of history at the moment. It is very hard to seize and understand the historical moment we are going through, particularly in the last ten or fifteen years, the post 1989 time, when nothing seems to stay stable for very long. Writers always go back to history when they are trying to understand the present and the present is particularly difficult to understand. I think the postwar British period was not difficult to understand. Now, with a new internationalism, we are very aware of other countries, thank God. We need to understand that, because you can try to find models in the past. So, *The Grace of Mary Travers*, which was set in the 1780s, came out of the Brixton riots, which happened in the 1980s, and there was this neat parallel. The fact is this was not the first time there had been riots. People were saying, 'We have never seen riots before', but you only had to look back at the eighteenth century. The Gordon riots interested me. I was fascinated by what makes a riot flare up and how it is interpreted. That fed into *The Grace of Mary Travers*.

Bigsby: Another of your historical plays was the best known of the plays you wrote in the 1980s, *Our Country's Good*, and that brings us back to the Royal Court Theatre because of the process whereby that play was developed. Could you say something about that?

Wertenbaker: It started with a two-week workshop. People think that at workshops all the actors start writing bits of plays, but that is completely wrong. I had ten actors and they researched anything I wanted them to. If I asked them to find out about superstitions they would do that or they would go and interview people who had been to prison. Then they would bring it back They would put themselves in the character of the person they had interviewed and several of us would sit around in a circle and ask questions. It wasn't exactly acting; it was putting yourself in someone's place. As a writer it is very useful because when you interview somebody yourself you tend to go completely to their side. If you can just sit back and watch somebody imitating somebody they have seen you get it at a remove, but you get the gist of it, particularly because actors are very good at emotions, at picking up certain things. They put their own imagination into it. This mishmash of things was very rich. The other thing I have to say, and I think it is something that British playwrights miss, is that I had a company: I had ten actors and I was writing for them and it was wonderful. This is what Shakespeare had and what Ayckbourn has. I had these wonderful actors, and I could write for a particular person because I knew what they could do. That was very rich. That was the great thing about having a company to work with, and it is so rare.

Bigsby: Like David Edgar with *Nicholas Nickleby* at the Royal Shakespeare.

Wertenbaker: Exactly, which is why that was such a great piece because he knew who he was writing for, which is great fun because you have a dialogue with the actors. Actors are very responsible and very committed as well. It doesn't always work, though. I did another one which was disastrous because somehow the actors and I never met, we never found common ground. But this particular group of actors, who are still my friends, went through something together which was an adventure. It was a kind of quest; it marked our lives in some ways.

Bigsby: *Our Country's Good* is set in Australia and was performed in prison in this country. When you saw that, did that change the play in any sense?

Wertenbaker: No, it didn't. The play was written from research done in prisons and I had gone to see a play by Howard Barker performed in Wormwood Scrubs, and that had really been the core of the play I was writing because, although it is set in the early eighteenth century, I wanted it to have a modern feel. It was in the middle of Thatcherism and the prevailing ethos was hard punishment. The idea was that anybody who had committed a crime was unredeemable, which is now happening again under Labour. A crime was not an accident; you were simply born a criminal. It is extraordinary that this is still being said in the twentieth century, but it is being said. Seeing this play performed by prisoners confirmed what I was looking for in this play. The actor who had performed in the Howard Barker play then put it on in a different prison. This actor, by the way, is now out and is an assistant director, directing plays; so the story has a happy end. You are not born a criminal. He had committed a serious crime by accident, as one does.

Bigsby: That is interesting because it feeds into one of the themes of the play. This is a play which has a play within a play, that is to say the characters are going to stage a play and this is presented as a redemptive process. The theatre within that play is redemptive for the criminals. You are suggesting that that proved true of the prisoners who later acted out that play. Is that how you feel about the theatre? You started by saying that the male playwrights who emerged in the 1960s and 1970s thought they would transform Britain. They wanted to move it to the left, though in fact it went to the right. Do you believe that theatre is about change and transformation, but not in that direct form?

Wertenbaker: I do believe it is redemptive, and it is redemptive because it is a dialogue. I think that if you can speak, if you have a dialogue, if you have a public debate or a dialogue, you are halfway there. It is the public aspect of this that is important, particularly in a society where so little is public any more. We watch television and films, but on the whole we have very little public debate. We don't have the marketplace. You have to be a newspaper columnist to get into the newspapers. Anybody can go to the theatre if they can afford it. I don't think it changes society. I think it is wrong to say I want it changed in my way. That was the big mistake of the 1970s playwrights, to say, 'We believe this is right and this is the way England should go', when maybe even if it should have, it didn't and didn't want to. What is important is to start a dialogue, and I keep insisting on that because it is so important to me. If there is that possibility, of thinking about something, talking about something you at least stop the silence. Therefore, you stop convention – which is a form of silence, which is the subtle form of silence where people fall into conventional ways of thinking and never question anything – and can stop oppression. This is why theatres were closed. There was an oppressive political regime. The first thing Mrs Thatcher did, and this is forgotten, was try to close the Royal Court. Within a few months the Arts Council withdrew its funds from the Royal Court. There were other reasons for it, but suddenly the theatre was being closed down and there was quite a battle to keep it open. It is extraordinary when you think about it that that was one of her very first gestures, not just starving the theatre, but actually trying to close down this particular theatre. She didn't in the end. Happily we live in a country where you can protest and stop these things happening. Theatre redeems and it can give a voice to people who feel they don't have a voice. You can put on a play. You can go into a pub or a room, and you can put on a play. You can always use theatre in some way and I think that is its great power.

Bigsby: What you say about giving a voice leads to *The Love of the Nightingale*, but before we talk about that, doesn't the theatre involve another kind of transformation in that acting itself is about the possibility of transformation? Also, as is evident in *Our Country's Good*, the theatre involves creating a provisional society on the stage, since no individual actor can do anything without acknowledging the fact that he or she is part of a group of people who are responding to them and to whom they respond. And this is at a time when Thatcher was saying there is no such a thing as society. Every night in the theatre you had a demonstration that there was, in fact, a functioning society.

Wertenbaker: Yes, and you can't function without it. You can't progress without it.

Bigsby: I mentioned *The Love of the Nightingale*, which reminds me slightly of a completely different play, Harold Pinter's *Mountain Language*, which is also about the silencing of voices. Is there something of your Basque experience coming through in this play?

Wertenbaker: Yes, very much. It is a terrible thing to have a language and therefore a culture silenced, really silenced. My generation in the Basque country, and the generation that came afterwards, suffered terribly. People were trying to learn Basque, which is one of the most difficult languages in the world. They were asking parents to teach it to their children. They wouldn't because the parents had been told: 'Don't speak Basque. It's bad. It makes you stupid.' This is what was said. There is a great resurgence of Basque culture at the moment, but some of it has been lost for ever. If you silence a culture and somebody's language or, indeed, their accents, if you impose the conventional on people who have another language, you are crushing something. I felt that very strongly, and it had a double significance in *The Love of the Nightingale* because women are also taught to keep quiet and not to speak their natural language. They are often told that they must not speak the way they do. Women's speech, after all, is slightly different. Probably you can hear it as I am talking. It is a little bit more circular. It avoids the grand statement. It tends to move around its subject. I doubt that this is true of all women or all men, but that kind of speech must be allowed as well, and it must indeed be allowed in writing. That was the background of that play. If you silence people you will have violence because that will be the only way they can express themselves. That goes back to the theatre and to language. As long as you have language, you are probably transforming the possibility of violence into something else. Stop the language and what else do you have? You see that in schools and we saw that in 1980s Britain. We will see it again. If you can't express anything then there is no other way to act.

The Love of the Nightingale is based on a Greek myth, the myth of Cinemel. Tereus, a northern king marries Philomele's sister and then goes to get Philomele. He falls in love with her, rapes her and after raping her – in my play it is because she mocks him and actually threatens to reveal him, to make what he has done public and to ridicule him particularly – he becomes so angry with this and so frightened by her speech that he just cuts out her tongue. In the original myth she weaves the story which her sister eventually finds. In my case she produces a mini-play: she produces a silent play during a Bacchic festival which her sister sees and understands, in the mime of this play, which is done with puppets, what has happened. And the sisters take a terrible revenge in that they kill Procne's child. I thought the feminists would accuse me of doing something terrible. In fact, it is the men who said, 'You are so violent and you are saying men are violent', and I said, 'But the greatest act of violence is a woman who kills her child.' They hadn't seen that. It is very curious what people see in a play. And the act of violence was because this child represented the future for these two women, for the mother. In a world where you can't speak, where tongues are cut out, it seems to me that this neglect or abuse of children derives from a total inability to conceive of a future which is worthwhile. I don't think it is just because people are crazy. I think it is despair that makes you abuse and neglect your children, because you are protecting this future. That is the gist of the play which ends pretty grimly with Tereus discovering his child.

Bigsby: You turn to the Greek theatre for this play, but the Greek theatre attracts you anyway, doesn't it? Why is that?

Wertenbaker: I am not quite sure. I don't think it is political theatre, but it is a theatre in which there is always debate. *Oedipus* is not just a family story, it is also a story about how you rule, what you do, what it means to be a king. All of the plays have that public element. That is what I love about them, this combination of the private and the public. Also, all these playwrights were writing at a time when democracy was being questioned. The abuses of democracy were beginning to be obvious, particularly in Euripedes, but also in Sophocles, and so they questioned the dangers of democracy, the possibility of abusing power. The Greeks prided themselves on this democracy but also went around raiding islands right, left and centre and there was a sense of despair in these playwrights, a questioning of where high civilization was going. I suppose I feel an affinity with that. We have to question democracy and we have to question what the dangers are. In play after play there is this tremendous questioning of the behaviour of the superpower. This is where I suppose my American past comes in, in that I feel responsible and devastated when there is abuse by the superpower, such as America. I think that is my fascination with the Greeks.

Bigsby: You have done a lot of translation, primarily from the French but also from the Greek. You speak Greek, don't you?

Wertenbaker: Not as well as I would like. I need help, but I can do it.

Bigsby: What is it that makes you set your own work aside to turn to translating Anouilh or Greek drama?

Wertenbaker: You find, when you translate, that there are not many faithful translators. There are adaptors who take a play, get it translated by somebody else and then write on the basis of that. I do translate from the original language. If I don't know it I learn it, I study it. It is wonderful to be in touch and it's the next best thing to being an actor. I would have liked to have been an actor and have all those words coming through me. If you can't do that at least you can translate. I have enjoyed it and I have learned a tremendous amount from all the playwrights I have translated. I tend to use it. There is always some influence.

Bigsby: In terms of style you resist naturalism. You are reaching for something else, aren't you?

Wertenbaker: Yes, I get bored with naturalism. You have so little time on the stage. You have two hours or two and a half hours, and to spend any of that time saying, 'Would you like a cup of tea, the kettle is boiling?' is a waste of time.

Bigsby: Your play, *Three Birds*, was staged at the beginning of the 1990s, but it seems to me to be really about the 1980s, the very period you have been talking about when there seemed to be no sense of values outside of money.

Wertenbaker: Yes, exactly. It was set in the art world, which was going crazy at the time. The only artists who were recognized were those with large pay cheques; the only writers those with large advances. The same thing was true in the theatre, and certainly in art. You no longer looked at a picture; the pay cheque was written underneath. You couldn't look at a painting any more, you couldn't look at a Van Gogh without thinking of the thirty-five million paid by Alan Bond or whoever it was, which turned out to be a great big scam anyway. It was very destructive for the artist. The original idea came from Mark Rothko who had, as I understood, been overvalued then undervalued by his agent and had subsequently committed suicide because he had lost faith in his own work. He didn't know what it was worth any more and felt this was a great danger for artists and for society, where nothing means anything. I don't think that England has recovered from this period. I think it is still a great problem.

Bigsby: Can I ask you a question about the process of staging a play? Edward Albee once said that a production doesn't improve the play, it simply proves it. My impression is that, for you, the rehearsal period is still a period of experiment and potential change. Is that right?

Wertenbaker: Yes. There are two schools of playwrighting. One is that you write the play, deliver it and don't change a word until you arrive at the first night. I think that particularly in the 1970s and 1980s there was a different approach and, in fact, the writers fought for this. They fought to be allowed into rehearsals and even to be paid to be in rehearsals, albeit a pittance. Even when I was something of an activist in the theatre, people would say, 'We can't have the writer in the rehearsal room because he will be drunk and the leading lady won't like it.' I think actors have changed as well. Then actors were thought to be stupid while writers were assumed to be intelligent. Really ridiculous. I find that I get a lot from actors if they are in tune with the play. I remember in *Our Country's Good* we had the first run-through and an actor looked very, very stormy. The actor playing the writer in the play suddenly said to me, 'You know, this is fine and it is not that I want a lot of lines, but I am not established. Nobody knows who I am. I must have a scene in the first act so that people will know who I am.' I wrote one of my favourite scenes in response to that, so it is not a negative process by any means as long as you are working with actors you like. I have had the opposite experience, though. It is dodgy, but usually it is positive. The great directors, Peter Hall, Max

Stafford-Clark and quite a few others, are incredibly sensitive to the audience. It is fascinating to watch them at work because they will say, 'The audience is going away right here. You won't get them back.' There are some writers who regard this as pandering to the audience, who regard themselves as avant garde, but I don't agree. Because my plays are complicated enough anyway I am very grateful for other people's contributions, for a director who can tell me when I am losing the audience.

Bigsby: You have also said you shouldn't make things easy for the audience.

Wertenbaker: It is a fine balance. You have to challenge an audience. You have to lead them somewhere. They are wasting their time if they are watching somebody make a cup of tea, and a lot of plays are just that. It is slightly frustrating for me to watch as a writer. You have to challenge. You have to bring them to you. If you lose them it is so difficult. You have wasted the opportunity, and I have done it in my plays. I have seen the audience moving away from the play. I could sit down and insist that the audience was wrong, but when I think about it more objectively I realize that it was my responsibility. I lost the audience and I shouldn't have. It is a balance. It is part of the craft of playwrighting. The great playwrights do take you with them. They take you into the most difficult areas, and it is wonderful when you see those plays.

Bigsby: At the beginning of this conversation you said that things have changed with respect to women playwrights. In what ways have they changed?

Wertenbaker: It is very hard to put a finger on it, but at the beginning of the 1990s a lot of young men started writing very domestic plays. And this is where one does become angry because they were writing plays of the kind women used to write, but something now made those plays acceptable and interesting. Critics seemed to think that it was wonderful and exciting that men should be writing domestic plays. Women, who were by then mostly writing big plays, said, 'What is this? We have spent all this time saying let's not have any more kitchen plays and suddenly you get the kitchen play, but because it is written by a young man it is interesting to the media.' It was suddenly fascinating, acceptable and wonderful, and it was infuriating.

Absolutely infuriating. The lads are writing plays about their mothers. There are those in this country still, and probably in all countries, who assume that if it is written by a man it is more real, more true, more interesting. This has to be fought against. I hate to be the one taking that position, because it is not actually a position I like. Women, women, women; I hate that position. I don't think women are better, more intelligent, write better plays in any way. But the assumption that there is nothing interesting about the epic or the political play because now only women are doing it, is just terrible and we are still fighting that one.

Bigsby: There was a period when theatre seemed primarily concerned with the state of England. Then there came a moment when playwrights realized there was a world elsewhere and they began to set their plays in Eastern Europe or the Far East, for example. You have always been interested in other cultures and other times. Is this cross-cultural element a transformation that you have observed going on in the theatre?

Wertenbaker: Yes, though it was only certain male playwrights who wrote about the state of England. Pinter very early on was writing about other countries, as indeed were other playwrights. It is partly because things were very boring in England and much more interesting in Eastern Europe, I have to say. I think that led playwrights to eastern Europe but it also seems a throw-back now to write about this one-culture Britain. It doesn't exist and it will exist still less and less. I certainly feel that very strongly. To set a play in a mythical England is odd and not quite true; it is nostalgic. One can write nostalgic plays, that is fine, and there is a place for them, but from my point of view I never really did except, perhaps, *Three Birds*, although that is an Anglo-American play. It is about Britain but it is also about America. Britain is changing. You can't live here any longer and think that England is an isolated, powerful country which rules the world. You would have to be crazy. I think we are even beginning to question British culture, what's known as British culture: that is, the male, white, middle-class culture of plays up until the 1950s. What people don't see is that from the 1950s to the 1980s it shifted from the middle class to the working class, but that was the only shift. It was still predominantly white and male. The power only shifted classes; it did not shift gender, culture or race. This is not recognized enough because everybody says, 'Oh, there was this great liberation.' There wasn't; there was simply a slight movement from one class to another. The tragedy of the theatre now is that most audiences and most plays are still predominantly white. It is incomprehensible. There is now a movement, particularly with smaller companies, to write bicultural plays, plays in different languages. The theatre is still a little bit behind.

Bigsby: Does it make sense any more to talk about British playwrights? The theatre, after all, is international. Richard Nelson, for example, is American, but for the last ten years at least he has opened his plays at the Royal Shakespeare Company and writes about this country or about the connection with America.

Wertenbaker: I think it is wrong to talk about the British playwright, or at least we need to redefine British. Richard Nelson is a very interesting example. He is American but I would say that culturally he is Anglo-American, and British culture is very anglo-American and has been for the last hundred years. The Churchills were Anglo-American. There is no pure Little England uncontaminated either by America, Europe or elsewhere. That idea is wrong. I think it would be wonderful to redefine what it means to be British. On the other hand, I accept the title of British playwright because the plays are staged in Britain, and Britain has been a great country for plays and still is despite setbacks and problems. What does it mean to be British? That is the question a lot of people are asking themselves.

IN CONVERSATION
WITH
ARNOLD WESKER

Arnold Wesker was born in the East End of London in 1932. He left school at sixteen and had a number of jobs, including that of pastry cook, an experience which he drew on for *The Kitchen* (1959). His first real recognition came with what has become known as the Wesker Trilogy, a series of plays exploring working-class life and political commitments: *Chicken Soup With Barley* (1958), *Roots* (1959), *I'm Talking About Jerusalem* (1960). Wesker's subsequent works include *Chips With Everything* (1962), *Their Very Own and Golden City* (1966), and *The Merchant* (1977), his version of *The Merchant of Venice*. Among his later works are community plays and a series of plays for women. In 1991, Wesker's play *Blood Libel* was staged in Norwich, where it was set. In 1994 he published the first volume of his autobiography, *As Much As I Dare*. This interview was conducted in May 1992.

Bigsby: You were born in the East End of London, in Stepney. Yours was a Jewish family. How Jewish was it?

Wesker: It was very Jewish, but Jewish in the sense of personality and temperament. We weren't orthodox. My parents were members of the Communist Party, as everybody in the East End seemed to be in those days. But, inevitably, we were Jewish. My mother came from Transylvania, my father from the Ukraine. They came to England at the age of about thirteen and brought with them the Jewishness of what is known as the *shtetl*, the little village. So, yes, very Jewish.

Bigsby: You were only just into your teens at the end of the war. Did you pick up any sense of there being a special threat to Jews?

Wesker: No, I didn't, but I think that I inherited from my mother a kind of unworldiness so I might not have detected it. For me it was a very happy childhood. I was a rogue and always up to mischief. I had a great deal of fun and I was loved by aunts, uncles, parents and sisters, so nothing seemed a threat to me. Even the quarrelling of my parents, which must have had some effect, didn't affect me as much as my sister who was eight years older.

Bigsby: You once said that you don't think of yourself as working-class in origin. Is that because a Jewish working-class life is rather different from British working class life in general?

Wesker: I think so. There are novels such as *Jews Without Money* and *East End My Cradle* which explore Jewish poverty, and Jews were poor, but I think that working class is a state of mind. If you are working class you have certain values, you imagine that certain things are not for you, that you wouldn't like this, you wouldn't like that, you don't want to involve yourself in this, that or the other. Jews never felt that. Jews were poor, but the world of literature, of thought, of debate, was constantly there. So, to that extent, I didn't feel myself working class.

Bigsby: Do you think that is why, in some of those early plays, there is a sense of frustration, irritation, with the British working class? After all, you were living in a house in which you could reach on to the shelf and there might by Dostoevsky, in a way that there would not be in a working-class house in Wigan, say.

Wesker: Yes, though irritation is not the word I would use. It didn't irritate me, and here it appears that I am contradicting what I said earlier. It worried me and I was aware of anti-Semitism, and I was aware of violence, and it seemed to me that the violence came from ignorance. I think I inherited that from my parents. Of course there are plenty of very cultured people, very wealthy people, who are guilty of violence against their wives. But, nevertheless, I did inherit from my parents, especially my mother, a sense that the lumpenproletariat got drunk in pubs and when they got drunk the Jews would be the first to go. I inherited this sense of fear of the lumpen mentality. That is, I suppose, why I was preoccupied with the role of education in society.

Bigsby: You mentioned your mother. I get the impression, from reading your plays, that she was a powerful influence upon you.

Wesker: She was, even though I fear I inherited this unworldiness from her, to a certain extent. But she had a kind of grace. She was sweet. Ugly things offended her and I don't mean aesthetically ugly, but ugly behaviour, ugly thinking. This doesn't mean that I am perfect. I am not saying that, but I inherited this. I do cringe. I don't quarrel, except with critics. I call that intellectual exchange, debate; it has an honourable history.

Bigsby: You ended your formal education at the age of sixteen. I suppose that must mean that you were largely self-educated, even while you were at school.

Wesker: Yes, I read a great deal and I was educated by the BBC. I heard music, lectures, talks, discussions, plays. I never went to the theatre, but I got my drama from the BBC and, of course, from cinema.

Bigsby: So what did a sixteen-year-old boy see as his future in 1948?

Wesker: Very specifically, I knew that I wanted to write. I said to myself that whatever I did I was going to be a writer. Of course, I had a responsibility to earn a living, so I had to go out to work. But I saw the future as being that of a writer. I say that with great certainty now but I was full of doubts and depressions, of course, and there was a period when I wanted to be an actor. I twice passed the entrance scholarship into the Royal Academy of Dramatic Art and twice failed to get a grant from the London County Council, as it was in those days. I thought, I am not a writer, I have no talent and I am going to stop writing and settle down to become a kitchen porter, or perhaps a cook, because I enjoyed working in kitchens. Then something very strange happened. I wrote behind my own back. I pretended I wasn't, but I did, and I wrote a trilogy of stories, which are not good but were certainly much better than anything I had done before. They had a strength to them that made me think, yes, I am going to keep at it.

Bigsby: But if they were stories, how did you end up in theatre?

Wesker: I'm not quite sure. I suppose the chronology was this: the other ambition I had was to be a movie director and so, working in the kitchens of a Paris restaurant, I saved up enough money to go to the London School of Film, which in those days was just beginning. While I was there I met with Lindsay Anderson, who I asked to read a short story, because I wanted to make it into a film. He did and he thought that it was very good and tried to help me get it made into a film, but it never happened. I spoke to him about *The Kitchen* and he wanted to read that. I said he could once it was returned from the *Observer* where I had sent it as an entry in the play competition with which Kenneth Tynan inaugurated his career as theatre critic. Then, while at the School of Film, which was in Brixton, a touring production of a play called *Look Back in Anger* came to the Streatham Theatre. I saw that and I thought, 'That's where it's happening.' The theatre and this play made an enormous impact on me and I thought, there has to be a sequel to it, so I went home and wrote *Chicken Soup with Barley* in six weeks. I read it to my mother and a friend of hers. It was about us, about the family, and my mother laughed and said, 'Oh, you are a silly boy. Who is going to be interested in any of that?' She could never understand that anyone was interested in it. I remember when I came back from Japan with a present from the actress who played the character based on my mother, she couldn't believe it: 'A Japanese actress playing me!' It was very strange to her.

Bigsby: That was the first of three plays which would constitute a trilogy, *Roots* and *I'm Talking About Jerusalem* being the other two. That trilogy has proved immensely popular and very durable. In print it has sold – what is it now – at the last count it was 350, 000. That would be astonishing for a novel, and yet those plays nearly didn't get staged.

Wesker: I wonder sometimes whether change takes place because it is time for change rather than because of anything we do. It is not that we created the change, but that we stepped into the moment. It didn't seem to me that I was doing anything innovative, except possibly in *The Kitchen*, which has thirty characters on stage, all working. But the plays which formed the trilogy were all conventional three-act plays, with beginnings, middles and ends, in that order. So, I don't know why they have lasted except I would like to think it is because they are not rooted in their time only. *Chicken Soup with Barley* is not simply about Jewish families. It is about political dissolution and the disintegration of a family, and that is a theme that can carry on for ever. *Roots* is not about farm labourers. It is about a voyage of discovery. So that will go on.

Bigsby: But while these plays have proved durable and extraordinarily successful they were not immediately snapped up for production, nor did they find an easy route directly on to the stage, or run for ever.

Wesker: That is true. Lindsay Anderson, who first warmed to *Chicken Soup*, took it to the Royal Court and George Devine never really liked it. He couldn't quite understand the enthusiasm for any of the plays. But he was a wonderful man. His great quality was that he would say, 'It doesn't matter that I don't respond to them, if someone else does, that I respect, then I have got to let it happen.' He said, 'Look, I am not sure about *Chicken Soup with Barley*, but we are going to have to have a fifty-year celebration of repertory theatre and the Belgrade Theatre in Coventry has presented us with a play we don't like so why don't we take your play there.' Lindsay took it to Coventry and they only offered two weeks' rehearsal. He said, 'I can't do it in two weeks, I need three weeks' rehearsal.' They wouldn't give him three weeks so Lindsay said, 'Look, I can't do it in that time but there's a young man at the Royal Court who loves the play and thinks he can do it in two weeks and he's prepared to go to Coventry and do it. His name is John Dexter.' John did it in two weeks. We got very good reviews. It came to London and then they commissioned *Roots*. They said, 'What are you doing next?' and I said, 'I've got this play called *Roots*', and they said, 'Well, we'll give you twenty-five pounds commission.' That seemed a lot of money in those days, to say nothing of the honour. So I wrote it and they didn't like it because the boy everyone is wanting to appear never does. It ends with a girl who finally discovers her own voice. They said, 'You know, everyone is so interested in this boy Ronnie that you ought to write a new third act. Make the first and the second act into one act, make the third act into the second act, and write a new third act in which Ronnie appears, because everyone wants to see him.' I said, 'I think you miss the point,' and I took it away. I thought that was the end of my career. But fortunately Peggy Ashcroft read it and she said, 'This is a wonderful play and it's just right for Joan Plowright,' and Joan said she'd go anywhere and do it. Coventry read it, and Dexter read it and said, 'Yes, we want to do it.' So it was staged. I found this with almost all my plays. I know they didn't want to do *Chips With Everything*. It was only because a commercial management said that they would go fifty-fifty that it was done. I don't know why it is that the plays have always had to fight to get on stage. It is an interesting question. Of course, some of them haven't got on stage yet in this country.

Bigsby: How long did the three plays in the trilogy run in London?

Wesker: I think no longer than three weeks.

Bigsby: Astonishing, isn't it?

Wesker: Yes, but *Roots* transferred to the West End in one of the hottest summers of all time and folded after four to five weeks. *Chips With Everything* was the only play that was a commercial success, and that by default because it ended up being perceived as a sort of Forces comedy.

Bigsby: When those first three plays had been produced, and indeed *The Kitchen*, those must have been enormously heady days, no matter how long they ran. There were awards; you were seen as being at the cutting edge of whatever was going on in British theatre. What did you see your future as being? Was your commitment to writing itself, or to using writing to bring about some transformation in the world?

Wesker: I don't think I ever believed that my writing – or any individual writer's work – would transform the world, though I was never quite sure what would. I don't know that I even thought in terms of transforming the world. I think that from a very early age I recognized that things happen in waves, that you take two steps forward and one step back. I had seen what had happened, for example, to the 1930s poets. They blossomed and then seemed to be dismissed. So I knew the way in which things went. I very quickly came to the conclusion that you are shaped by a whole spectrum of art over a long period of time, though I suppose there are individual works which many of us could say had a very special impact upon us. I think if you look at the early essays you will see that I was saying exactly the same thing. I was resisting this notion that we were revolutionaries.

Bigsby: Not revolutionaries, perhaps, but there was a strong utopianism in you. You were prepared to go to prison to protest against nuclear warfare.

Wesker: I don't see that as utopian.

Bigsby: In 1963 you said that by 1984 you hoped the arts would be as free as the health service and education would be.

Wesker: Yes, but I think that I was a little canny. I knew that what you had to do was make certain declarations which would stand as measurements. But in private I would say, 'Look, I don't know whether it's going to happen. But we are here for a short time and we are famous for a short time and really I have a responsibility to use that fame.' I thought so, anyway, and so I used it over a period of ten years trying to set up Centre 42, which I couldn't make work.

Centre 42 was an organization which I, and a number of other people, set up in order to create an arts organization for a popular audience, not, as was often perceived, an arts organization of popular art for a popular audience. I wanted to see the best that was available in the arts, the best that was being produced and had been produced in the arts, being made available to a popular audience. I started off by giving a lecture to students at Cambridge, called 'Oh Mother, is it worth it?' Here I was writing these plays, but was anybody listening? I concluded that the answer was no: despite the wonderful full audiences at the Royal Court, this was not the popular audience that I would have liked. I sent this essay as a pamphlet to every trade union secretary in the country, saying, 'I don't know what you think of this, but I made this statement in which I've suggested that the Labour movement ought to show more responsibility towards the arts, and what do you say? Let's have some debate, some discussion.' Then I thought that it was not enough to criticize, I should make some suggestions. I worked out a number of suggestions and made that into a second pamphlet, which again I sent to nearly two hundred unions.

One central suggestion was that the Trades Union Congress should conduct an enquiry into the state of the arts, because it seemed to me that that would focus attention on the arts in a way that had not happened before. One union picked up that suggestion, the Association of Cinema and Television Technicians. They made it a resolution at the 1960 Trade Union Congress, calling for a paper, an enquiry into the arts, and that was resolution 42. We said, OK, they passed the resolution, now if you want to take it any further we will create an arts organization which you can use if you want to. That was the simple framework, and in 1961 we were invited to put on a festival in Wellingborough, as a result of which we were invited in 1962 to put on six festivals which we did with a grant from the Gulbenkian Foundation. After that I said, right, now we need a base because if we are going to do it, it has to be done to the highest possible standards. We looked around and we found the Roundhouse and I spent the next eight years trying to raise £650,000 to convert the Roundhouse into an arts centre. I failed and it folded in 1970. That's a quick history.

Bigsby: But the curious thing about it was that it seems that your play, *Their Very Own and Golden City*, predicts that failure. You were presenting yourself at that time as a socialist writer, but if you look at those plays there is a counter-current in nearly all of them. The plays are partly to do with disillusionment, failed dreams.

Wesker: I suppose I began my career disillusioned. Being the son of a communist family, although I was never a member of the Communist Party, or any political party for that matter, I had the same expectations from the Soviet Union. Then came 1956 and the Hungarian uprising. Indeed, even before then, someone had introduced me to Richard Crossman's *The God That Failed*, in which former communist writers explained their disillusionment, and that was seminal. I read that when I was in the Air Force. So my disillusionment began fairly early on and 1956 sealed it.

But I was young and my mother was very influential in this respect. She was resilient. She didn't really understand. She didn't believe what had happened but I quarrelled and fought and bludgeoned and finally she delivered what is virtually the last speech in *Chicken Soup with Barley*. And this impressed me. I mean it impressed me that there is this in human beings: that despite all the failures, all the disappointments and disillusionment, there is a spirit which they hang on to. Survival has been a very strong theme in my work. David Hare is constantly quoting Oscar Wilde as saying that no map of the world is complete without utopia, by which he means that the dream of paradise, of the Garden of Eden, is a pretty powerful myth. On a personal level, on a social level, I have been concerned with the human spirit that wants to reach out for some sense of completion, unity, some way of making sense of life. You never do, I realize that you never do, but the need to and the effort to is always impressive to me.

Bigsby: The line that Sarah has in *Chicken Soup with Barley* is that if you don't care you'll die. Is that a line that you would echo today?

Wesker: Yes, it was her line.

Bigsby: Your mother's line?

Wesker: Yes. I can remember the Salvation Army picked it up. They had posters. I think that is where the 'Caring Society' began, because the Salvation Army picked it up and used it on their posters. Everybody began talking about a 'Caring Society'. It is all due to my mum.

Bigsby: Well, we have got you through the late 1950s and the 1960s, periods of some triumph for you. Then you came into the 1970s and there seemed to be a series of disasters of one kind or another waiting for you.

Wesker: Yes. I suppose you are really referring to *The Journalists*.

Bigsby: Indeed, you had problems with *The Journalists*, and also with *The Merchant*, later renamed *Shylock*, though the problems there were of a different order.

Wesker: In the case of *The Journalists* it was the actors in the Royal Shakespeare Company and in the case of *The Merchant* it was God. If you don't have God on your side, it really is tough.

Bigsby: But with *The Friends* it was probably neither God nor the Royal Shakespeare Company.

Wesker: *The Friends* had very mixed reviews. I persuaded the producer to print an advert giving both the good and the bad reviews and they balanced, but that play actually ran longer than *Roots* in the Roundhouse. It was, however, an occasion for me to write a long, very thoughtful, if contentious, essay about critics. My belief has always been that criticism is so important that really critics must themselves be subject to criticism, and the nature of criticism must be thought about. That is what that essay was about. I see that as a battle in the normal course of events. *The Journalists* and the Royal Shakespeare Company were a completely different kettle of fish, and there I do consider my fortunes took a disastrous turn. I am very angry with the people concerned. Some people would say it was my own fault because I should not have sued the Royal Shakespeare Company, but do you want to know the history? The actors refused to perform the play.

Bigsby: Has that ever happened before?

Wesker: It has never happened before, and I don't think it has ever happened since. I have my own theory as to why they did that but we will never know. I have documents with the reasons they gave but I believe that at that time the Worker's Revolutionary Party was very strong among the acting profession, particularly among the Royal Shakespeare Company, and *The Journalists* features four very intelligent Tory cabinet ministers. Remember, this is before Margaret Thatcher and the Tory party came into power and the left often thinks that the enemy must always be stupid. Then, it was about journalists, and journalists are very flippant about serious subjects and I echoed this in the play. Actors don't have the most subtle powers of political perception and I think they confused what the characters said with what they imagined I felt. They reacted violently against the play. In other countries it is called censorship. But, anyway, I was very angry and sued the Royal Shakespeare Company, who had contracted the play and really damaged the play's reputation, because it had been bought by three other countries and the RSC had said they couldn't do it until the RSC had done it. They wanted the world première. So they waited and then, when it wasn't done, they didn't do it either. It lost me a lot of money.

Bigsby: But it wasn't just the loss of that play, was it? It seems to have done something to the continuity of a career.

Wesker: Yes, because I heard that Trevor Nunn, who was running the theatre at the time, had written to every theatre management saying,

'You've got to come in on our side against Wesker because if he wins it will set a precedent that will damage us all.' I think it created the image of me as a troublemaker, and that is not true. I am really very easy to get on with. But people think you are trouble if you disagree with them sometimes. I think, to that extent, people stayed away and it was very difficult for me to get plays on.

Bigsby: On the other hand, you say you are not a troublemaker, but you certainly deal in polemic. You have talked about the way critics stand between you and an audience. You have insisted that, in this case, actors stood between you and an audience, and elsewhere you have suggested that directors stand between you and the audience. How did you manage to sustain the conviction that the audience was there on the other side of these people waiting for you?

Wesker: I don't know that I did, and I don't know that that is what makes one right. You don't write because you know there is an audience. A writer's got to do what a writer's got to do! You write regardless of whether you think there is an audience. You hope that the entire world is your audience when you have finished, but the audience is not what you think about as you are writing. I give readings of plays and the readings get a very warm and vivid response. This is very encouraging and so you think, well, maybe what I am writing does touch people. For the last five or six years I have been attending the British Council's Cambridge Seminar, which brings writers, academics, publishers and journalists from around the world to a Cambridge college where they meet British writers, and last year I read this new play called *Letter to a Daughter*. It is the sixth play in a cycle of plays for one woman. There was a professor from the University of Seoul, Korea, who fell in love with it, went back and persuaded one of the leading theatres in Korea to do it. As a result, the world première of *Letter to a Daughter* took place. This makes me think that if I can touch Korean, Brazilian and Latin American audiences, then I am not whistling in the wind.

Bigsby: But you have written some very tart things about directors: either you have accused them of being necrophiliacs, more interested in dead than living authors, or being concerned to foreground their own role. What should a director's relationship be to the text?

Wesker: First of all, it is not simply me saying it. I wrote an article for

The Times which I called 'The Necrophiliacs', though they didn't use that title for obvious reasons. I did this because there had been a statement made by one of the younger generation of directors saying that they would sooner direct the classics, while Jonathan Miller had said, a long time before, that he would sooner work with dead authors. So I just gave them a name for what they described as their preference.

What do I think? I suppose I have an old-fashioned view of the director *vis-à-vis* new work, which is that you take it very carefully in your hand and carry it on to the stage, offer it to an audience, saying, this is the play of Jack, Jean, Joan, and not saying, as one did to me of *The Journalists*, 'You don't leave me any room to say anything.' The answer was, 'I don't really want you to say anything. I would like you to help me get this play on the stage. If you start saying things on top of what I am saying there is a confusion of voices, and if you actually get in the way of what I am saying it is a kind of censorship.' I think all I am calling for is a certain modesty, a certain humility on their part. What they do with the classics is quite another matter.

Bigsby: But the theatre is a collaborative art. The director, the actors are going to bring to that performance qualities which are in them and distinctive to them. Surely you would be writing novels if you wanted to avoid that aspect?

Wesker: The fact that you need other people to help your work on to the stage is really no excuse, it seems to me, for them to impose themselves. To offer their skills and imagination to help your work get on the stage, in the best possible way, seems to me a very honourable thing to do. When I directed John Osborne's *The Entertainer* at the Theatre Clwyd, I wasn't concerned to impose upon it what I thought he should have written. I tried to deliver the play that I thought he had written, and I felt that was my modest task.

Bigsby: But your production would have been different from somebody else's production. What is the nature of that difference?

Wesker: The difference is that I am a different person, my intelligence is greater or lesser, my imagination is greater or lesser, my powers of directing are greater or lesser. It is not a difference of interpretation. That is my quarrel with them. They all say, we are all different so it has got to be a different interpretation. They are making a vice out of a virtue.

Bigsby: Do you imply that there is a stable meaning which has to be served?

Wesker: We shouldn't get on to this, because it is a very, very big question. I have a sneaking suspicion that somewhere there is the one right way to deliver a line, the one right way to play that Beethoven quartet. I have heard the best musicians say it is not a question of interpretation. There is a mystery and we are trying to understand it, we are trying to find the way in which Beethoven really heard this music. That is what we are trying to do when we play it and that is what I think directors should do when they are approaching a new work.

Bigsby: Have you, as a director of your own plays, discovered things in those plays which you did not know as a writer? Has the act of directing given you insights which were perhaps closed to you when you were originally creating the play?

Wesker: Yes, but not to do with intention, maybe to do with the melody, the way in which I heard a line. Let me get this absolutely clear, when I direct I do not direct, as many directors do, by coming to the stage with an absolutely clear vision of what it is I want and then forcing it on actors and everybody concerned. I don't do that. Paradoxically, what I say is, look, I think there is a spectrum of right ways, of possible right ways to deliver this line, and my task is to keep you within that spectrum and to stop you from going outside it. I don't come singing the melody. I come to rehearsals every morning thrilled to see what it is an actor has thought about overnight and brought to that morning's rehearsal.

Bigsby: Your plays have found audiences in this country, but they have also found audiences elsewhere: in France, Japan and America, but especially in Scandinavia. Do you have an answer as to why especially there?

Wesker: I think this is a myth; it isn't especially Scandinavia.

Bigsby: A number of your plays have received their première there.

Wesker: Yes, but that doesn't mean that they are done more there. That is just chance. *Shylock* was done there and *The Wedding Feast* was done there, but *Love Letters* had its première in the States. *Letter to a*

Daughter had its in Seoul while I directed the world première of *The Mistress* in Rome. In fact, Japan is the country that possibly has done most of my work. There was a time when it was Germany, and at this particular moment it is Latin America. An extraordinary number of requests have come through in the last months from Brazil, Argentina, Uruguay and Mexico.

Bigsby: Is there any logic to this?

Wesker: No. *The Four Seasons* was done in Mexico some years ago, and was actually the best production of that play that I have ever seen, and I have seen quite a lot of them in different countries. The actor who played the part of Adam fell in love with my work and has been translating it. This is the way my work gets done. A director, an actor or a translator falls in love with it and pushes it.

Bigsby: What led you to write your own version of *The Merchant of Venice*? I know that you saw a production directed by Jonathan Miller, but what was it about that production that got under your skin sufficiently to provoke you to write?

Wesker: Two things. Firstly, it obviously didn't work. Jonathan tried to show that Shylock was a dealer, like everybody else, by setting the play in a capitalist Victorian England, and it didn't work. It still came out not as an anti-Semitic play, but a play in which the Jew is very unpleasant. I had just had enough of it. It struck me that when Portia, in that particular production, said, hold on, wait a minute, you can't take a pound of flesh without blood, what Shylock should have said, and the kind of Jew that I knew would have said, was, 'Thank God, thank God. I've been relieved of the sin of taking life.' I thought, well, yes, that makes much more sense. I mean, it is not part of the Jewish personality to be vengeful, otherwise there would have been a quite different relationship between Jews and Germany, Israel and Germany. My first thought was, one day I will do a production of *The Merchant of Venice* which will bring this out, and someone said you will have to do a lot of rewriting. I thought, why not? But I didn't rewrite. My play is not a rewriting of *The Merchant of Venice*. I simply took the same three stories that Shakespeare used and wrote a completely different play, using the same names for the characters and adding some historical characters.

Bigsby: How important to your work in general has Jewishness been?

Wesker: It has grown in importance over the years. Although I was never a member of a political party, except the Young Communist League for about six months between the age of fifteen and sixteen, I was, in my early years, a member of a Zionist youth organization. That was in the days when Zionism wasn't a dirty word, when the PLO hadn't gone to work with its public relations and made it a dirty word. It was a leftwing Zionist youth movement and that set the seeds of a Jewish awareness, a Jewish consciousness. I think that as the years have passed, and I have seen that there is a reaction to the plays, a reaction against the plays, I had to ask myself why and I have come to the conclusion that there is an un-English voice that comes through. It jars. It doesn't sit comfortably on the English scene, and this has made me feel very much more Jewish than I might otherwise have been.

Bigsby: What does that Jewishness consist of? You are not Jewish in a religious sense, are you? You don't celebrate the festivals of the Jewish faith. You don't embrace many of the myths, so what does Jewishness mean in that context? What is it that you are defending or speaking out of?

Wesker: You are first aware of a sense of history. You are very aware of what that history is. It is a history of persecution, which everyone knows by now. It is also a history of a race of people that seems to attract irrational persecution. This hurts. It is offensive and unjust, and so being Jewish is to be on the side of a certain justice, a sense of justice. There are also certain inherited values, and it would take too long to attempt to think them through now. But you have ways of looking at the world; there is a certain sense of humour, often black humour, a sense of self-mockery. You don't really feel comfortable if there isn't a little bit of anti-Semitism around. It is an appetite and a curiosity and, essentially, a generosity of spirit about life and other human beings, and I like that. I am proud of Jewish achievements.

Bigsby: But you once said something which strikes me as very strange. You said that you personally had never experienced anti-Semitism because you think that to suffer it requires a fearful state of mind, which you don't possess. Now, if that is an accurate quotation, that is akin to accusing the Jews of being responsible for their own persecution.

Wesker: Did I really say that? It sounds very interesting, actually. But is it true?

Bigsby: If that is accurate, it is saying that the Jews are collaborators in their own persecution.

Wesker: I don't know that you can come to that conclusion from that statement. It does sound familiar. I think I was talking personally. The fact is that there is something about anti-Semitism that I can't believe. I mean, if anyone says anything anti-Semitic it makes me laugh. It's silly. You could say that it is because Jews persist in believing in the one God and pursuing their own religious rituals that they attract hostility, but I think there are reasons other than that. As I make my Shylock say: 'I think it's to do with their invention of God.' They were the first ones to invent God and I say that very deliberately because I don't believe in a creator in that religious sense. I think they not only invented God, they said this God, whom we have invented, has chosen us. This is not because we are better people, though this is another myth that I don't suppose will ever be got rid of. People imagine that the concept of the chosen race implies that they think they are better than other people, not that they are chosen in order to take on a responsibility, chosen to look after God's laws and God's creation. If you believe that this is your task as a people, this does make you uncomfortable to live with because it means you are always saying, 'I don't think that's just. I don't think that is right.' The response is often, 'What do you mean, you don't think that is right? This is our country.' Somewhere in all that is the cause of anti-Semitism. I think if you carry on doing that it does make you an uncomfortable partner; and I would like to be more of a comfortable partner, but I don't mind too much being that uncomfortable.

Bigsby: It strikes me that few British writers have written as many major works for women as you have done, from the figure of Sarah through the central character of *Caritas* to the one-woman plays. I get the feeling that you regard women as somehow having a greater strength, a greater resilience than men.

Wesker: Yes, I don't know what more to say to that. I was surrounded by very strong women – aunts, mother, sister. I am more comfortable in the company of women than men. I do find them in a strange way more courageous, more remarkable, more honest. They generally tend to bring more out of me than men. Men are meaner. Mind you, when a woman is mean she is mean like no one else. But, by and large, I prefer the company of women.

Bigsby: I have seen you give dramatized readings of your one-woman plays. Does performing the role of a woman, in such readings, lead you to further understanding, beyond the writing of the work? Does speaking the words and making the gestures bring you closer to an understanding of a woman's sensibility?

Wesker: Something does occur to me as you ask that question. Being male, certainly being a Jewish male, I am full of guilt, both justified and unjustified. When I am reading these roles I do get a sense of self-flagellation, and I quite enjoy being self-critical in that way, through the mouth of the women that I have created. I don't think I have ever said that before.

Bigsby: One thing strikes me about your women characters and that is that they are all survivors. When the men have given up they carry on. Even at the end of their tether they are survivors.

Wesker: I got that from my mother and from all the women around me. I think that that kind of remarkable strength has to be re-created. I think it is valuable.

Bigsby: You wrote a play, with a woman at its centre, called *Caritas*, which is about a young anchoress who, as a gesture of her faith, asks to be walled up. She then loses her faith and asks that the walls be taken down, but her request is denied. It is a play about people being trapped, in some sense, in their own beliefs. Does that have any personal bearing on you, either on your own beliefs or the tendency of people to trap you in your own earlier beliefs?

Wesker: I am as prone to self-imprisonment as anyone, but not in terms of my political beliefs. Those I was able to slough off.

Bigsby: That is an interesting remark. You mean that your political beliefs of the 1950s and early 1960s have now gone, been sloughed off?

Wesker: Oh, very early on. I am talking about the communist ethos that I grew up in. The ability to slough things off that don't any longer belong to me is there. I was very conscious, though, every so often of thinking, wait a minute, why am I doing this? I no longer want to do this. I no longer think this. Why do I think this? Why am I saying this if I no longer believe it? Over a whole area of activities, I realized that we take time to catch up with who we have become, and some of us never do. *Caritas* was sparked off by people I knew, individuals, but also by that whole era of flower power, of people attaching themselves to Buddhist beliefs. I thought, why are they attaching themselves to these alien beliefs? They couldn't get rid of them once they walked into them. They couldn't let go and it damaged and destroyed their lives. So it was more rooted in that than something specifically personal in my life.

Bigsby: At the beginning of your career you said you would like the man in the street to be able to come into your plays and understand immediately what was going on. You invoked Pasternak going into a factory and the workers asking for more. That is not what has happened. Do you regret that, or was it always an unreal objective?

Wesker: No, it used to happen. I can remember driving my car once and pulling up at a traffic light and the bus driver leaned out and said, 'It's almost as bad as *The Kitchen*, isn't it?' Encounters like that are very gratifying. I have come to recognise that art is a difficult language and as you develop as an artist you set more difficult tasks for yourself. It is a language that has to be learned and, as the writer in *Annie Wobbler* says, quoting Johnson, people have a great aversion to intellectual activity. They do, so I suppose that I have come to recognise that the arts probably only have a small minority audience. What I am never certain about is how large that minority is, and nor do I think that the recognition of that fact should do anything to hold back state subsidy for the arts.

Bigsby: You have written many plays, very different in form, very different in the number of actors. Looking at the whole of that work up to this moment, can you see any central unifying theme?

Wesker: I am interested in bringing things together. There is a character in *Annie Wobbler* who talks about great poetry. She quotes a Thomas Hardy line and then changes the order of its words. It falls to pieces. That is what I would like, she says, to be able to assemble the right words in the right order. In one way or another – whether it is

Christine in *Caritas* trying to get divine revelation, to get it right, or Andrew Cobham in *Their Very Own and Golden City* trying to build beautiful cities in which people would be happy – it is getting the right words in the right order that seems to preoccupy a lot of the characters in my plays.

Bigsby: Every writer has a voice, a distinctive voice. If you picked up a Pinter play and the name was taken off the cover, you would know it was Pinter's. If somebody picked up a Wesker play, how would they know it was a Wesker play?

Wesker: They would have to work very hard. It is not there in the style, because I believe that material should dictate the style of the play. So, a love story like *Four Seasons* dictates a lyrical style. But I think that if you looked at the characters you would find preoccupations that they have, ways of looking at the world, certain values that they hold and weigh in their hands. That is where you would find the tone of voice, not in the style.

Bigsby: You are on the verge of sixty. Looking back, what has given you the greatest pleasure in your career to date?

Wesker: The fact of an audience's response, always. It is the word coming back that tells you it has touched someone in some way. It is very special to be in an audience and to know that they have warmed to someone you have struggled to put together over a long period of time. Then there is the much more private sense of gratification which comes simply from output. When I am feeling very low, I look at those seven Penguin volumes and I think, well, if I die tomorrow, it's not bad. I don't know what posterity will do with it, but I have done it and it is a lot of work. Then there is the diary. Since 1963 I must have written the equivalent of fifty novels. It is a lot of work and just the knowledge that I have been working non-stop is gratifying.

In Conversation With Tom Wolfe

Tom Wolfe was born in Virginia in 1931, and holds a PhD in American Studies from Yale. He started his career as a conventional journalist and, indeed, won an award for his foreign reporting but, turning to the domestic scene, he came to see himself as part of a new literary movement, borrowing techniques both from the novel and from journalism. He became a principal voice of what came to be known as the new journalism, a genre which he suggested had challenged the novel on its home territory and won. His books include *The Kandy-Kolored Tangerine Flake Streamline Baby* (1965), *The Pump House Gang* (1968), *The Electric Kool-Aid Acid Test* (1968), *The Painted Word* (1975), and his account of American astronauts, *The Right Stuff* (1979). This interview was conducted in December 1980, before the publication of his novel, *Bonfire of the Vanities* (1988). His second novel, *A Man in Full*, appeared in 1998.

Bigsby: How far did your upbringing prepare you for your career?

Wolfe: A lot of the stylistic qualities that I have somehow picked up along the way have come from my background without my knowing it. I grew up in the South and as I look back on it all, through school days in Virginia, there is a great rhetorical tradition with people constantly getting up and giving speeches. At a very young age we were forced, almost at bayonet point, into debating societies. There was a lot of Bible reading, a lot of going to Sunday school, and things of that sort. You end up picking up a lot of rhetorical methods running through your sleep and this certainly crept back into my work as a journalist.

Bigsby: You then studied for a degree and later took a doctorate at Yale, in the American studies programme, which seems extremely appropriate since you have, in effect, been doing American studies ever since?

Wolfe: In my opinion, the American Studies programme is best suited for journalists. I did not go into it with that in mind at all. I was going to teach, but I spent five years getting my doctorate, which no one should do. There were a few who spent even longer, but I took an awful lot of time doing it. It became something of an academic trap. In fact, I finished my dissertation in August one year when it was already too late to get a job teaching anywhere. I took a job as a truck-loader, because all the proletarian novels that I had read in American studies taught me that the beginning of wisdom was taking a working-class job. So I took a job as a truck-loader, waiting for the insights that were going to come to me. They never came.

The day of a working-class labourer seemed to be one of very boring work all day long, then heading off to the one place in town that served ten-cent draught beer. It was called Utika beer and there was a television set over the bar and there were these shows where girls with pleated skirts were whirling around – a very stroboscopic sight with these skirts going round, very hypnotic, and you would slip into a Utika beer coma. And that was the day: the insights never came. Then I went off looking for a newspaper job, that being the only work, other than truck-loading, that somebody with nine years of college education could qualify for.

Bigsby: You went on to write a great deal about the 1960s and the 1970s, but almost nothing about the 1950s except, I think, that you once said they were fuliginously flat. Do you have a clear sense of that decade, when you were in your twenties?

Wolfe: I have a clearer sense of the 1950s now, to tell you the truth, than I did when I was living in them. After working on the *The Right Stuff*, which was about the Mercury astronauts, men who were chosen as astronauts in 1959, I went back to the library and started reading magazines and newspapers from that period. It was a startling thing to do. It seemed so much like another world. To give one obvious example, in all the pictures in *Life* magazine men's ears stuck out and the hair was cut so close to the head that sometimes the sun would shine through them. There were a lot of pictures where you could see the sun through these ears, but at the time it never dawned on me. Now, if you can take that image into politics, it never dawned on me at that time how patriotic we all were in America. Journalists were very patriotic. James Reston wrote a column in which he said, 'Here in Washington, which is supposed to be a cynical town, our hearts beat a little faster yesterday at the sight of seven brave young men who spoke unashamedly of home and hearth, of God, country, family and the verities of American life.' Now if anyone, for any perverse reason, wanted to finish off James Reston they should just go to his house in Martha's Vineyard and read him this column and I am sure he would slice his wrists because the atmosphere of journalism and, in many respects, of the country, has changed so much since the 1950s.

Bigsby: Did you go into journalism in the way you were describing primarily because you were interested in journalism or because you were waiting around to produce a novel?

Wolfe: I wanted to write a novel. When I was in college – now we are going back to the late 1940s – if you were interested in writing you assumed that you were going to go out and light up the skies with a novel, and that was the only way it was going to be done. Newspapers were full of people like myself who, in their own minds, were stopping at the newspaper for a cup of coffee on the road to the final triumph, which was going to be the novel. The idea was that at some point in your career in journalism, after working the fat off your style and your soul, you would quit journalism, go into a shack somewhere and work hard for six months or a year and come out with a brilliant first novel. My contention has always been that there should be no difference in the techniques that are going to be effective in fiction or non-fiction.

It is just that in non-fiction, in journalism, you have the difficulty of getting the material in the first place or getting enough detail about the mental life of someone you are writing about to do this accurately.

Bigsby: What is it that made you suggest, as you did, that the new journalism – I know that's a phrase that turns you white nowadays – had displaced the novel as the principal literary genre?

Wolfe: I overstated the case. That piece was, in a way, like a manifesto. It never displaced the novel, as I look back on it, but it did do this: it shook the foundations underneath the novel so that the novelists were no longer nearly so secure in their status as the kings of the literary world. There was a period in the 1960s, and to a certain extent in the early 1970s, in which the excitement in prose was in journalism. As evidence of that I point not to my work but to the work of someone like Truman Capote and *In Cold Blood*. It is difficult to remember now what an impact that book had. Then there was Norman Mailer's *Armies of the Night*.

If prominent novelists begin to turn to non-fiction that in itself causes a kind of status quake of some sort, and it interests me today to see experimental novelists – you almost have to put the words in quotes and add a snigger these days – backing into realism. I am thinking of people like E.L. Doctorow, whose work had always been typical of what I call New Fabulism, which was a totally unrealistic sort of fiction, adding real names to his fables. Suddenly he introduces a name like Leon Trotsky or Sigmund Freud or Stamford White, the architect, into a fantasy and, as time goes by, with his new novel, *Loon Lake*, he introduces more and more realism, still trying to run up a flag and say, well I am still experimental, don't get me wrong. It is like backing out of the throne room of a king who you know is about to fall from power. You don't dare really turn your back on him but you want to get out of there fast, so you learn to walk backwards at a rapid clip. That is what so many of the experimental novelists do. I think they are beginning, reluctantly, to agree with my position about realism: that it is a plateau that you can't retreat from.

Bigsby: I think of you as rather like Holden Caulfield in *Catcher in the Rye*, someone who goes around attacking phoneys and phoniness. But from what position are you doing that? Is there a populist streak in you somewhere?

Wolfe: I never pictured myself as going around attacking phoneys, but I can see that in many cases that has been the end result, that is what it has boiled down to. In many cases it was perversity. If everybody in the world that I live in, to give you one example, thought that the Black Panthers was just a marvellous organization and the people like Leonard Bernstein, who were giving parties for the Black Panthers, were just wonderful people, and this was the way of the future, to me it was irresistible to take an artist's look – and that's the way I thought I was looking – at what this really amounted to. So I did go to a party that Leonard Bernstein gave for the Black Panthers and as I saw this man, who lives in a nineteen-room duplex apartment on Park Avenue and 79th Street, raising his fist and saying 'Right on!' as the Field Marshall of the Black Panthers announced the ten-point revolutionary programme under which there would be no more privately owned duplexes on Park Avenue and 79th Street, I could not resist writing it. Now in my own defence I must say, having admitted to perversity, that I always try to write these pieces from the inside-out; that is to say, I have tried to bring the scene alive, let the people talk and, from inside the whale, to use Orwell's phrase, steer the mind of the reader rather than pulling back and passing moral judgement.

Bigsby: You accuse the novelist in 1960s America of having ignored substantial cultural realities, yet you look at the Panthers and write an amusing essay about styles, manners of approach. At the same time, of course, America's cities were burning. You went to a colloquium once and tried to explain to people that they were undergoing a 'happiness explosion'. On the other hand, the 1960s also consisted of Vietnam, riots, assassinations, but you weren't drawn to write about them. I have read one piece you wrote about Vietnam which was from the perspective of a pilot. On the whole, though, it is an issue that does not appear.

Wolfe: I'm glad you mentioned that piece. I was much criticized for that, incidentally. In fact, I was compared to Céline in an unflattering way, meaning that I was a Fascist for writing about the war in Vietnam through the eyes of a pilot flying a fighter bomber off a carrier. The criticism was, where are all the napalmed children? Well, the napalmed children had been quite well written about, it seemed to me, by lots of people. The military officer – and that is, after all, who was carrying out the war in Vietnam for the United States – was treated as an abstract brute, a Fascist, a protofascist, who you didn't have to describe because you knew his essence. I said, well, what is the essence of such a person? And I found it was something quite different. For a start, the ones that flew over North Vietnam didn't carry napalm; there was plenty of napalm used, obviously, but not in North Vietnam.

These were people who suffered agonies and had the strange pride of a sportsman, which is not altogether admirable. Nevertheless, I felt it quite well worth taking a look at and writing about sympathetically – no, that makes it sound like a partisan performance – let's say empathetically from the inside-out again. That piece was called 'The Truest Sport: Jousting with Sam and Charlie'. It was about American fighter pilots and was written, in so far as I could do it, from inside the central nervous system of a pilot who felt that at any moment he was going to be blown to smithereens. In fact, he was finally shot down.

Bigsby: Does the new conservatism of the environment in which we are now living create particular problems for you? In the 1960s you were gunning for the New Left. The New Left has not only disappeared, its representatives now come back wearing pinstriped suits and broadcasting for religious groups. Do you see, stretching ahead of us in the 1980s, the same kind of fuliginously flat world that existed in the 1950s and which you didn't address then? Is there a risk that you are going to be reduced to silence by living in this vapid world?

Wolfe: You are quite right. If everybody starts suddenly agreeing with your own thoughts, which may have come out of a perverse desire to rock the boat, it would certainly take a lot of the fun out of things. But I don't think the human comedy is ever going to let us down, and I should mention one thing that is responsible for this so-called turn to the right. I don't see so much a turn to the right as a disappearance of the left, which are two quite different things. I think people should be very careful about looking at the election of Ronald Reagan. It is not a turn to the right as much as it is a disappearance, a fleeing, of the left.

At the heart of this is the discovery of concentration camps in socialist countries, one after the other, starting with the publication of *The Gulag Archipelago*. Since that time we have found concentration camps in China, in the new united Vietnam, in Cambodia, where they became horrible beyond belief, in Cuba. And now any time there is socialism – and by socialism I am talking about real socialism, monolithic socialism – we find concentration camps and we are in a century in which it is no longer possible to have an ideological detour around concentration camps. You cannot argue your way around that block in the road.

This being the case, Marxism no longer exists anywhere, I think, as a spiritual force. It exists as a political force. There are still ideologues, but it no longer exists as a spiritual force. Even in the US, the Marxist idea that beyond the next hill, or beyond the rubble of the next burnt-out city, there is an Eldorado called socialism, generated opposition to the institutions of the United States, whether the criticism came from within the American literary world or from abroad.

Bigsby: You are speaking with a certain kind of passion, which you evacuate with some care from your essays.

Wolfe: Very unkind of you to point that out, but you are right. I suppose one reason that I have been called a conservative more and more in the last four or five years is that I have finally got fed up with what I think of as the intellectual corruption of fashionable attacks on democracy. That is the way I look at it. These fashionable attacks on democracy begin to get more than silly after a while; they become disturbing. We have been living, for a long time in the intellectual community, in the situation of the French businessmen who, in the last election in France (which was really Giscard against the coalition which would be led by the communists), found it impossible, in polite conversation, in cultivated circles, to be pro-Giscard. On the night of the election there were rooms full of businessmen, in marvellous suits, sitting around saying, 'Oh, my God, we lost, we lost.' But in their heart of hearts they were saying, 'And thank God we did.' Because in their heart of hearts they knew that the position they were taking, intellectually and in conversation, was ruinous. I think my confrères in the literary world in the United States had that same kind of relief. We don't have to keep harping on with this fashionable criticism of American institutions any longer; the wind has shifted and now we can do something. And I think what they can do is to become, for the first time in a long time, intellectually honest.

Bigsby: Would it be wrong of me to detect that you look as though you are poised to jump in one of two directions – one is to go back to being that award-winning foreign correspondent, the other is to write the novel that you had promised yourself that you would write?

Wolfe: You are very prescient. I do intend to write a novel as my next book. I want to write a novel about New York, the city I have lived in for almost twenty years now, because I think that the last twenty years in New York has been a period that will be looked back to centuries from now. I suddenly think of Céline who, when asked by an interviewer what he thought his position would be in French literary history in the year 2050, said, 'My dear fellow, what on earth makes you think the Chinese will be interested in French literature of the twentieth century?' That aside, I think people will look back to this period in New York, and for that matter other metropolises of America, in the way they look back to Regency England, or back to Paris in the 1840s, as a period that fostered excesses you can't help but wonder at.

Now I hope that my performance in writing such a book will transcend any particular personal passions that I might have. I would much prefer to be like Balzac. Balzac was also called a conservative. In fact, he wrote plenty of pamphlets in support of the monarchy, and things of that sort. Balzac, though, through his depiction of life in the 1820s and 1830s and 1840s in France, ended up being the writer who, probably more than any other in France, helped bring on the revolution of 1848, because he couldn't resist being honest in his descriptions of industrial bourgeois society in France. He couldn't hold back. No matter what it was, he had to present the whole thing. I hope, and without trying to put myself in the same room with Balzac, that I might be able to do the same thing.